Centre-Right Parties in Post-Communist East–Central Europe

This book is of profound importance for it is the first to cover the centre-right in post-communist Eastern Europe. It makes a vital contribution to the broader research agenda on the Central and East European centre-right by focusing on one specific question: Why strong and cohesive centre-right formations have developed in some post-communist states, but not others. It delves into the attempts to develop centre-right parties after 1989 in four nations: the Czech Republic, Hungary, Poland and Slovakia.

The authors of the case studies use a common analytical framework to analyse and provide fascinating insights into the varying levels of cohesion in centre-right parties across the region.

This volume was previously published as a special issue of *The Journal of Communist Studies and Transition Politics*.

Aleks Szczerbiak is Senior Lecturer in Contemporary European Studies at the Sussex European Institute, University of Sussex, specialising in Central and East European politics.

Seán Hanley is Lecturer in East European Politics at the School of Slavonic and East European Studies, University College London. He has published a number of articles on both party development and the right of the Czech Republic.

90 0655585 6

7 Day

University of Plymouth Library

Subject to status this item may be renewed
via your Voyager account

http://voyager.plymouth.ac.uk

Exeter tel: (01392) 475049
Exmouth tel: (01395) 255331
Plymouth tel: (01752) 232323

Centre-Right Parties in Post-Communist East–Central Europe

Edited by

Aleks Szczerbiak and Seán Hanley

 Routledge
Taylor & Francis Group

LONDON AND NEW YORK

First published 2006 by Routledge
2 Park Square, Milton Park, Abingdon, Oxon OX14 4RN

Simultaneously published in the USA and Canada
by Routledge
270 Madison Avenue, New York, NY 10016

Routledge is an imprint of the Taylor & Francis Group

© 2005 Aleks Szczerbiak and Seán Hanley

Typeset in Times by Techset Composition Limited
Printed and bound in Great Britain by Antony Rowe Ltd, Chippenham, Wiltshire

British Library Cataloguing in Publication Data
A catalogue record for this book is available from the British Library

Library of Congress Cataloging in Publication Data

A catalog record for this book has been requested

ISBN 0-415-34781-5

CONTENTS

Notes on Contributors

Aleks Szczerbiak is Senior Lecturer in Contemporary European Studies at the Sussex European Institute, University of Sussex, specializing in comparative Central and East European politics. He is author of *Poles Together? The Emergence and Development of Political Parties in Postcommunist Poland* (2001).

Seán Hanley is Lecturer in East European Politics at the School of Slavonic and East European Studies, University College London. He has published a number of articles on party politics in the Czech Republic and is currently working on a book dealing with the rise and fall of the new Czech Right.

Brigid Fowler is a PhD candidate at the Centre for Russian and East European Studies (CREES), European Research Institute, University of Birmingham, where her research concerns the impact of domestic political factors on Hungary's EU accession process, focusing on the 1998–2002 government. She has been a Research Fellow at CREES and has published on aspects of Hungarian politics and EU enlargement.

Tim Haughton is Lecturer in the Politics of Central and Eastern Europe at the University of Birmingham. His main research interests are party politics in Eastern and Central Europe and the impact of European Union membership on the domestic politics of the region.

Marek Rybář is Assistant Professor of Political Science at Comenius University in Bratislava. His main research interest is party politics.

Paul G. Lewis is Reader in Central and East European Politics in the Faculty of Social Sciences at the Open University, where he specializes in comparative politics. He is the author of *Political Parties in Post-Communist Eastern Europe* (2000), editor of *Political Development and Democratic Change in Post-Communist Europe* (2001), and co-editor of *Pan-European Perspectives on Party Politics* (2003) and *Developments in Central and East European Politics 3* (2003).

Introduction: Understanding the Politics of the Right in Contemporary East–Central Europe

ALEKS SZCZERBIAK and SEÁN HANLEY

Despite their importance in contemporary European politics, parties of the centre-right remain a strikingly under-researched area in both West European and post-communist Eastern European comparative politics. Compared with the voluminous literature on the left-wing communist successor parties or on the extreme right, little has been written on post-communist centre-right formations in terms of either empirical case studies or attempts to develop explanatory frameworks. The reasons for this paucity of research appear to be both pragmatic, reflecting the personal preferences and interests of individual researchers, and methodological, reflecting intrinsic problems of definition and comparison. Whereas communist successor parties, for example, constitute an easily identifiable bloc, defining who is on the centre-right from amid an array of nationalist, conservative, Christian, liberal and populist groupings is a much more difficult task. As Hanley notes later in this collection, in addition to the vague boundaries between far right and centre-right in the region, liberal and agrarian parties, which have been absorbed into consolidated centre-right blocs in most West European democracies, often appear as small 'centrist' groups in a post-communist context. Further unresolved questions concerning the origins of the post-communist centre-right; its social bases, ideologies and responses to the new challenges of Europeanization and globalization combine to make it a particularly rich, if complex, vein of comparative research that has so far gone largely unaddressed.

The Limits of Historical–Structural Explanation

Most comparative frameworks explaining the emergence of centre-right parties (and parties generally) in post-communist Europe, and national variations among them, stress broad structural and historical factors. The highly influential work of Kitschelt, for example, argues that the incomplete nature of social modernization in pre-communist Hungary and Poland and the coercive nature of their subsequent modernization under communism led to the conservation of populist, ruralist and conservative discourses and debates. These constituted a cultural and ideological reservoir for reconstituting the Right after 1989, but preserved the historical division with liberals committed to free markets and lifestyle pluralism. Lack of social support for communism in such semi-modern societies, Kitschelt argues, created weak 'national-accommodationist' ruling parties, whose successors initiated and embraced economic reform after 1989, blurring the socio-economic dimension of left–right competition. The free-market, liberal-conservative character of the Czech Right, by contrast, is explained by the pre-communist social modernity of the Czech lands, which left traditional sectors intellectually and socially marginal, but produced an authoritarian 'bureaucratic–authoritarian' form of communism that was averse to any element of market reform. In Bulgaria and Romania, Kitschelt suggests, extremely low levels of pre-communist modernity created clientelistic 'patrimonial communist' ruling parties, able to dominate both the transition from communism in 1989 and the early post-communist period through the use of nationalism and economic populism. Faced with strong ex-communist elites, centre-right groupings in these states therefore fuse pro-market stances with militant anti-communism, in many ways resembling the broad opposition coalitions elsewhere in the region that briefly mobilized against communist regimes in 1989–90, but then fragmented.[1]

Milada Anna Vachudová, by contrast, plays down the differences identified by Kitschelt between the conservative and neo-liberal centre-right in Hungary, Poland and the Czech Republic, regarding both as 'moderate right'. She attributes the emergence of the 'moderate right' in some states in the region to the existence of strong organized opposition groups under communism, which, she claims, furnished the intellectual basis of such parties and the alternative elites for them. Conversely, she attributes the weakness of the moderate Right in states such as Slovakia, Bulgaria, Romania and Croatia to the weakness of such opposition which, she suggests, allowed former ruling parties or extreme nationalists to appropriate the nationalist discourses of the traditional pre-communist right and emerge as a dominant force.

Such structural–historical analyses paint a broadly convincing picture in explaining *patterns* of left–right competition across the region. However, they have a number of significant weaknesses. First, they do little to address issues relating to the *strength*, *cohesion* and *success* of centre-right parties in individual states. There has, so far, been relatively little consideration in the literature of why some post-communist centre-right formations are electorally and organizationally more successful than others.[2] However, what is clear is that the levels of success can often appear anomalous when viewed against a historical backdrop. As Szczerbiak makes clear in this collection, despite the existence of deep-rooted political divisions in Poland dividing a large Catholic–nationalist constituency from secular Poles and a marked urban–rural divide – and despite the short-lived success of Solidarity Election Action in the mid-1990s – centre-right forces have remained organizationally weak and politically divided. In the Czech Republic, by contrast, as Hanley describes, despite the historic strength of the left in the Czech lands and weakness of authoritarian nationalism, political Catholicism and aristocratic conservatism, a powerful and durable neo-liberal 'Thatcherite' centre-right emerged.[3] Second, like many accounts of party formation in West European settings, the structural–historical bias of such approaches leads them largely to avoid consideration of the course of post-communist politics. Most contributors to this volume are broadly in sympathy with the aspirations for 'contextualized comparison' that underpin such work – a reaction against both the thick description of some area studies and the 'radical decontextualization' of quantitative methodologies and rational choice approaches that dominate US political science.[4] However, such work, we would argue, has tended to produce analysis that is too deterministic, broad-brush and static to address key aspects of comparative politics in contemporary Central and Eastern Europe. In the present case, such work has tended to ignore the strategies and interaction of political actors, the uncertainty of outcomes and the problems of political organization, whose effective solution is necessary to translate even the most powerful structural determinant into a concrete result. Even Vachudová's analysis, which relates the type of 'Right' that emerged to more proximate causes, namely the strength of organized opposition under communism and competition from the post-communist left after 1989, ultimately relies upon regime type and regime legacies as the key explanatory variable. However, as Fowler and Szczerbiak note in this collection, even subsequently successful communist successor parties such as those in Hungary and Poland were politically marginal and electorally unpopular in the early 1990s and are *themselves* arguably still adapting. Indeed, as Fowler notes, despite narrowly losing the 2002 election, Fidesz–Hungarian Civic Alliance (Fidesz–MPSZ) has remained a formidable competitor for power precisely because of its capacity for *continued rapid strategic learning*, which it has effectively translated into well-disciplined reorganization and realignment. Finally, as contributions to this collection make clear, *the power of regime legacies to explain political variation even in broad terms may be rapidly fading*. For example, as Haughton and Rybář suggest, the polarized party politics of state building in Slovakia, identified by many as a path-dependent regime legacy, may be a relatively transitory phase in the country's post-communist politics, which may now be giving way to more conventional programmatic competition between left and right.

Bringing Politics Back In

Arguably, then, the re-emergence of the centre-right in post-communist Central and Eastern Europe can be more fully understood only by considering a range of 'political' factors marginalized or reduced to structural variables in existing comparative analysis. As well as examining legacy-based explanations, and in particular Vachudová's linking of weak communist regime and strong democratic oppositions with the emergence of strong moderate centre-right parties (and vice versa), contributions to this collection have systematically explored a number of propositions stressing 'political' factors:

- that choices made by political actors during the critical junctures of the 1989–91 period could determine the development of strong and cohesive centre-right parties;
- that a less proportional electoral system would produce strong and cohesive centre-right parties (and vice versa);
- that a parliamentary regime would be more likely to produce successful centre-right bloc than a (semi-)presidential system;
- that successful centre-right parties will be formed centrally and institutionalize on the basis of territorial penetration, rather than territorial diffusion; and
- that the presence of ideologically and socially cohesive political elites would lead to the formation of strong and united centre-right parties (and vice versa).

Critical Junctures and Formative Moments

The actions and decisions of political actors at moments of uncertainty and indeterminacy can be seen as shaping patterns of party development for many years to come. In post-communist politics, such critical junctures have often been identified as occurring in and after the period of transition in 1989–90. Grzymała-Busse, for example, while drawing on the structural–historical regime legacies approach developed by Kitschelt and his collaborators, introduces the notion of critical junctures into her work on communist successor parties.[5] She argues that the organizational, ideological and electoral-strategic choices taken by reform-minded elites in communist successor parties in the key 1989–91 period played a decisive role in determining their future developmental path. However, the extent to which such leaders possessed the know-how to make such choices was, in large part, determined by the legacy of political skills that they inherited from the previous communist regime, a tension between structure and agency never fully resolved. However, the contributions to this volume suggest that in a number of cases unstable patterns of party competition and/or party institutionalization caused critical junctures to occur several years after regime transition and its immediate aftermath.

Institutional Approaches

Institutional approaches stress the importance of the institutional frameworks within which parties emerge and develop as being the key factors determining their strength and cohesiveness, as well highlighting parties' own status as meso-institutions. *Macro-institutional factors* stress the importance of broader structural–institutional incentives and include factors such as the nature of executive structures, the spatial distribution of power within a state and, in particular, electoral systems. The logic of these approaches is fairly straightforward. For example, a more proportional electoral system will discourage party cohesion because it will encourage political entrepreneurs who find themselves marginalized within their political formation to pursue a strategy of 'exit' rather than 'voice', and vice versa.[6] Similarly, it has been suggested, a (semi-)presidential system will encourage actors to rise above party politics and thereby undermine party development and institutionalization. According to this approach, a particular post-communist state's broader institutional configuration, particularly the proportionality of its electoral system and whether or not it has a powerful presidency, will determine whether or not it develops cohesive centre-right parties.[7] However, as a number of the case studies in this collection suggest, post-communist elites have often not behaved rationally in relation to institutions. Moreover, as Fowler's study of the Hungarian right in particular implies, a strong parliamentary regime can be regarded as much an *effect* of strong political parties as a *cause*. Finally, as Szczerbiak argues, semi-presidentialism should perhaps be viewed as offering a complex mix of incentives and can in certain circumstances, as in Poland in the mid-1990s, *favour* party formation by uniting a previously fractured right into a broad electoral coalition.

It is, therefore, also necessary to consider the micro-institutional level of party development. *Micro-institutional* approaches stress the importance not only of a party's organization and internal power dynamics but also its origins as key variables accounting for whether it can successfully institutionalize itself. A classic statement of this position can be found in the work of Panebianco, who identified the role of external sponsors and patterns of territorial penetration or diffusion as critical determining factors.[8] Once again, the logic is simple. An organization with a weak institutional power centre and where key leaders owe a higher degree of loyalty to a pre-existing faction or external sponsor rather than the organization as a whole will inevitably be more organizationally brittle. According to this approach, therefore, a successful centre-right party will be formed centrally and develop on the basis of territorial penetration. Such an approach, as Szczerbiak suggests, may explain the puzzling institutional weakness of Poland's Solidarity Election Action – an organization formed by an external trade union sponsor as a loose confederal grouping – which contrasts markedly with the apparent durability of parties created by political entrepreneurs on the Czech and Hungarian centre-right. Such an analysis may bode ill for the newly ascendant Slovak right-wing coalition and its key component, the Slovak Democratic and Christian Union (SDKU), whose early disintegrative tendencies are analysed by Haughton and Rybář.

Elite Cohesion and Ideological Construction

Finally, there is the role of *elite cohesion and ideological construction*. To some extent this overlaps with the theme of critical junctures in stressing the importance of political agency. However, we believe that the origins and internal cohesion of political elites and the broader strategic and ideological visions that political entrepreneurs develop can be regarded as sufficiently distinct to represent a separate variable. The presence or absence of ideologically and socially cohesive political elites, often but not always drawn from the counter-elites outside (or marginal to) the communist party-state during late socialism, appears a critical factor in accounting for the relative success or failure of centre-right parties in post-communist states. Gil Eyal, for example, has traced both the break-up of the Czechoslovak federation in 1992 and the varying patterns of party political development in the Czech Republic and Slovakia after 1992 to the nature of the counter-elites in the Czech lands and Slovakia under late socialism.[9] However, as this collection suggests, the role of party-forming elites must be seen as comprising more than simply endowment with resources, skills and assets, however broadly conceived. As the country studies by Fowler and Hanley suggest, the relative success of dominant centre-right formations in Hungary and the Czech Republic partly reflects the ability of political entrepreneurs that founded them to craft distinct 'civic' ideologies relating older nationalist or national-populist discourses to current issues in post-communist transformation. Such successful ideological construction – which may also embrace *shifts* in party ideology – arguably enhances party cohesion and purpose by framing issues into a coherent narrative, thereby facilitating policy choice, intra-party communication, party–voter links and strategic realignments. In both cases, the emergent centre-right benefited from charismatic leadership and a cohesive generationally defined elite with a common educational and social background. By contrast, the inability of the Polish right to unite on any other basis than its common heritage in the Solidarity movement, and the concomitant diversity of its right-wing elites, appears a source of further weakness. Once again, these factors also appear to be evident for the emergent Slovak centre-right which, despite its electoral success, seems closer to the Polish pattern of elite fragmentation and ideological vagueness, although its modernizing project would seem to provide a more favourable basis for ideological construction.

The Prospects for the Central and East European Centre-Right

At the time of writing, centre-right formations are in a period of electoral retreat in many Central and Eastern European states. Hungary's Fidesz–MPP narrowly lost the April 2002 election, although it has clearly emerged as the dominant force on the right of the political spectrum in Hungary. In the Czech Republic, the Civic Democrats have lost the last two elections and been in opposition since 1997, despite remaining a powerful, popular and well-institutionalized party. In Slovakia, by contrast, while centre-right parties have been more organizationally and electorally fragmented, this has not prevented them from winning the last two elections and being in office since 1998. In Poland, on the other hand, the centre-right groupings that emerged from the Solidarity opposition movement have been weak and divided, although recent developments point to a possible upturn in their fortunes. Notwithstanding Hanley's Scandinavian analogy, there seem few really clear discernible trends in the development of the centre-right in the four countries surveyed, not otherwise explicable in terms of national electoral cycles. Nevertheless, we believe, this collection represents a small but significant step forward in understanding an important, but hitherto neglected, area of politics of the region.

NOTES

1. This approach has subsequently been refined to explain differing organizational, political and strategic development of individual parties, specifically communist successor parties. See A. Grzymała-Busse, *Redeeming the Communist Past: The Transformation of Communist Parties in East Central Europe* (Cambridge: Cambridge University Press, 2002); H. Kitschelt, 'Constraints and Opportunities in the Strategic Conduct of Post-Communist Successor Parties: Regime Legacies as Causal Argument', in A. Bozoki and J.T. Ishiyama (eds.), *The Communist Successor Parties of Central and Eastern Europe* (Armonk, NY: M.E. Sharpe, 2002), pp.14–40.
2. The question of what constitutes 'success' is itself debatable. Although it depends, in part, on what the parties' actual objectives are, for the purpose of this research we view it as a combination of office seeking and vote maximization (the latter being arguably a prerequisite of the former) for any broad-based party seeking to play a dominant role in a coalition government.
3. Still more surprisingly, in Bulgaria, despite socio-economic backwardness, a weak liberal tradition and a repressive 'patrimonial communist' regime, the main centre-right grouping, the Union of Democratic Forces (SDS), later broadened into a wider grouping the United Democratic Forces (ODS), proved surprisingly effective electorally and organizationally robust throughout the 1990s, before partially disintegrating in 2001. See S.M. Fish and R.S. Brooks, 'Bulgarian Democracy's Organizational Weapon', *East European Constitutional Review*, Vol.9, No.3 (Summer 2000), pp.62–71.

4. See P. Pierson, 'Epilogue: From Area Studies to Contextualized Comparisons', in G. Ekiert and S. Hanson (eds.), *Democracy and Capitalism in Central and Eastern Europe: Assessing the Legacy of Communist Rule* (Cambridge: Cambridge University Press, 2003), pp.353–66.
5. See Grzymała-Busse.
6. See, for example, C. Nikolenyi, 'From Fragmentation Towards Unity: The Center-Right in the Hungarian Party System, 1994–1998', paper presented at the European Consortium for Political Research General Conference, September 2003; J. Hopkin, *Party Formation and Democratic Transition* (Basingstoke: Macmillan, 1999), ch.1.
7. See S. Saxonberg. 'The Influence of Presidential Systems: Why the Right Is So Weak in Conservative Poland and So Strong in the Egalitarian Czech Republic', *Problems of Post-Communism*, Vol.50, No.5 (Sept.–Oct. 2003), pp.22–36.
8. See A. Panebianco, *Political Parties: Organization and Power* (Cambridge: Cambridge University Press, 1988).
9. See G. Eyal, *The Origins of Postcommunist Elites: From Prague Spring to Breakup of Czechoslovakia* (Minneapolis and London: University of Minnesota Press, 2003).

Getting the Right Right: Redefining the Centre-Right in Post-Communist Europe

SEÁN HANLEY

Introduction

The existing literature on the centre-right in Eastern and Central Europe is small and fragmentary. Current published research amounts to an edited collection,[1] one book-length treatment, which largely reviews prospects for democratization,[2] several monographs on national cases,[3] and a small number of comparative papers.[4] A number of other works discuss the centre-right in the region as a subsidiary theme within accounts of topics such as economic transformation and the break-up of Czechoslovakia.[5] Critical, left-wing scholarship has also sometimes focused on the East and Central European centre-right as the key political vehicle for the restoration of capitalism and agent of transnational capital after 1989.[6] The paucity of literature on the centre-right in post-communist Europe contrasts with the voluminous, detailed and often sophisticated comparative literatures on the left – usually focused on communist successor parties – and, to a lesser extent, the far right.[7] In this study, therefore, I seek to bring together the fragmented existing literature and to suggest in outline the basis of a workable definition of the right and centre-right in Central and Eastern Europe, which can both accommodate its undoubted diversity and provide a common framework for analysis. Broadly speaking, I will suggest that the centre-right in the region can be understood as neither an atavistic throwback to a pre-communist past nor a straightforward assimilation of Western identities and ideologies. Rather, it is a product of the politics of late communism, domestic reform, European integration and post-Cold War geo-political realignment, which has powerfully reshaped historical influences and foreign models.

Defining the Centre-Right

As Hanley and Szczerbiak suggest in the introduction to this collection, one of the greatest stumbling blocks is the lack of a clear, agreed operational definition of what the political 'right' is. Leaving aside definitions which view the right as a set of enduring philosophical tenets or inherent psychological predispositions,[8] the most coherent accounts of the development of left and right in Europe have been constructed by scholars working on parties and party systems. On the basis of comparative analysis of their historical and social origins, these stress the national and cultural specificity of parties (and party families) which make up competing blocs of 'right' and 'left' in any given party system.

Historically, the emergence of the political right in Western Europe and in North and South America can be associated with distinct property-owning classes, the defence of social institutions such as the Catholic Church and the rise of a bourgeois civil society linked to the development of capitalism. The same links can be identified in the re-emergence of the right in new or restored democracies such as West Germany, Italy and France after 1945 or Spain after 1975.[9] However, in Eastern and Central European countries the emergence of an organized political right after 1989 largely *preceded* the laying of social bases and the 'transition to capitalism', making class and clea-vage-based definitions problematic. Moreover, in one case – that of Poland – the right had a substantial working-class base, having largely emerged through the Solidarity movement.[10] As noted in the introduction to this collection, ana-lysts using a historical sociological approach, such as Kitschelt, have resolved this difficulty by re-conceptualizing 'cleavages' into terms of state–society relations derived from regime–opposition dynamics and patterns of socioeco-nomic modernization. However, whereas families of communist successor parties on the 'left' can be easily identified through organizational continuities with former ruling parties, parties of the 'right' pose considerable problems of definition and conceptualization (see Table 1).

Comparativists have identified three groups of parties in the region as 'right-wing':[11] (1) mainstream centre-right parties with ties to the West Euro-pean centre-right, which Vachudová terms the 'moderate right' and others subdivide into 'traditionalist conservatives' and 'liberal conservatives'; (2) broad populist–nationalist groupings, which played a dominant role in the politics of new nation-states, such as Slovakia and Croatia, in 1990s – termed the 'independence right' by Vachudová; and (3) former ruling commu-nist parties, with a 'chauvino-communist position', combining nationalism, social conservatism and economic populism – termed the 'communist right' by Vachudová and 'communist conservatives' by Chan (see Table 2).

Moreover, actors across the region have themselves generated their own national discourses of 'rightness', which represent a further set of definitions to be considered. In the Czech Republic, for example, the Civic Democratic Party (ODS) of the former prime minister (and recently elected president), Václav Klaus, not only defined itself in terms of economic liberalism and

TABLE 1
KEY CENTRE-RIGHT PARTIES IN SELECTED STATES IN CENTRAL AND
EASTERN EUROPE

Country	Parties	% vote (last national election)	Incumbent	International affiliation
Bulgaria	Union of Democratic Forces (SDS)	18.2 (2001)	No	EPP/EDU
Czech Republic	Civic Democratic Party (ODS)	24.5 (2002)	No	EPP/EDU
	'Coalition' between Freedom Union (US), Czechoslovak People's Party– Christian Democratic Union (KDU–ČSL)	14.23 (2002)	Yes	
Estonia	Union for the Republic–Res Publica (RP)	24.6 (2003)	Yes	EPP
	Estonian Reform Party (ER)	17.7 (2003)	Yes	ELDR
Hungary	Fidesz-Hungarian Civic Party (Fidesz–MPP)	41.1 (2002)	No	EPP/EDU
Latvia	New Era (JL)	23.9 (2002)	Yes	EPP
	Latvia's First Party (LPP)	9.6 (2002)	Yes	EPP
	People's Party (TP)	16.7 (2002)	No	EPP
	Fatherland and Freedom (TB/ LNKK)	5.4 (2002)	Yes	EPP
Lithuania	Homeland Union– Lithuanian Conservatives (TS)	8.6 (2000)	No	EDU
	Lithuanian Liberal Union (LLS)	17.3 (2000)	No	ELDR
	New Union–Social Liberals (NS)	9.6 (2000)	Yes	ELDR
Poland	Solidarity Electoral Action of the Right (AWSP)	5.6 (2001)	No	EPP
	Law and Justice (PiS)	9.5 (2001)	No	EPP
	League of Polish Families (LPR)	7.8 (2001)	No	?
	Civic Platform (PO)	12.7 (2001)	No	EPP
Romania	National Liberal Party (PNL)	6.9 (2000)	No	ELDR
	Romanian Democratic Convention 2000 (CD)	5.0 (2000)	No	?

(Continued)

TABLE 1   *CONTINUED*

Country	Parties	% vote (last national election)	Incumbent	International affiliation
Slovakia	Christian Democratic Movement of Slovakia (KDH)	8.3 (2002)	Yes	EDU/EPP
	Slovak Democratic and Christian Union (SDKU)	15.1 (2002)	Yes	EPP
	Alliance for the New Citizen (ANO)	8.0	Yes	?
Slovenia	Liberal Democracy of Slovenia (LDS)	36.3 (2000)	Yes	ELDR
	Slovenian People's Party (SLS)	9.6 (2000)	Yes	EDU/EPP
	Social Democratic Pty of Slovenia (SDS)	15.9 (2000)	No	EPP
	New Slovenia-Christian People's Party (NSI)	8.6 (2000)		EPP

Sources: P.G. Lewis, *Political Parties in Post-Communist Eastern Europe* (London: Routledge, 2000); <http://www.parties-and-elections.de/indexe2.html> <http://www.election world.org> (both accessed 1 June 2003).

anti-communism, but also saw itself as bringing the 'tried and tested' neo-liberal approaches of the Western right to a provincial society over-inclined towards collectivism.[12] In states such as Hungary and Poland, by contrast, 'right-wing' politics are understood at both mass and elite level in terms of Christian, conservative–national, national–populist or radical anti-communist positions, with free-market parties constituting as a distinct 'West of centre', liberal camp.[13]

Similar problems are posed by small agrarian parties, which were a feature of both the Hungarian and Polish party systems during the 1990s, and which recently made important electoral gains in Croatia, Estonia and Latvia. As the Scandinavian experience demonstrates, agrarian formations have the potential to evolve into ideologically distinct centre parties.[14] In Romania and Bulgaria the initial dominance after 1989 of 'chauvino-communist' former ruling parties – or groupings that emerged from them – saw the 'right' emerge as heterogeneous 'democratic' alliances of traditionalist nationalists, historic parties, liberals and radical anti-communists.[15] A similar pattern seems observable in Serbia. However, here the oppressive nature of the Milošević regime and a historic split between liberals and traditional nationalists made opposition alliances more unstable and thus lacking even a loose 'right-wing' identity.[16]

TABLE 2

TYPOLOGIES OF 'RIGHT-WING' PARTIES IN POST-COMMUNIST EUROPE

Vachudová Chan Lewis	'Communist Right' 'Communist-Conservatives' 'Post-Communist'	'Moderate Right' 'Traditional Conservatives' 'Conservative'	 'Liberal Conservatives' 'Liberal-Conservative'	'Independence Right' – 'Nationalist'
Hungary		Hungarian Democratic Forum (1990–94) Fidesz–Hungarian Civic Party*		None
Poland		Solidarity Election Action (1996–2001)		
Czech Republic			Civic Democratic Party (ODS)	
Slovakia				Movement for a Democratic Slovakia (HZDS)
Croatia				Croatian Democratic Union (HDZ)
Serbia	Serbian Socialist Party (SPS)			
Romania	Social Democracy of Romania (PSDR)		Romanian Democratic Convention (CDR)**	
Bulgaria	Bulgarian Socialist Party (BSP)		Union of Democratic Forces (SDS)**	
Russia	Communist Party of the Russian Federation (KPRF)			

*Categorized by Paul Lewis as 'liberal-conservative'.
**Lewis's categorization.

Sources: P.G. Lewis, *Political Parties in Post-Communist Eastern Europe* (London: Routledge, 2000); M. Vachudová, 'Right-Wing Parties and Political Outcomes in Eastern Europe', paper presented at the APSA annual meeting, San Francisco, 2001; K. Chan, 'Strands of Conservative Politics in Post-Communist Transition: Adapting to Europeanisation and Democratisation', in P.G. Lewis (ed.), *Party Development and Democratic Change in Post-Communist Europe* (London: Frank Cass, 2001), pp. 152–78.

Meanwhile, in new national states such as Slovakia and Croatia, despite the existence of strong nationalist, liberal and Christian forces, a self-identifying discourse of the right was largely absent from party politics in the 1990s. Instead, political competition was polarized around a single set of issues relating to national autonomy and national statehood and its stewardship by Vladimír Mečiar's Movement for Democratic Slovakia (HZDS) and Franjo Tudjman's Croatian Democratic Community (HDZ) – what Vachudová terms the 'independence right'. A similar pattern can be detected in the Baltic states, where, despite not enjoying the degree of dominance of HZDS or HDZ, conservative nationalists have tended to present themselves as champions of recovered national independence against a Russophone 'left'.[17]

Interestingly, however, since losing power in 1998 and 2000 to broad coalitions of parties with more conventional ideologies of left and right, both HZDS and HDZ have expressed a desire to reinvent themselves as Christian Democratic 'People's Parties' of the West European type.[18] However, Christian Democratic and liberal groupings in the opposition alliances that displaced them also claim to be on the centre-right and have links with centre-right groupings in Western Europe.[19] Moreover, as Zake's study of the neo-liberal People's Party (TP) in Latvia suggests,[20] new centre-right parties with more conventional programmatic appeals can make significant electoral breakthroughs, partially realigning such party systems away from ethnicity and issues of state building. Similar trends may be observable in the emergence of the liberal, business-oriented Alliance for the New Citizen (ANO) as a parliamentary force in Slovakia in 2002 and of the conservative NGO-cum-party *Res Publica* as Estonia's largest party in 2003.[21] However, the recent electoral breakthrough in Latvia by another technocratically led, pro-market party – 'New Era', led by former central bank president Einars Repse – emphasizes the instability of such party systems.[22]

A number of provisional conclusions emerge from this survey. First, it is clear that the 'right' is a culturally and historically contingent category that has rooted (or re-rooted) itself in the political discourse of many, but not all, post-communist societies. In the main, these societies appear to be those geographically and historically closest to core West European states. However, while local understandings of the political 'right' are important, serious comparative analysis clearly requires a more stable and elaborated framework. The identification by both Vachudová and Chan of such a variety of 'right-wing' forces is valuable in pointing to different patterns of post-communist development and the way nationalist and conservative discourses were appropriated by different forces in different contexts. However, in other respects it is confusing and unsatisfactory. 'Chauvino-communist' former ruling parties, for example, while clearly 'conservative' in reacting against change, fall most comfortably within the comparative study of communist successor parties.

Parties of the 'independence right' such as the Croatian HDZ and Slovak HDZ – despite the nostalgia of a radical nationalist fringe for wartime clerico-fascism – are regarded by most other scholars as simply populist or national-ist.[23] This reflects their inconsistency or indifference towards issues unrelated to state building and the possibility that their dominance may prove transitory, ultimately giving way to more conventional patterns of programmatic compe-tition. The most recognizable centre-right forces from a West European per-spective are the group of moderate conservative or liberal-conservative parties, all of which define themselves as (centre-) right formations and have been accepted into the main organizations of the European centre-right.[24]

As Vachudová notes, while their relationship with pre-communist right-wing traditions varies,[25] these parties have a common historical and organizational origin in opposition to communist regimes before 1989 or mobilization against them in 1989–90. They must, therefore, be understood as *essentially 'new' pol-itical forces, shaped by late communism and the subsequent politics of post-communist transformation*, rather than a simple throwback to the authoritarian conservatisms and integral nationalisms of the past. At the same time, however, contrary to the assumptions of some writers,[26] the liberal, neo-liberal, conserva-tive and neo-conservative identities and ideologies adopted by such forces are more than hasty borrowings from the West or diktats from international financial institutions.[27] Even where Western neo-liberal and neo-conservative ideologies were consciously imported, as in the cases of Poland and the Czech Republic, this was *already* being undertaken in 1970s by dissident and technocratic counter-elites – usually in response to the failure of reform communism or as a means of modernizing national political discourses.[28] Systematic underestimation of the role of domestic social and political forces in creating the Eastern and Central European centre-right, and consequently its broader legitimacy and appeal, is characteristic of much critical left-wing scholarship on the region.[29]

The need, in some cases, to consider liberal, social-liberal and agrarian parties as forces outside the Eastern and Central European centre-right appears a complicating factor, given that the defence of agricultural interests and economic liberalism are part of the broad centre-right in most West Euro-pean party systems. To some extent this problem is offset by the limited elec-toral support of such parties,[30] and the trend, over time, for them to become aligned with (or absorbed into) broader centre-right or centre-left blocs, Hungary being the clearest example of this tendency. However, we should also note the success of *new* centrist, liberal groupings in rapidly reoccupying the political space vacated by older, discredited liberal and neo-liberal groupings. Such newly ascendant liberal centrist parties include the Freedom Union (US) in the Czech Republic, which entered parliament in 1998, or the Civic Platform (PO) in Poland, which did so in 2001. Similarly, whereas in Hungary the Independent Smallholders (FKGP) have disappeared as an electoral force and been absorbed into the dominant centre-right grouping Fidesz, the unstable Polish party system now contains *two* agrarian parties: the Polish Peasants' Party (PSL) and the radical–populist protest party, Self-Defence.[31] This suggests that patterns of competition that separate the liberals and agrarians from the broader centre-right are more durable than individual parties themselves.[32] Underlying this, it can be argued, is a distinct pattern of Eastern and Central European party and party-system formation, in which centre-right parties, in the absence of a strong class base, lacks the broad appeal and integrative ability of their West European counterparts. In certain respects, this is comparable to the historic pattern of party formation in Scandinavia, where weak, sectorally and regionally divided bourgeoisies produced an array of weak conservative–liberal, agrarian and denominational parties, rather than a unified centre-right.[33]

A further issue of definition is that of delineating the centre-right from the extreme right. In West European party systems, although the nature of the extreme right is disputed, this distinction seems empirically and conceptually clear. Most West European centre-right parties draw on the historic cleavages identified by Lipset and Rokkan[34] and on the experience of post-1945 re-democratization. Extreme right, 'new populist' parties, by contrast, emerged only in the 1970s in response to cultural and social shifts in advanced capitalist societies.[35] It is, therefore, possible to define the extreme right in terms of a family of parties with its own distinct origins and characteristics.[36]

In post-communist East and Central Europe, it has been suggested, the distinction between the centre-right and the far right is conceptually considerably less clear. This reflects both the legacy of the integral nationalism, authoritarian conservatism and collaboration with fascism that defined the right historically in many states of the region,[37] and the fact that both centre-right and extreme right are products of post-1989 democratization. In many cases, however, it appears possible to make a clear *empirical* distinction, identifying the centre-right by its larger and broader electorate (generally in the range 20–45 per cent), its catch-all electoral appeal and status as a potential participant in government, and its membership of European groupings of mainstream conservative and Christian Democratic parties. However, in Poland, where the dominant centre-right grouping, Solidarity Election Action (AWS), collapsed as an electoral force in 2001, to be effectively replaced by number of new conservative and Christian parties with a more radical rhetoric of protest and medium-sized electorates of about ten per cent,[38] such empirical yardsticks seem difficult to apply. One possible conceptualization is to view the centre-right as *seeking to reconcile liberal–capitalist modernization with traditional moral values and specific local and national identities*, and the extreme right as seeking to mobilize a radical minority behind alternatives to such modernization.[39]

Ideologies of the East–Central European Centre-Right

Some have argued that the prominence of social-cultural divisions in the politics of both key post-communist states and more established Western democracies has subverted and voided older notions of 'left' and 'right' rooted in the class politics and distributional conflicts of the nineteenth and twentieth centuries.[40] Others have suggested for Central–East European states in particular that the constraints of globalization and conditionalities of European integration – or shared goals of post-communist modernization – have robbed ideology of any significance for practical policy making in the region, providing only an illusion of choice and alternation.[41] Such issues are beyond the scope of this study. What does seem certain, however, is that ideology plays an important role in both framing political action and giving cohesion and identity to political organizations. This is particularly the case, it may be argued, in periods of far-reaching social and political change, such as post-communist transformation, when structural determinants may be weaker, levels of uncertainty higher, and political identities less well defined. The ideologies of Eastern and Central Europe's new centre-right combine both historic discourses and newer ideas imported from Western contexts or developed locally during the post-communist transformation. These ideologies can broadly be broken down into three key strands: anti-communism, conservatism (including, for the purpose of this discussion, nationalism and populism) and liberalism (plus neo-liberalism).

Anti-communism is one of the few ideological tenets shared almost without exception across the diverse Eastern and Central European centre-right. Calls for radical de-communization – often linked to vaguer aspirations of speeding up reform through decisive action – were among the most characteristic demands of emergent right-wing forces in Eastern and Central Europe in the early 1990s. In many states in the region, de-communization was also a key issue promoting differentiation in broad anti-regime coalitions and prompting the foundation of political parties, including parties of the centre-right. Centre-right parties have subsequently been among the keenest advocates of lustration procedures intended to screen those holding high public office for past collaboration with the communist security apparatus (and in some cases to debar them).[42] At a deeper level, anti-communism has been used by many centre-right parties as an ideological device to depict left–right competition as a continuation of the struggle against communist one-party regimes that began before 1989. Right-wingers in Hungary, for example, speak of a 'thick' or 'permanent' transition,[43] while in the Czech Republic the same notion is expressed through the concept of a struggle against 'Third Ways' supposedly drawing on the heritage of 1960s reform communism. Centre-left opponents are thus viewed as continuing communist ideology in an attenuated form, ensuring the dominance of elites drawn from *nomenklatura* structures, or themselves personifying links with the communist past. At the same time, however, de-communization has been a divisive issue *within* the emergent centre-right in the region, given the conflicting imperatives of historical justice and broader socio-economic reform. Although in most cases traditional liberal or conservative agendas won over the demands of small, vocal groups of radical anti-communists, in at least one instance – that of the Union of Democratic Forces (SDS) in Bulgaria – the division proved crippling for much of the early 1990s.[44]

A further ideological fault-line is that between liberals – including both the established civic-minded intelligentsia and neo-liberals influenced by Western economics and public choice theory – and conservatives, usually committed to a moral order rooted in traditional discourse of the Nation (or the People) as a historic community. Most large, established centre-right parties in Western Europe combine these conflicting elements both in their ideologies and in the range of sub-groups and factions represented within them. As many observers have noted, however, there is often a tension between the two, especially at times of marked political and social change.[45] The relationship between liberal and conservative ideas – and liberal and conservative actors – can therefore be seen as highly significant for the consolidation and development of Eastern and Central Europe's centre-right. This is particularly the case given that, in a number of states in the region, there is a historic cleavage between liberal and conservative–national (national–populist) camps, which appears to have weakened non-socialist forces. In Poland, for example, the coalition government formed in 1997 between the liberal Freedom Union (UW) and the larger, conservative–national Solidarity Election Action (AWS) bloc proved fraught and collapsed in 2000, ultimately resulting in the electoral demise of both parties.[46] Similar, although less acute, tensions are at present emerging in Slovakia's governing centre-right coalition between the liberal, pro-business Alliance for the New Citizen (ANO) and the Christian Democratic Movement (KDH) over proposed changes to the country's abortion law.[47]

Nevertheless, such divisions, however historical or structural in origin, cannot be regarded as set in stone. As Hall notes, even where such cleavages *were* ultimately reflected in post-1989 party systems, under late communism there were often observable – if often abortive – attempts at intellectual *rapprochement* between liberals and conservative–nationalists (or national–populists). These usually entailed liberals rethinking their earlier rejection of the importance of historic questions relating to the nation.[48] This tendency can be seen to have resumed in the mid-1990s in *the growing nationalization of key liberal and neo-liberal forces* in the region. In Hungary, the disinte-gration of the Hungarian Democratic Forum (MDF), the main political vehicle of the national–populists and winner of the first post-communist multi-party elections, after a difficult period in office, created important opportunities for realignment. These opportunities were taken by the Federation of Young Democrats (Fidesz), under the leadership of Viktor Orbán. Originally an anti-communist youth party considered to be in the liberal camp, Fidesz successfully repositioned by Orbán in 1994–95 as a right-wing formation, combining aspects of its earlier liberalism and anti-communism with the traditional nation- and family-centred agenda of the national populists.[49] The resultant Fidesz–Hungarian Civic Party (Fidesz–MPP) is the dominant party of the Hungarian right, having successfully drawn in the Christian, rural and nationalist electorates of smaller parties, and, in electoral terms, is the strongest centre-right party in the region.

Similarly, in the Czech Republic, for much of the 1990s Václav Klaus's governing Civic Democratic Party (ODS) presented itself as a neo-liberal party inspired by the British and US New Right, albeit with a nationalist subtext stressing the congruence of the Czech character and the free market.[50] As such, it explicitly rejected traditional Czech political thought, including its conservative, liberal and nationalist strands, as provincial, collectivist, messanistic and irrelevant to contemporary society. However, after losing office in November 1997 and being outpolled by the centre-left in elections in 1998, the party – still under the leadership of Klaus – realigned itself, moving away from a stress on free markets towards a more nationalistic stance stressing the need to defend Czech national interests. This, in part, represented an intensification and elaboration of the party's Eurosceptic stance (see below), but was also notable for its revival of the nationalist paradigm, juxtaposing the interests of the Czech nation to those of Germany and the German-speaking world. This was made explicit by the party's resolute defence of the legal status of the 'Beneš Decrees' – post-war emergency measures expelling Czechoslovakia's 2.5 million ethnic German population and some ethnic Hungarians. Many Austrian and German politicians, as well as much of the Czech liberal intelligentsia, considered that the decrees should be repealed or modified before Czech entry into the EU. However, ODS dismissed such claims as a threat to Czech statehood. In their 2002 programme, the Civic Democrats also took up new, socially conservative themes such as the need to restrict immigration.[51]

The Czech case is interesting and potentially significant, because, unlike in Hungary, in the Czech lands there is no deep historical divide between a commitment to liberalism and a commitment to nationalism and 'national' values. There was apparently no strong electoral incentive for Klaus and his party to adopt a more traditionally nationalist inflection. Indeed, it might be argued that it even lost them support.[52] Many journalistic commentators have suggested that the revival of historic issues such as the Beneš Decrees by right-wing politicians in the Czech Republic, Germany, Austria and Hungary[53] marked a return to regional traditions of petty chauvinism and populist nationalism.[54] However, beyond the electoral opportunism of certain politicians and parties, they gave little explanation of why such a revival might be taking place. Others have identified the beginnings of a Central European form of 'alpine populism' seen in Northern Italy, Switzerland and Austria during 1990s, based the defence of small, provincial, relatively prosperous societies against migration from poorer neighbouring states.[55] However, 'alpine populists' such as Italy's Northern League or Austria's Freedom Party were protest parties, which successfully preyed upon established centre-right parties in long-standing clientelistic or cartel-like arrangements,[56] rather than key players in national party systems like the Czech ODS or Hungary's Fidesz.

The Challenge of Europeanization and Globalization

Many centre-right parties in Western Europe emerged on the basis of cleavages associated with classical socio-economic modernization and nation-state formation. Centre-right parties in post-communist Eastern and Central Europe have, by contrast, formed against a background of social, cultural and technological changes that can broadly be termed 'post-modernization', many of which call into question the importance of the nation-state.[57] Of these, globalization and the related process of European integration are by far the most significant.[58]

These processes not only aggravate historical sensitivities in a region where the formation of national states was historically belated, contested or incomplete, they also pose particular challenges to many parties of the centre-right in the region.[59] Although few centre-right formations are actively opposed to EU membership, early comparative research on party-based Euroscepticism has highlighted a tendency for them to be more Eurosceptic than their counterparts in Western Europe.[60] Many dislike the far-reaching transfer and restriction of national sovereignty required by EU membership; the bureaucratic centralization and likely power of large West European states (in particular, Germany) in an enlarged EU; the marginalization of local businesses and elites; and the erosion of national and local identities under the competitive pressures of the single market. Parties with strong free market commitments, such as the Czech Civic Democrats (ODS), have also argued that the EU is over-regulated and 'socialist' or 'collectivist' in its economic thinking. Beyond a loosely shared set of Eurosceptic concerns, however, centre-right parties in the region seem to have differing geo-political and European orientations, reflecting both ideological differences and older historical alignments. Both the Czech ODS and the Bulgarian ODS have tended to view themselves as conservative parties on British or US lines and are strongly Atlanticist. In the Czech case this may also reflect historic anxieties about German domination of the Central European region at the expense of Czech interests. By contrast, conservative-national parties, if they have a vision going beyond the preservation of national distinctness and independence, have closer affinities with Gaullism and German Christian Democracy. They are more suspicious of the US role in Europe and, notwithstanding reservations over European political integration, show a greater willingness to accept the Franco-German axis. In the case of Hungary's Fidesz, this again can be seen as continuing historic national alignments – in this case Hungarian co-operation with Austria and Germany. The war in Iraq threw these divisions into sharp relief. Conservative nationalist formations such as Fidesz–MPP in Hungary and the League of Polish Families (LPR) opposed both US–British intervention and own their governments' political, logistical and military support for it.[61] Liberal, anti-communist, centre-right groupings, by contrast – such as the Bulgaria's ODS and, with the notable exception of their former leader President Klaus, the Czech Civic Democrats (ODS) – firmly supported the Coalition and criticized their governments' stances on Iraq as lukewarm and half-hearted.

The Eclipse of the Post-Communist Centre-Right?

Already by the mid 1990s, some broad centre-right groupings such as the national–populist Hungarian Democratic Forum (MDF) and the Romanian Democratic Convention (CD) had experienced electoral and organizational disintegration.[62] The period 2001–2002 saw the electoral failure of centre-right parties in Poland, Hungary, the Czech Republic and Bulgaria. In the three Central European cases, social democratic parties outpolled their main centre-right rivals and formed centre-left coalitions with smaller agrarian or liberal parties;[63] in the fourth (Bulgaria), the 2001 elections saw both the incumbent Union of Democratic Forces (SDS) and the Bulgarian Socialists swept aside by the National Movement–Simeon II (NDSV), an ad hoc reform movement headed by Simeon Saxe-Coburg, the former king, who had spent the communist period living abroad as an exile. In two of these cases – Poland's AWS and Bulgaria's SDS – electoral defeat was also accompanied by partial or total party collapse. The re-election of Slovakia's centre-right coalition was an exception to this trend, although, as noted above, this may be explained as a continuation of the pattern of competition characteristic of some new national states in the region: broad coalitions mobilizing against a dominant nationalist party.

In all four states where the centre-right was defeated, far-reaching discussions are now under way about the nature and future of the right in the region. While in Poland the issue seems a case of the right seeking basic programmatic and organizational cohesion, elsewhere discussion has focused on *broadening* the centre-right's electoral appeal and acquiring a deeper level of social implantation – a strategy often depicted by its advocates as a move towards to the West European Christian Democratic model. In the wake of its election defeat, Hungary's Fidesz, for example, has sought to reinvent itself as 'civic movement from below', connected to sympathizers in local communities through a network of 'civic circles', which would be open to right-wing voters of small, weakened or defunct Christian, agrarian and extreme right parties. Accordingly, it has renamed itself Fidesz–Hungarian Civic Alliance (Fidesz–MPSZ) and wishes, according to its leader Viktor Orbán, to become a 'People's Party' on the West European Christian Democratic model.[64] Similar ideas have been circulating since at least the mid-1990s in the Czech Civic Democratic Party (ODS) and were most recently championed by the unsuccessful leadership contender, Petr Nečas.[65]

Although the importance of electoral cycles should not be underestimated, it may also be necessary to consider whether there are underlying factors behind the recent decline of the Eastern and Central European centre-right. It is possible, for example, that the origins of many centre-right parties as engines of regime change leave them vulnerable to ideological exhaustion and crises of party identity, as the fundamental institutional and political choices of post-communist transformation recede in importance. It may also be the case that the social structure of Eastern and Central European states – and, in particular, distributions of transition 'winners' and 'losers' – is now making it difficult to sustain strong centre-right parties in the region, leaving nationalist mobilization, Euroscepticism and anti-communism as generally unsuccessful default strategies. In this respect, the underlying parallel with the Scandinavian experience – a structurally weak and divided centre-right with a limited support base – may be instructive.[66] Alternatively, there may be broader factors at work affecting not only the mainstream right in the region, but also the far right which has suffered a parallel, but much more precipitate, decline.[67] Still more broadly, one could speculate that the problems of the Eastern and Central European centre-right may be part of a broader political malaise affecting the mainstream right across many Western democracies rooted in globalization, cultural shifts and the adaptive capacities of the centre-left.

Conclusions

The comparative study of centre-right parties in post-communist Eastern and Central Europe represents a significantly under-researched field, but one that poses considerable challenges to scholars. Notions of the 'right' have varied both historically and cross-nationally as well as in popular and academic usage, and they require considerable clarification. This study has suggested that the 'centre-right' in the region should be broadly understood as a set of parties seeking broad electoral support for programmes fusing elements of liberalism (including neo-liberalism) and varieties of conservatism, which balance the demands of post-communist social transformation, modernization and Europeanization with older historical identities and ideologies.

However, even comparative analysis of the centre-right thus understood faces significant methodological difficulties. In contrast to the limited range of post-communist successor party types, a diverse range of parties has emerged on the new Eastern and Central European centre-right. These, moreover, seem to lack any single, identifiable, common point of origin. Nevertheless, this study has argued, it is significant that the origins of most electorally successful centre-right parties in the region, such as, for example, Hungary's Fidesz, Bulgaria's SDS or the Czech ODS, seem to lie in opposition to and mobilization against communist regimes in the late 1980s and early 1990s. The success of parties across such a range of cases – and indeed the failure of centre-right in countries with such a rich history of anti-communist opposition as Poland – calls into question the explanatory power of the influential structural–historical literature on party-system formation. Rather than a stress on regime legacies and state–society relations, it appears that a renewed focus on the political strategies during late communism and the early transition period may be necessary in order to explain the varied success of the centre-right in the region.

In some states in Central and Eastern Europe, however, although discourses of the centre-right – and, indeed, attempts to build broad centre-right groupings – can be found, no consolidated centre-right appears to exist. This, taken in conjunction with recent electoral defeats of major centre-right formations in Poland, Hungary, the Czech Republic and Bulgaria, raises questions of whether the centre-right in the region may be facing a structural crisis. However, although there are a number of plausible hypotheses to account for such a decline – centre-right parties' origins as engines of regime change; the absence of pre-existing propertied classes or the challenge of Europeanization to nationalist and conservative ideologies – further research is clearly needed. An interesting and significant counter-trend to this apparent decline seems to be found in newly created national states, such as Estonia, Latvia, Slovakia and Croatia. Here the eclipse of broad nationalist movements, defined by issues of independence and statehood, is offering electoral opportunities to a range of new centre-right groupings with more conventional programmatic appeals.

ACKNOWLEDGEMENTS

Earlier versions of this contribution were presented to an informal seminar at the School of Slavonic and East European Studies, University College London, 20 June 2003, and published as a Sussex European Paper. I would like to thank all participants their comments and observations. I would also like to thank Professor George Schöpflin for his thoughtful written comments.

NOTES

1. J. Held (ed.), *Right-Wing Politics and Democracy in Eastern Europe* (Boulder, CO: East European Monographs, 1993).
2. T. Hellen, *Shaking Hands with the Past: The Origins of the Right in Central Europe* (Helsinki: The Finnish Academy of Sciences, 1996).
3. S. Roper, 'From Opposition to Government Coalition: Unity and Fragmentation in the Democratic Convention of Romania', *East European Quarterly*, Vol.31, No.4 (1998), pp.519–42; M. Wenzel, 'Solidarity and Akcja Wyborcza "Solidarność": An Attempt at Reviving the Legend', *Communist and Post-Communist Studies*, Vol.31, No.2 (1998), pp.139–56; S. Hanley, 'The New Right in the New Europe? Unravelling The Ideology of "Czech Thatcherism"', *Journal of Political Ideologies*, Vol.4, No.2 (1999), pp.163–89; D. Brown, 'The Development of the Union of Democratic Forces', paper presented at 'One Europe or Several?' programme workshop on Bulgaria, Lucas House, University of Birmingham Conference Park, 15 March 2001; C. Kiss, 'From Liberalism to Conservatism: The Federation of Young Democrats in Post-Communist Hungary', *East European Politics and Societies*, Vol.16, No.3 (2003), pp.739–63.
4. See K. Chan, 'Strands of Conservative Politics in Post-Communist Transition: Adapting to Europeanization and Democratization', in P.G. Lewis (ed.), *Party Development and Democratic Change in Post-Communist Europe* (London: Frank Cass, 2001), pp.152–78, and M. Vachudová, 'Right-Wing Parties and Political Outcomes in Eastern Europe', paper presented at the American Political Science Association annual meeting, San Francisco, 2001.
5. See for example, A. Innes, *Czechoslovakia: The Short Goodbye* (New Haven, CT: Yale University Press, 2001); M. Orenstein, *Out of the Red: Building Capitalism and Democracy in Postcommunist Europe* (Ann Arbor, MI: University of Michigan Press, 2002).
6. See for example, Alex Callinicos, *The Revenge of History: Marxism and the East European Revolutions* (Cambridge: Polity, 1991); P. Gowan, 'Eastern Europe, Western Power and Neo-Liberalism', *New Left Review*, No.21 (1996), pp.129–40; S. Saxonberg, *The Fall: A Comparative Study of the End of Communism in Czechoslovakia, East Germany, Hungary, and Poland* (Amsterdam: Harwood Academic Press, 2001), pp.387–95.
7. See, for example, A. Gryzmala-Busse, *Redeeming the Communist Past: The Transformation of Communist Parties in East Central Europe* (Cambridge and New York: Cambridge University Press, 2002), and A. Bozóki and J.T. Ishiyama (eds.), *The Communist Successor Parties of Central and Eastern Europe* (Armonk, NY: Sharpe, 2002). On the extreme right see for example P. Hockenos (ed.), *Free to Hate: The Rise of the Right in Post-Communist Eastern Europe* (London, Routledge, 1994); L. Cheles (ed.), *The Far Right in Western and Eastern Europe* (London: Longman, 1986); S. Ramet (ed.), *The Radical Right in Central and Eastern Europe Since 1989* (University Park, PA: Pennsylvania University Press, 1999); and M. Minkenberg, 'The Radical Right in Post-Communist Central and Eastern Europe: Comparative Observations and Interpretations', *East European Politics and Societies*, Vol.16, No.2 (2003), pp.335–62.
8. Such an approach is taken by most of the contributors to R. Eatwell and O'Sullivan (eds.), *The Nature of the Right: American and European Politics Since 1789* (London: Pinter, 1989).
9. F. Wilson (ed.), *The European Center-Right at the End of the Twentieth Century* (New York: St Martin's Press, 1998).
10. Wenzel.
11. This section refers primarily to the work of Chan, 'Strands of Conservative Politics'; Vachudová; P.G. Lewis, *Political Parties in Post-Communist Eastern Europe* (London: Routledge, 2000).
12. Hanley, 'New Right in the New Europe?'.
13. As Kitschelt notes, such patterns of competition to some extent resembled the threefold division between socialist, liberal and Catholic blocs in West European party systems such as those of

Holland and Belgium: H. Kitschelt, 'The Formation of Party Cleavages in Post-Communist Democracies: Theoretical Propositions', *Party Politics*, Vol.1, No.4 (1995), pp.447–72.

14. N. Sitter and A. Batory, 'Cleavages, Competition and Coalition Building: Agrarian Parties and the European Question in Western and Eastern Europe', *European Journal of Political Research*, Vol. 43, No. 4 (2004), pp.523–46.

15. V. Tismaneanu and G. Klingman, 'Romania's First Postcommunist Decade: From Iliescu to Iliescu', *East European Constitutional Review*, Vol.10, No.1 (2001); R. Peeva, 'Electing a Czar: The 2001 Elections and Bulgarian Democracy', *East European Constitutional Review*, Vol.10, No.4 (2001), available at <http://www.law.nyu.edu/eecr> (accessed 1 June 2003).

16. T. Garton Ash, *A History of the Present* (London: Penguin, 1999), pp.254–74.

17. I. Zake, 'The People's Party in Latvia: Neo-Liberalism and the New Politics of Independence', *Journal of Communist Studies and Transition Politics*, Vol.18., No.3 (2002), pp.9–31.

18. See S. Cvijetic, 'And What Now?', *Central Europe Review*, 17 January 2000, online at <http://www.ce-review.org> (accessed 15 May 2003); T. Haughton, 'HZDS: The Ideology, Organisation and Support Base of Slovakia's Most Successful Party', *Europe–Asia Studies*, Vol.53, No.5 (2001), pp.745–70; D. Hipkins, *Croatia: HDZ Confident of Revival*, Balkan Crisis Report, No.322, 8 March 2002, available at <http://www.iwpr.net> (accessed 15 May 2003); and *RFE/RL Newsline*, 22 and 23 April 2002, Part II.

19. Indeed, following the disappearance of its social-democratic component from the Slovak parliament in the 2002, many Czech and Slovak commentators now refer to Slovakia's current governing coalition of liberal, Christian Democratic, pro-business parties as 'right-wing'.

20. Zake.

21. See E. Mikkel, *Europe and the Estonian Parliamentary Election of March 2003*, Opposing Europe Research Network Election Briefing No.12, 2003, available at <http://www.sussex. ac.uk/Units/SEI/oern/ElectionBriefings/index.html>; K. Grunthal, 'Juhan Parts: From Political Watchdog to Estonia's Prime Minister', *Helsingin Sanomat* (Helsinki), on-line international edition, 15 April 2003.

22. L. Raubisko, 'Latvia: It's Out With the Old and In With the "New Era"', *Radio Liberty Feature*, 5 Oct. 2002, available at <http://www.rfrerl.org/nca/features/2002/10/07102002160412.asp> (accessed 15 May 2003).

23. See, for example, Lewis, *Political Parties*; C. Mudde, 'Another One Bites the Dust: Democracy and Extremism in Eastern Europe', *RFL/RFE Newsline*, 10 April 2000, available at <http://www.rferl.org/newsline/2002/04/5-not/not-100402.asp> (accessed 15 May 2003); C. Mudde, 'In the Name of the Peasantry, the Proletariat, and the People: Populisms in Eastern Europe', *East European Politics and Societies*, Vol.15, No.1 (2001), pp.33–53.

24. These parties also co-operate regionally and have in the past three years attended an annual conference of centre-right parties in Central and Eastern Europe; the last such conference took place on 27–29 September 2002 and adopted a common declaration. See <http://www.zahradil.cz/html/4.html>, accessed 10 Feb. 2004.

25. See Held.

26. For example, M. Dangerfield, 'Ideology and Czech Transformation: Neoliberal Rhetoric or Neoliberal Reality?', *East European Politics and Societies*, Vol.11, No.3 (1999), pp.436–67.

27. Callinicos; Gowan.

28. See J. Szacki, *Liberalism After Communism* (Budapest: CEU Press, 1995); Hanley, 'New Right in the New Europe?'; S. Shields, 'The "Charge of the Right Brigade": Transnational Social Forces and the Neoliberal Configuration of Poland's Transition', *New Political Economy*, Vol.8, No.2 (2003), pp.225–44; G. Eyal, *The Origins of Postcommunist Elites: From Prague Spring to Breakup of Czechoslovakia* (Minneapolis, MN and London: University of Minnesota Press, 2003).

29. Callinicos; Gowan; Saxonberg, pp.387–95; for a broader critique of neo-Marxist analyses of the decline and the fall of communism see N. Robinson, 'Marxism, Communism and Post-communism', in A. Gamble, D. Marsh and T. Tant (eds.), *Marxism and Social Science* (Basingstoke: Macmillan and Champaign, IL: University of Illinois Press, 1999), pp.302–19.

30. See K. Lang, 'Falling Down: The Decline of Liberalism', *Central Europe Review*, Vol.2, No.1 (8 September 2000), available at <http://www.ce-review.org/00/31/lang31.html> (accessed 15 May 2003); Sitter and Batory.

31. See B. Fowler, 'Notes on Recent Elections: The Parliamentary Elections in Hungary, April 2002', *Electoral Studies*, Vol.22, No.4 (2003), pp.799–807; A. Szczerbiak, 'Poland's Unexpected Political Earthquake: The September 2001 Parliamentary Election', *Journal of Communist Studies and Transition Politics*, Vol.18, No.3 (2002), pp.41–76; C. McManus-Czubinska, W.L. Miller, R. Markowski and J. Wasilewski, 'The New Polish "Right"?', *Journal of Communist Studies and Transition Politics*, Vol.19, No.2 (2003), pp.1–23.

32. See N. Sitter, 'When is a Party System? A Systems Perspective on the Development of Competitive Party Systems', *Central European Political Science Review*, Vol.3, No.1 (2002), pp.75–97.

33. See G. Luebbert, *Liberalism, Fascism, or Social Democracy: Social Classes and the Political Origins of Regimes in Interwar Europe* (Oxford: Oxford University Press, 1991); see also M.D. Hancock, 'Sweden's Nonsocialist Parties: What Difference Do They Make?', in Wilson, pp.171–98; L. Svasand, 'The Center Right Parties in Norwegian Politics: Between Reformist Labor and Radical Progress', in Wilson, pp.225–46.

34. S.M. Lipset and S. Rokkan (eds.), *Party Systems and Voter Alignments: Cross National Perspectives* (New York: Free Press, 1967).

35. See H. Betz, *Radical Right-Wing Populism in Western Europe* (Basingstoke: Macmillan, 1994); P Taggart, 'New Populist Parties in Western Europe', *West European Politics*, Vol.18, No.1 (1995), pp.34–51; H. Kitschelt and A. McCann, *The Radical Right: A Comparative Analysis* (Ann Arbor, MI: University of Michigan Press, 1997).

36. Mudde, 'Another One Bites the Dust'.

37. H. Rogger and E. Weber (eds.), *The European Right: A Historical Profile* (Berkeley, CA: University of California Press, 1966); H.J. Wolff and J.K. Hoensch, *Catholics, The State and the Radical Right 1919–1945* (Boulder, CO: Social Science Monographs, 1987); N. Blinkhorn (ed.), *Fascists and Conservatives: The Radical Right and the Establishment in Twentieth Century Europe* (London: Unwin Hyman, 2000).

38. See Szczerbiak; McManus-Czubińska et al.

39. This idea is implicit in M. Minkenberg, 'The Radical Right in Post-Communist Central and Eastern Europe: Comparative Observations and Interpretations', *East European Politics and Societies*, Vol.16, No.2 (2003), pp.335–62; see also G. Schöpflin, 'New-Old Hungary: A Contested Transformation', *East European Perspectives*, Vol.4, No.10 (2002), 15 May, available at <http://www.rferl.org/eepreport/2002/05/10–150502.html> (accessed 24 Jan. 2004).

40. For example, V. Cable, *The World's New Fissures* (London: Demos, 1993), or I. Christie, 'Three Visions of Politics Europe in the Millennial World', *OpenDemocracy.net*, 30 May 2002, at <http://www.opendemocracy.net/debates/article-3–55-386.jsp> (accessed 20 Jan. 2004). Fowler's discussion of the 'neo-liberalisation' of post-communist social democratic parties in Hungary and Poland in this collection provides a provocative illustration of this thesis.

41. For example, A. Innes, 'Party Competition in Post-communist Europe: The Great Electoral Lottery', *Comparative Politics*, Vol.35, No.1 (2002), pp.85–104.

42. See K. Williams, A. Szczerbiak and B. Fowler, *Explaining Lustration in Eastern Europe: A 'Post-Communist Politics' Approach*, Sussex European Institute Working Paper No.62, March 2003.

43. For an example of this perspective in its Hungarian variant by a Budapest-based British sympathizer of Fidesz, see J. Sunley, 'Old Ideas for New Elites: Hungary and the Politics of Permanent Transition', *OpenDemocracy.net*, 12 June 2002 (accessed 1 June 2003).

44. See S.M. Fish and R. Brooks, 'Bulgarian Democracy's Organizational Weapon', *East European Constitutional Review*, Vol.9, No.3 (2000), pp.63–70.

45. D. Edgar, 'The Free or the Good', in R. Levitas (ed.), *The Ideology of the New Right* (Cambridge: Polity Press, 1986), pp.55–79.

46. See Szczerbiak. As Wenzel notes, the fact that even Catholic-national groups in Poland were able to unite only on the basis of the symbolic identity of the Solidarity movement, rather than any forward-looking programmatic or ideology, indicates deeper problems.

47. *RFE/RL Newsline*, Part II, 25 and 29 April, 20 May 2003.
48. See R.A. Hall, 'Nationalism in Late Communist Eastern Europe: Comparing the Role of Diaspora Politics in Hungary and Serbia', Parts 1–3, *East European Perspectives*, Vol.5, Nos. 5, 7 and 9 (2003), 5 March, 2 April and 30 April 2003, available at <http://www.rferl.org/eepreport> (accessed 15 May 2003). This tendency may also have been obscured both by the ideological breadth of opposition initiatives and by the fact that many prominent liberal opposition intellectuals, such as Jacek Kuroń and Janos Kis, came to liberalism via reform communist or radical-left positions.
49. Kiss; I am grateful to Brigid Fowler for numerous helpful discussions concerning some of these points.
50. See K. Williams, 'National Myths in the New Czech Liberalism', in G. Hosking and G. Schöpflin (eds.), *Myths and Nationhood* (London: Hurst, 1997), pp.132–40; Hanley, 'New Right in the New Europe?'.
51. S. Hanley, 'Europe and the Czech Parliamentary Elections of June 2002', Opposing Europe Research Network Election Briefing No.5, July 2002, available at <http://www.sussex.ac.uk/Units/SEI/oern/ElectionBriefings/index.html> (accessed 1 Aug. 2003).
52. Ibid.
53. Orbán and Fidesz supported calls for the cancellation of the decrees.
54. For example, J. Rupnik, 'The Other Central Europe', *East European Constitutional Review*, Vol.11, No.1–2 (Winter–Spring 2002), available at <http://www.law.nyu.edu/eecrvol111-num1–2/special/rupnik.html>, and J. Pehe, 'Back to Instability in Prague', *Prague Post*, 27 March, online edition.
55. See M. Perrault and I. Hall, 'The Re-Austrianisation of Central Europe? Assessing the Potential of the "New" Far Right after Haider', *Central Europe Review*, 1 April 2000, available at <http://www.ce-review.org/00/13/essay13.html> (accessed 1 June 2003); Vachudová.
56. Betz; Taggart.
57. See R. Inglehart, *Modernization and Postmodernization: Cultural, Economic, and Political Change in 43 Societies* (Princeton, NJ: Princeton University Press, 1997); A. Giddens, *Runaway World: How Globalisation is Reshaping Our Lives* (London: Profile, 2002).
58. See A. Bieler, *Globalisation and Enlargement of the European Union: Austrian and Swedish Social Forces in the Struggle Over Membership*, Warwick Studies in Globalisation (London: Routledge, 2000).
59. However, as Zake suggests, particularly in small states with open economies, globalization and Europeanization can open opportunities for new parties of the right or centre-right, by creating new social constitutencies with an interest-maximizing integration into the global economy.
60. P. Taggart and A. Szczerbiak, 'Contemporary Euroscepticism in the Party Systems of the European Union Candidate States of Central and Eastern Europe', *European Journal of Political Research*, Vol.43, No.1 (2004), pp.1–27; see also P. Kopecký and C. Mudde, 'The Two Sides of Euroscepticism: Party Positions on European Integration in East Central Europe', *European Union Politics*, Vol.3, No.3 (2002), pp.297–326.
61. *RFE/RL Newsline*, Part II, 21 and 24 March and 6 May 2003.
62. A. Mungiu-Pippidi and S. Ionita 'Interpreting an Electoral Setback: Romania 2000', *East European Constitutional Review*, Vol.10, No.1 (2001), at <http://www.law.nyu.edu/eecr/vol10num1/features/interpreting.html> (accessed 12 June 2004).
63. Szcerbiak; Hanley, 'Europe and the Czech Parliamentary Elections'; Fowler.
64. 'Fidesz Facelift Aims to Broaden Appeal', *Budapest Sun*, 6 Feb. 2003, and *RFE/RL Newsline*, Part II, 7 Feb., 15 and 24 April and 19 May 2003.
65. P. Nečas, 'Základní teze k budoucímu směřování ODS', 2 December 2002, available at <http://www.ods.cz> (accessed 15 May 2003).
66. Given the pressures of Europeanization and globalization, however, it seems unlikely that centre-left governments in the region will have the resources or the opportunities to pursue projects of national welfare capitalism.
67. Mudde, 'Another One Bites the Dust'.

Blue Velvet: The Rise and Decline of the New Czech Right

SEÁN HANLEY

Introduction

This article seeks to give an analytical overview of the origins, development and comparative success of the Czech centre-right since 1989. It will focus principally on the most successful party of the Czech right, the Civic Democratic Party (ODS) of the former Czech prime minister (and current president), Václav Klaus. However, it will also discuss the fortunes of a number of smaller Christian Democratic, liberal and anti-communist groupings, insofar as they have, with varying degrees of success, sought to provide right-wing alternatives to Klaus's party. In comparative terms, the article will suggest, the Czech centre-right represents an intermediate case. Although in Klaus's ODS, the Czech centre-right has been represented from an early stage by a large, stable and well-institutionalized party, avoiding the fragmentation and instability of the Polish right, it has failed to achieve the degree of ideological and organizational concentration seen in Hungary. Indeed, since the mid-1990s, the Czech right has become increasingly divided and has in successive general elections since 1996 proved unable to withstand the electoral challenge of the Czech Social Democrats (ČSSD).

After discussing the evolution and success of Czech centre-right parties between 1991 and 2002, the article reviews a number of factors commonly used to explain party and party-system formation in the region as they relate to the Czech centre-right. These include both structural-historical explanations and 'political' factors such as macro-institutional design, strategies of party formation in the immediate post-transition period, patterns of party institutionalization, charismatic leadership and ideological construction. It will argue that both the early success and subsequent decline of the Czech right are rooted in a single set of circumstances, which distinguish the Czech Republic from the other cases studied in this collection. Key factors among these were the early institutionalization of a dominant party of the mainstream right and the right's rapid and successful adoption of the mantle of technocratic, market-led modernization.

The Rise and Decline of the Czech Right

The Czech 'New Right'

The first notable party of the right founded in post-communist Czechoslovakia was the Civic Democratic Alliance (ODA), created on 17 December 1989 by a group of neo-conservative dissidents and free-market economists. However, the Alliance's lack of resources, its theoretical preoccupations and its immediate absorption into the broad Civic Forum movement, which oversaw Czechoslovakia's transition to democracy in 1989–90, limited its impact. Nevertheless, through its foundation and subsequent sponsorship of the Inter-parliamentary Club of the Democratic Right (MKDP) within Civic Forum, it served to define the emergent Czech 'democratic right' in terms of Western-oriented, pro-market conservatism, whose primary goal was the dismantling of communism and the enactment of social and economic transformation.

The principal and best-known party of the centre-right in the Czech Republic is the Civic Democratic Party (ODS), formed in early 1991 on the basis of the free-market, anti-communist right wing of a disintegrating Civic Forum. ODS is closely identified with its charismatic founder, the former Czechoslovak finance minister (1990–92) and former Czech prime minister (1992–97), Václav Klaus, who led the party from its foundation until December 2002, when he stood down to launch his successful bid for the Czech presidency. Like its smaller precursor, Klaus's party identified itself as a Western-style conservative party defined by issues of post-communist transformation. In the early and mid-1990s the ODS was the dominant force in Czech politics and the linchpin of the 1992–97 centre-right coalition governments, which negotiated the division of Czechoslovakia in late 1992 and implemented many key policies of post-communist transformation in the Czech Republic. Its smaller coalition partners were the Civic Democratic Alliance (ODA) and the Christian Democratic Union-Czechoslovak People's Party (KDU-ČSL). The People's Party had existed as a 'satellite' party under communism, but its origins dated to the nineteenth century. Drawing on historic bastions of support in rural Catholic regions of South Moravia and East Bohemia, KDU-ČSL was the only historic party other than the communists to gain representation independently in the Czech and Czechoslovak parliaments after 1989 (see Table 1). However, its broader appeal was initially weakened by its confessional character and perceived collaboration with the old regime.[1]

The Decline of the Czech Centre-Right

By the mid-1990s it had become evident that, rather than producing the post-communist economic miracle some had expected, the policies of the Klaus government had created an under-regulated, under-capitalized, inefficient private sector, dominated by politically connected, rent-seeking groups.

TABLE 1
ELECTION RESULTS TO LOWER HOUSE OF CZECH PARLIAMENT, 1992–2002

Party	1992 % of vote	Seats	1996 % of vote	Seats	1998 % of vote	Seats	2002 % of vote	Seats
Civic Democratic Party (ODS)*	29.73	76	29.62	68	27.74	63	24.47	58
'Coalition'	—	—	—	—	—	—	14.27	31
Freedom Union (US)	—	—	—	—	8.60	19	—	(9)
Christian Democratic Union-Czechoslovak People's Party (KDU-ČSL)	6.28	15	8.08	18	9.00	20	—	(22)
Civic Democratic Alliance (ODA)	5.93	14	6.36	13	—	—	—	—
Czech Social Democratic Party (ČSSD)	6.54	16	26.44	61	32.32	74	30.20	70
Communist Party of Bohemia and Moravia (KSČM)**	14.04	35	10.33	22	11.03	24	18.51	41
Association for the Republic-Republican Party of Czechoslovakia (SPR-RSČ)	5.98	14	8.01	18	—	—	—	—
Society For Moravia and Silesia-Movement for Self Governing Democracy (HSD-SMS)	5.87	14	—	—	—	—	—	—
Liberal Social Union (LSU)	6.52	16	—	—	—	—	—	—

Notes: Results show parliamentary parties only. Centre-right parties italicised. Total seats = 200.
    *Joint list with Christian Democratic Party (KDS) in 1996.
    **Left Bloc coalition in 1992.

Source: <http://www.volby.cz>.

The resultant economic malaise added to the momentum of the Czech Social Democratic Party (ČSSD), which emerged as the principal party of the Czech centre-left following the failure of the Czech communist successor party, the Communist Party of Bohemia and Moravia (KSČM), to adopt a reformist course in 1993. The Czech Republic's economic problems also aggravated relations between Klaus's party and its coalition partners, both of which developed new programmatic positions critical of ODS. Whilst the Christian Democrats stressed their commitment to a 'social market', the Civic Democratic Alliance called for greater reliance on market forces to transcend the semi-private, semi-public 'bank socialism' of the Klaus era.

Such conflicts intensified when in elections held in June 1996, against most expectations, the centre-right coalition narrowly failed to retain its parliamentary majority, continuing as a minority administration 'tolerated' by the opposition Social Democrats. In November 1997 the incipient crisis facing the Czech centre-right was brought to a head by a party-financing scandal in ODS that led to the collapse of the Klaus government. Klaus's alleged complicity in the scandal prompted his coalition partners to withdraw from the government and caused a split in ODS itself, when senior figures in the party called his integrity and political judgement into question. Similar irregularities concerning anonymous donations were then uncovered in the smaller Civic Democratic Alliance, igniting tensions between neo-conservative former dissidents and liberal pragmatists in the Alliance, which saw it rapidly disintegrate as a political force.[2] Factional conflict also broke out in Klaus's Civic Democratic Party (ODS), but proved less destructive. At a special party congress in Poděbrady in December 1997, the former prime minister – who claimed to have been unaware of the irregularities – successfully mobilized grassroots support to resist (by a decisive majority) pressure for his resignation.

Klaus's defeated opponents, who included a significant section of ODS's parliamentary and party elite, left to found a new party, the Freedom Union (US), in February 1998. In early parliamentary elections in June 1998, despite recovering much apparently lost support, Klaus's ODS was outpolled by the Social Democrats, who became for the first time the largest Czech party. Although centre-right parties of the outgoing coalition regained a theoretical parliamentary majority, such were the tensions between ODS and its former allies that Klaus unexpectedly opted to allow a minority Social Democratic government under Miloš Zeman to take office, on the basis of a written pact, the 'Opposition Agreement'. After losing office, Klaus's party attempted to realign itself by combining neo-liberal demands with conservative and nationalist themes, such as defending national interests against the EU, restricting immigration and resisting German demands to revise the legal status of the 'Beneš Decrees' expelling Czechoslovakia's ethnic German population in 1945–46.[3] The Christian Democrats and Freedom Union responded to the new political situation by founding a new electoral alliance, the Quad-Coalition (4K), with the much diminished Civic Democratic Alliance and the small Democratic Union (DEU) party, which identified itself as pro-European and committed to completing unfinished reforms.

Despite growing public dissatisfaction with its cartel-like character, the 'Opposition Agreement' endured until scheduled parliamentary elections in June 2002. These were won by the Social Democrats under a new leader, Vladimír Špidla, who subsequently became prime minister. Špidla abandoned co-operation with ODS to work with the Freedom Union and the Christian Democrats, who became junior partners in a coalition government with a narrow parliamentary majority, on the basis of a shared opposition to the euroscepticism of ODS.

The 2002 election results seemed to mark the failure of ODS's post-1997 realignment. Internal recriminations focused on Klaus, whom many powerful regional ODS organizations had come to consider an electoral liability rather than an asset. In October 2002 Klaus announced that he would not stand for re-election as ODS chairman at the party's December 2002 congress, ostensibly to facilitate his campaign for the Czech presidency due to be vacated Václav Havel in February 2003. The election of Klaus as president by a joint session of the Czech parliament in February 2003 with the support of Communist deputies – attracted by his resolute defence of the Beneš Decrees and promise to normalize relations with their party – provided a further political surprise. Some argued, however, that the presidential election result was more a personal triumph for Klaus and his informal team of advisers than a victory for his party or the broader centre-right.[4] Klaus's successor as ODS leader, Senator Miroslav Topolánek, a pragmatic politician with a regional power base in the industrial city of Ostrava, seemed to lack both personal authority and a clear political vision, leading to suggestions that Klaus's party might simply become a coalition of local politicians and business interests.[5] As even sympathetic observers conceded, after the 2002 election, the Civic Democrats appeared ideologically and politically disunited and uncertain of their future role in Czech politics.[6] Despite being in government, both the Christian Democrats and Freedom Union (US) also experienced difficulties. As well as dissolving their electoral alliance, both parties suffered internal splits and changes of leadership related to their collaboration with the Social Democrats.[7] Recent polling has consistently suggested that the Freedom Union's support has fallen below the level necessary to re-enter parliament.[8]

Assessing the Success of the Czech Right

Overall, the success of the Czech centre-right appears to represent an intermediate case between those of equivalent formations in neighbouring Poland and Hungary. Despite two electoral defeats and one major internal party crisis, the Civic Democratic Party (ODS) has avoided the organizational and electoral fragmentation and collapse of the centre-right in Poland. However, equally it has failed to gain the levels of support or concentration of the centre-right achieved by Hungary's Fidesz through alliance building and the absorption of smaller organizations. Although in 1996 Klaus's party absorbed the tiny ex-dissident Christian Democratic Party (KDS) and elements of the influential anti-communist grouping, the Club of Committed Independents (KAN),[9] it failed to take in more significant groupings, even those ideologically close to it such as the Civic Democratic Alliance (ODA).

As in Poland, an ideological and cultural division between neo-liberals and conservatives has represented a barrier to encompassing right-wing unity, although in the Czech case it is the neo-liberal right that is the dominant partner and the conservative Christian Democrats the minor player. Perhaps more significantly, ODS also failed, it can be argued, to maintain the broad alliance between neo-liberals and anti-communists (discussed below) that underpinned it at its foundation. As early as 1994, radical anti-communists who had previously been supportive of Klaus founded the Democratic Union (DEU), which polled three per cent in the 1996 elections, to campaign for a more 'moral' approach to transformation showing greater sensitivity to issues of historical justice. In the case of the Civic Democratic Alliance (ODA), despite merger discussions and informal understandings with Klaus's ODS in 1991 and 1992 – and, reportedly, a renewed offer to members of the ODA elite in 1996 – alliance building was obstructed by policy disagreements, failure to agree merger terms and Klaus's dismissal of small, elite-based groupings as unimportant.[10] Divisions among high-ranking ODS members in 1997–98 over the direction and management of the party led to a significant split and the foundation the Freedom Union (US), which rapidly took up the role played by the disintegrating Civic Democratic Alliance as spokesman for a less statist brand of centre-right liberalism. As recently as 2002, the European Democrats (ED), a grouping founded by the former Civic Democrat Mayor of Prague, Jan Kasl, broke away from the party and successfully contested local elections.[11] In purely political terms, despite the departure of Klaus and considerable leadership change within the Freedom Union, the participation of smaller centre-right parties in the current coalition government – itself a legacy of the divisions generated by the break-up of the Klaus government – further rules out initiatives at promoting centre-right co-operation.

Longer-term electoral trends also appear unfavourable for the Czech centre-right. As Table 2 indicates, ODS's support has declined in every parlia-

TABLE 2

VOTES AND SEATS WON BY PARTIES OF THE RIGHT IN ELECTIONS TO THE LOWER HOUSE OF THE CZECH PARLIAMENT 1992–2002

	1992 %	No. of seats	1996 %	No. of seats	1998 %	No. of seats	2002 %	No. of seats
Civic Democratic Party (ODS)	29.93	76	29.62	68	27.74	63	24.57	58
Neo-liberal parties (ODS + ODA + US)	35.36	90	35.98	81	36.36	82	n/a*	n/a*
Centre-right (Neo- liberal parties + Christian Democrats)	41.84	105	44.06	99	45.34	102	38.74	89
All right-wing parties (centre-right + anti-communist and far right*)	50.52	119	54.87	117	49.24	102	40.48	89

*Freedom Union ran a joint list with Christian Democrats.
**Votes for the Republicans (SPR-RSČ), Club of Committed Independents (KAN) and Democratic Union (DEU).

Source: <http://www.volby.cz>.

mentary elections to the lower house of the Czech parliament since 1992 from a peak of 29.62 per cent in 1992 to 24.57 per cent in 2002.[12] Moreover, calculation of the combined votes and seats won by liberal free-market parties suggests that, until 1998, this bloc's support remained significant, but static at about 35 per cent of the electorate. A similarly stable picture emerges for the broad Czech centre-right, including both liberal groupings and the Christian Democrats, which, with aggregate support of more than 40 per cent between 1992 and 1998, represented the minimum winning coalition capable of generating a parliamentary majority. However, leaving aside their well-known problems of inter-party co-operation, the 2002 election saw a sharp decline in the combined vote of centre-right parties that would have left them far short of a parliamentary majority. Given the absence of shared intellectual milieux and the pronounced economic populism of the Czech far right, in the Czech Republic it is perhaps not realistic to think in terms of a single bloc of 'right wing' parties extending from the fringe to the mainstream as in Hungary.[13] Nevertheless, as Table 2 indicates, the parallel decline of the Czech extreme right as an electoral force since 1998 would render even a hypothetical strategy of right-wing inclusion of the type pursued by Fidesz irrelevant in a Czech context.

However, despite the decline in electoral fortunes and loss of national office, the key parties of the Czech centre-right remain stable and well established. The Civic Democrats are well represented in local and regional government and play a key role in governing large municipalities such as Prague and Brno and regional authorities elected for the first time in 2000, where the ODS holds a majority of the governorships (*hejtmanství*). This reflects the party's success in building and maintaining a national organizational network with a presence in most major population centres and a stable national membership of approximately 20,000.[14] The Christian Democrats, too, have a dense local organizational network and, particularly in regions of traditional support, are well established in communal and municipal politics.[15]

Explaining the Czech Right

The Historical Weakness of the Czech Right

In many ways, the Czech lands were an unlikely setting for the emergence of a strong centre-right. In contrast to Hungary and Poland, where the post-1989 right was able to draw on powerful traditions of populism, conservative nationalism and political Catholicism dating back to the nineteenth century, 'right wing' forces in the Czech lands were historically weak and divided. Czech party development before 1938 broadly conformed to the pattern of cleavage-based party formation seen in Western Europe, albeit in a way strongly crosscut by the struggle for Czech national self-determination.[16] However, the social forces that formed the bases of the traditional right in many European countries, such as conservative aristocratic landowners or the Catholic Church, were politically weak or absent in the Czech case.[17] Political forces that might have coalesced into a broad conservative or liberal Czech 'right wing' were impeded from doing so both by the prominence of the 'National Question' in Czech politics and by the framing of a 'progressive' Czech national identity by the dominant nationalist discourse. Before 1918 conservative land-owning and liberal middle-class elites therefore tended to found parties as 'national' formations, which by the late nineteenth century were easily pushed aside by.the rise of mass confessional, class- and interest-based parties.[18]

The 'right wing' of the historic Czech party system inherited by Czechoslovakia in 1918 was both divided between an array of nationalist, Catholic and agrarian parties and disadvantaged by the progressive and left-liberal bias of Czechoslovakia's founding 'state idea'. To some extent, this pattern of party system development paralleled that in Scandinavia.[19] However, the presence within the new state of disaffected national minorities meant that governing coalitions in interwar Czechoslovakia, although shifting in ideological composition, tended to oppose 'state-forming', Czech-based parties to parties of the German and Slovak minorities, rather than blocs of left or right.

After the collapse of democratic inter-war Czechoslovakia following the 1938 Munich Agreement, some figures from the inter-war 'right' attempted to create an authoritarian, pro-German Czech corporate state through the creation of a Party of National Unity (SNJ),[20] further weakening and discrediting the historical right. As elsewhere in Europe, the perceived collaboration of traditional right-wing parties in the 'Second Republic' (1938–39) and the Nazi-controlled Protectorate of Bohemia and Moravia (1939–45) prompted the Czech electorate to swing markedly to the left after 1945. Moreover, even in the relatively democratic post-war conditions before the communist takeover in February 1948, two of the three historic 'right-wing' parties – National Democracy and the Agrarians – were banned for alleged collaboration. After 1948 official communist historiography assimilated the historic Czech 'right' to fascism and reactionary foreign rule. After the collapse of the Prague Spring reform movement in 1968–69 official media extended the label 'right wing' to proponents of radical reform and dissident critics of regime.

Regime Legacies and Historical Pathways

At the elite level, Czech political debates are often dominated by crosscutting issues such as civil society, national identity and European integration. Nevertheless, at the party-system level there is overwhelming evidence that left–right party competition has since its inception in the early 1990s been predominantly structured by divisions over the role of the state and the market.[21] This has been underpinned by growing correlation between social class and party choice. Although parties on the Czech centre-right and centre-left draw support from a range of social groups, there has been a clear tendency for better-educated, more urban and more prosperous groups of 'transition winners' to support the centre-right, and 'losers' the left and centre-left.[22] Kitschelt and his collaborators see such patterns of left–right competition in the Czech Republic as conditioned by the repressive, reform-averse nature of the 'bureaucratic-authoritarian' version of communism in Czechoslovakia. This in turn is seen as a product of relatively high levels of pre-communist socio-economic modernity in the Czech lands, which, it is argued, furnished the communist regime with both an effective state apparatus and mass support from a sizeable and well-organized working class. Left–right division after 1989, it is argued, thus centred on distributive issues, rather than moral or social issues, producing a free market, liberal-conservative centre-right, rather than a national-populist bloc.

However, for all its strengths such broad structural-historical analysis does little to account for the *strength* of the Czech right after 1989, the nature of its institutionalization or *changing* patterns of inter-party competition and co-operation, which seem difficult to reduce to regime legacies. Moreover, even within an explanatory framework of regime legacies, as Fowler suggests elsewhere in this issue, it may be necessary to *note how such legacies were transmitted* through the structural location and intellectual discussions of counter-elites under late communism. Although conscious of the Czech lands' democratic heritage, the dissident movement that emerged in the 1970s developed an innovative, philosophically laden discourse of human rights, 'civicness' and anti-politics, sometimes overlapping with West European ideological models as points of reference, rather than seeking to build on pre-communist intellectual tradition. Indeed, it tended to be critical not only of communism – including the abortive reform era of the 'Prague Spring' – but also of historic Czech nationalism, which had ultimately been appropriated by the Left. Paradoxically, the 'transfer' of the Sudeten Germans in 1945–46, the subject of much *samizdat* criticism and reassessment,[23] in removing the historic focus for right-wing Czech nationalism further undermined any prospect of its intellectual revival. Thus, despite isolated attempts by some dissident intellectuals to re-evaluate Austrophile Catholic conservatism and the National Democrat tradition of the 1920s,[24] emergent 'right-wing' counter-elites chose largely to draw their inspiration from Anglo-American neo-liberalism and neo-conservatism. The informal dissident grouping around Pavel Bratinka and Daniel Kroupa, for example, established contacts with leading Western (neo-)conservative intellectuals in the 1980s and subsequently crystallized into a right-wing 'civic current' within the Movement for Civil Liberties (HOS) formed in 1987 by leading figures within Charter 77.[25]

An equally significant counter-elite can be found in the generation of younger neo-liberal technocrats, who emerged on the margins of the 'Prague Spring'.[26] Rather than being co-opted into the reformist wing of the regime or marginalized in opposition milieux strongly defined by historical nationalism, as in Hungary and Poland, under Czechoslovakia's repressive post-1968 'normalization' this group formed part of an outwardly uncommitted 'grey zone' between official power structures and independent political opposition. The presence of cohesive counter-elite groups as a product of the failure of the Prague Spring and the 'normalization' regime,[27] rather than the strength of opposition per se or longer term legacies of historical modernity, created the potential for the emergence of a Czech New Right (but did not guarantee that it would take place). This right was to be 'new' both in the sense of importing Anglo-American New Right ideology and in seeking to make a conscious break with historical Czech political traditions, including those of the defunct historic Right.

The Right as Vehicle for Technocratic Modernization

A further mediated 'legacy' specific to the Czech Republic was the centre-right's inclination and ability to project itself as an agent of political professionalism and technocratic modernization. The literature on political parties in Eastern and Central Europe has often explained the renewed political appeal of reformed successor parties in states such as Hungary and Poland as the result of their donning the mantle of professionalism and technocratic efficiency.[28] As Fowler observes in this collection, in the post-communist context, such commitments amount in practice to the 'neo-liberalization' of these parties. However, there has been relatively little consideration of such factors in relation to the centre-right.[29] In the Czech case, in view of the failure of the old regime to co-opt technocrats who might furnish the basis of reformed, pro-market successor party, and given the absence of a conservative-national right seeking to frame regime change as a return to traditional moral and national values, it was the right that first underwent 'neo-liberalization', inventing (or re-inventing) itself as the agent of socio-economic modernization and transformation.

A pronounced clash between the political and organizational culture of neo-liberal technocrats and former dissidents was evident from the earlier days of Civic Forum.[30] A stress on political professionalism and businesslike efficiency originated as a reaction against the ethos of non-bureaucratic, non-professional, informal civic participation prevalent in Civic Forum. Petr Havlík, the first chief secretary of the ODS's head office, promised members that the party would 'remove all irrationalities and revolutionary habits and gradually establish a good system of a professional standard', describing ODS as 'an enterprise [*podník*] on a green-field site. . . . our shareholders are our members'.[31] This extended to a broader conception of the party as being primarily an efficient coordination device linking people – the political elite and rank-and-file activists and voters – who shared common goals and interests.[32] This end was the transformation of Czech society, which as the 1992 ODS programme noted was 'beyond individuals, . . . it requires the institutionally based co-operation of people with common interests and a similar way of thinking'.[33]

There is an extensive literature on economic and social transformation in the Czech Republic in the 1990s. Much of it highlights the limitations, contradictions and unintended consequences of the coupon-based privatization programme of the 1992–97 Klaus governments and, in particular, its failure to create effective ownership structures. Other writers have noted the Klaus administration's neglect of legal and regulatory frameworks and its failure to reform public administration. Others have contrasted ODS's strident neo-liberal rhetoric with the reality of strong state influence in the economy, an extensive welfare state, and continued regulation of rents and utility prices. Diverse explanations for such uneven policy performance have been advanced. Some cite ideological belief in market forces,[34] submerged nationalism,[35] and calculations of electoral self-interest on the part of Klaus and his party.[36] Others have highlighted the constraining legacies of a social liberal compromise forged by the 1990–92 government, led by Civic Forum; the blocking of policy learning as a consequence of stable, majority government;[37] or the need to utilize pre-existing managerial networks.[38] Such debates are beyond the scope of this study. Nevertheless, what does emerge clearly is that early dominance of Klaus's Civic Democrats was closely linked with their perceived ability to act as the only credible vehicle for successful post-communist transformation. This dominance was undercut by the gradual accumulation of policy failures, and by the re-composition of the Czech centre-left and its formulation from the mid-1990s of a credible transformation project of its own, sharing the same broad goals of modernization and Europeanization.[39]

Macro-Institutional Factors

Electoral Systems and Strategies for Party System Redesign

Although writers stressing regime legacies dispute its importance,[40] institutional design – and, in particular, the choice of electoral system – is widely considered a crucial influence on the formation of parties and party systems in new democracies. Since the fall of communism, parliamentary elections to the lower house of the Czech parliament have used proportional representation based on closed party lists, large multi-member electoral districts and a five per cent threshold for representation.[41] However, the electoral system appears to have only a limited bearing in explaining the success of the Czech right. There is, however, significant evidence suggesting that the Czech electoral system may have blocked the consolidation and concentration of the centre-right on the pattern seen in Hungary, whose mixed electoral system offers a very different set of incentives.

While erecting insuperable barriers to the electoral viability of some tiny ex-dissident groupings, the electoral system did permit the continued parliamentary existence of small parties of the centre-right, such as the Christian Democrats, Civic Democratic Alliance (1992–98) and Freedom Union (1998 onwards). It has also made launching (and voting for) small anti-communist formations appear a viable choice. The far-right Republicans (SPR-RSČ), for example, successfully broke into parliament in 1992 with slightly less than six per cent of the vote. The more moderate Democratic Union, founded in 1994, failed to enter the Czech parliament in both 1996 and 1998, polling 2.80 and 1.45 per cent respectively, possibly drawing votes from the centre-right.

Under Klaus, the Civic Democrats had a long-standing commitment to a bipolar model of party competition of alternating blocs of left and right as a 'standard' and desirable form of politics.[42] An important understanding of ODS and the Social Democrats in signing the 'Opposition Agreement' on 9 July 1998 – an understanding made explicit in its successor, the 'Patent of Toleration', signed on 14 January 2000 – was that the two parties would engineer such an outcome through the introduction of a more majoritarian electoral system for elections to the lower house of parliament.[43] Electoral reform was intended to 'reinforce the importance of the results of competition between political parties in accordance with the constitutional principles of the Czech Republic' by decreasing the representation (and hence the bargaining power) of smaller parties, in effect creating a two-party system.[44] Counterfactual analysis of the impact of the proposed amendments to the electoral law would have, which used votes cast in 1998, suggested that, even without any transfers of votes to larger parties, a two-party system would effectively result.[45] However, although an electoral reform bill agreed by Klaus's party and the Social Democrats was passed by the Czech parliament in 2000, the Constitutional Court ruled the law unconstitutional on 24 January 2001.[46]

Parliamentarianism and Successful Right-Wing Party Formation

In a recent paired comparison of the Czech Republic and Poland, Saxonberg has argued that the relative success of the Czech centre-right derives, in part, from the absence of incentives for charismatic leaders to pursue alternatives to party formation. By contrast, the relatively powerful, directly elected presidency in Poland, he suggests, led a charismatic leader such as Wałęsa to avoid founding or consistently supporting a party.[47] Such institutional effects can be seen as particularly significant, given that, unlike communist successor parties, centre-right parties are typically 'new' formations, which will experience early problems of stabilization and institutionalization.

At an aggregate level, there is compelling evidence correlating weak party structures in new democracies with moderate and strong presidentialism.[48] Anecdotal evidence from Romania and Russia of the fractiousness and weakness of pro-reform centre-right blocs in semi-presidential post-communist states confirms this association. However, detailed analysis of the Czech case suggests that, as in other cases discussed in this collection, such institutional effects may be more apparent than real. Saxonberg is undoubtedly correct to argue that, in both Czechoslovakia and the Czech Republic, strong parliamentarianism and a weak presidency elected by parliament made party-building the only realistic route to executive power for ambitious politicians.[49] However, the implicit assumption that all charismatic leaders were ambitious politicians capable of 'rationally' reading and responding to institutional incentives is flawed. Despite the popularity of figures such as Klaus, Václav Havel was the dominant political personality in the Czech lands, having acquired an almost mythic status as a symbol of regime change.

Havel's distaste for formal political organization and, in particular, party political organization led him, upon becoming a presidential candidate in December 1989, to break all contact with the Civic Forum movement he had co-founded. Thereafter, he made no direct intervention in the movement's internal affairs until September 1990 and also declined to stand for the movement's chairmanship – a post he himself had proposed – which he would probably have won without difficulty. Havel's 'irrational' behaviour in refusing to seek power through involvement with a political party thus opened the way for the 'more rational' Klaus to win the post. This suggests that a more critical factor in explaining successful party formation are the cognitive frameworks through which new political elites approach post-transition politics.

Micro-Institutional Factors

The Break-Up of Civic Forum: Crafting Party Formation

As moderate centre-right parties in Central and Eastern Europe are typically the 'successor parties' of opposition movements, the break-up of the broad civic movements formed in 1989–90 represented a critical juncture in the formation (or non-formation) of centre-right parties. Much of the literature on civic movements in Eastern Europe attests to the difficulty of transforming broad, loose movement-type organizations into lasting political structures.[50] However, Klaus's Civic Democratic Party emerged in 1990–91 in precisely this way.

Civic Forum (OF) was formed in Prague on 19 November 1989 as an ad hoc committee-like grouping of counter-elite and opposition groups, bringing together Prague-based dissidents, striking actors and students, and social scientists and economists from the 'grey zone'. As mobilization increased and the regime ceased to resist, local Civic Forums were created across the Czech Lands, and by early 1990 the movement was a powerful, if loosely structured, national organization heading a transitional government. In the succeeding months, the Forum formalized its organizational structures and identity, seeking to reconcile the horizontal, spontaneous, non-ideological movement structure developed during the Velvet Revolution with the demands of office-holding and contesting parliamentary elections in June 1990. The movement's overwhelming victory in these elections, and the expectations that the elected Czechoslovak and Czech government it headed would rapidly deliver coherent reform, exacerbated these contradictions and rapidly exposed internal divisions.

As Hadjiisky's research has impressively demonstrated, these divisions concerned not only ideological differences over the pace of market reform, de-communization or the constitutional relationship of Czechs and Slovaks, but also conflicts between organizational interests within the Forum.[51] Principal among these were (1) growing pressures from OF's full-time paid regional officials and elected representatives to recognize them as political professionals; and (2) discontent amongst grassroots activists that their views (especially on de-communization) were not represented by the movement's former dissident leaders. Such tensions were expressed from mid-1990 in the emergence of a 'right wing' within the movement initially articulated by Bratinka and Kroupa's Civic Democratic Alliance (ODA), which defined the 'right wing' position in terms of rapid economic reform, radical de-communization and resistance to Slovak demands for greater autonomy for Czechoslovakia's two national republics.[52]

However, leadership of the 'right' was rapidly taken over by the federal finance minister, Václav Klaus. Klaus's unexpected election as chairman of Civic Forum in October 1990 marked the rise of the Czech right as a majority coalition of dissatisfied, anti-communist grassroots activists, neo-liberal technocrats and right-wing dissident intellectuals not attracted by former dissident groupings such as ODA or the tiny Christian Democratic Party (KDS). Klaus's project to transform the Forum into an ideologically and organizationally well-defined party of the centre-right oriented towards electoral competition and the delivery of a programme of social and economic transformation rather than citizen participation, although not realized as envisaged, led to the movement's break-up in February 1991 and the foundation of the Civic Democratic Party (ODS) two months later.[53]

The creation in ODS of such a broad and diverse coalition, albeit on smaller scale than that of OF itself, and its transformation into a durable political party represented a significant and unusually successful piece of political crafting. To some extent, this was conditioned by the repressive nature of Czechoslovakia's communist regime and by the mode of transition from communism. The suddenness of the 'Velvet Revolution' and numerical weakness of opposition groupings allowed Civic Forum to emerge as a unitary organization, rather than a coalition of more developed opposition groups or the 'civil' wing of a trade union. The large number of grassroots Civic Forum participants with no ties to the pre-1989 opposition and in search of political identity also favoured transformation. Czechoslovakia's relatively late transition process also enabled Klaus and others to learn from the break-up of Solidarity in Poland in mid-1990. However, to a considerable extent the successful formation of ODS must be regarded as the result of contingent choices rather than a predetermined outcome. As Klaus's chief aide recalls, in October 1990, hours before the election for the chairmanship of Civic Forum, which was to launch his career as a party leader, a reluctant Klaus had to be persuaded to stand.[54]

The Decline of the Czech Centre-Right as Problem of Institutionalization

A newly founded political party can be regarded as an organizational solution to a collective action problem, in which participants (members, voters) exchange resources (financial, material, technical, time) to generate political outcomes that would not be achievable by individuals. A party becomes organizationally stabilized relatively quickly when such resource flows and exchanges are regularized and settle into some kind of equilibrium. In the longer term, however, members and voters may begin to identify with the party to such an extent that the party is seen as an end in itself, leaving behind the instrumental goals of its founders and initial supporters. Such a process – and the air of permanence and durability it produces – is widely termed institutionalization.[55]

ODS's formation (and its own view of its formation) was as a rational response to the problem of coordinating and mobilizing political support for market reform and other policies. By the mid-1990s ODS had apparently delivered these public goods and had at the same time stabilized itself organizationally, acquiring enough votes and resources to sustain itself and maintaining a rough balance between internal interests, competing elites and elite and grassroots actors. However, despite generating electoral support and a degree of voter identification unusual for a 'new' party in Eastern and Central Europe, the party could not be regarded as institutionalized in the sense described above. ODS's internal party crisis of the mid-1990s, which culminated in the split of 1997–98, represented a breakdown in the institutionalization process. Paradoxically, this breakdown was caused by the same factors that had initially allowed ODS to form and stabilize so quickly and so successfully: charismatic leadership, internally democratic organization and ideological militancy. In choosing to support Klaus almost regardless of the circumstances of the funding scandal or the party's record in office, the majority of ODS members in effect chose to make the party a formation based increasingly on a bond of trust with its charismatic founder and leader. Rather than outgrowing its founder, the party in crisis saw the reassertion of Václav Klaus's personal authority and prominence, allowing him to develop his personal policy agendas (on, for example, Europe) without being checked by rivals. ODS was both too stable to expand the centre-right through party breakdown – the model described by Fowler in the case of the MDF and Fidesz – and too weakly institutionalized to expand through a more normal process of replacing its leadership, renewing its ideology and identity and embracing new alliance-building tactics.

Critical Elections as Critical Junctures

1992 and 1998: From Breaking the Left to Braking the Left

Klaus's Civic Democratic Party not only took over the bulk of the Civic Forum's local and regional assets and organization, but in the 1992 Czechoslovak and Czech elections also attracted some 55 per cent of its voters.[56] In successfully taking over the resources, the electorate and the pro-reform mission of Civic Forum, Klaus's ODS thus established itself as the dominant force on the right. In doing so, it blocked off the growth potential not only of small ex-dissident parties such as ODA and KDS, but also of more dynamic rivals threatening to create an alternative right. Principal amongst these were the Christian Democrats and a newly emergent militant and populist anti-communist right, which was in 1991–92 able to attract growing levels of publicity, popular interest and electoral support. In the event, the electoral breakthrough achieved in June 1992 by Miroslav Sládek's far-right Republican Party (SPR-RSČ) was limited. Moreover, in rapidly agreeing to the dissolution of the Czechoslovak federation after the election with Vladmír Mečiar's Movement for a Democratic Slovakia (HZDS), now the dominant force in Slovak politics, Klaus's Civic Democrats closed off a further possibility. With the passing of the federal, Czecho-Slovak party system, the fragmented Czech left was cut off from more economically populist Slovak parties with which it might have made common cause.[57]

Six years on, the 1998 election marked a further critical juncture for the Czech centre-right. In its 1998 election campaign ODS had called for a mobilization of its supporters against a centre-left which it once again depicted as a danger to reform and democratic development. However, when the election results failed to produce a viable majority government – principally, because of the Freedom Union's unwillingness to enter a coalition with either ODS or the Social Democrats – Václav Klaus negotiated the Opposition Agreement. The agreement and its successor, the Patent of Toleration, were formal pacts, which committed ODS to support the continuation in office (but not all the legislation) of a minority Social Democratic government. The agreements also guaranteed ODS key posts in parliament, and informally in the management structures of public bodies. As noted above, the two signatories also agreed to enact a number of mutually beneficial constitutional and legislative changes, principally electoral reform.[58]

ODS justified the Opposition Agreement as a pragmatic and realistic arrangement, which would maintain political stability and exercise a 'braking' effect on the Social Democrats. In this view, the agreement did not mark the suspension of left–right competition, but merely transferred it to a new setting.[59] Critics saw it as a cynical exercise in clientelistic power politics, which made nonsense of pretended ideological divisions.[60] Such discussions are, however, beyond the scope of this study. What nevertheless does seem clear, in hindsight, is that Klaus's strategic initiative in July 1998, even if originally intended as a pragmatic response to temporary political deadlock, weakened the possibility of a resumption of bi-polar left–right competition.

First, the Opposition Agreement provided a focal point for ideological rethinking within the Civic Democratic Party, which led it to stress differences with smaller centre-right parties, rather than with the left. The most important such difference was the party's new stress on 'national interests', a stress whose traditionally nationalist framing of Czech interests in juxtaposition to those of Germany was widely shared on the Czech left. As the Czech presidential election of 2003 graphically illustrated, in the Czech context, in marked contrast to the Polish and Hungarian cases, the revival of traditional nationalism can tend to blunt left–right, ideological divisions even where, as in relations with the Communists, they are rooted in the regime–opposition divide. Second, and paradoxically, the Opposition Agreement has legitimized left–right co-operation even for those centre-right groupings opposed to the agreement. In entering into coalition with the Social Democrats in 2002, Freedom Union politicians deployed essentially the same arguments, namely that the coalition would promote Czech accession to the EU and avoid making the centre-left dependent on the Communists.

The 2002 Election as Critical Juncture: The Failure of the Quad-Coalition

From the mid-1990s, under the chairmanship of Josef Lux, the Christian Democrats sought to reposition themselves as a third force in Czech politics offering a form of moderate conservatism, which would appeal to voters beyond the party's traditional rural Catholic and regional constituency. Although partially successful in diversifying the party's electorate, this strategy failed to increase the Christian Democratic vote significantly, leaving the dream of building a 'Czech CDU' unrealized.[61] However, the breakaway of the Freedom Union as a liberal anti-Klaus formation and the signing of the Opposition Agreement, which sought to exclude small parties from the party system through electoral reform, created the basis of a new alliance. After initial pragmatic co-operation in the November 1998 local and senatorial elections, in mid-1999 four smaller centre-right parties – the Freedom Union, Christian Democrats, Civic Democratic Alliance and Democratic Union (now shorn of much its earlier radical anti-communism) – agreed to form an integrated electoral bloc, the Quad-Coalition (Čytrkoalice, or 4K).[62]

Although deeply critical of Klaus's ODS, 4K nevertheless framed itself within the liberal, anti-communist discourse of reform, modernization and Europeanization characteristic of the Czech centre-right. Its founding 'St. Wenceslas Day Agreement' of 28 September 1999 thus pledged it to 'tackling political drift [marasmus], effectively countering growing communist influence, solving our country's current problems and leading it to the European Union'.[63] As Lux had foreseen in 1998 before leaving politics through illness, the grouping also seemed to have the potential to create an influential fusing of liberalism and moderate conservatism through its commitment to civil society, decentralization and European integration.[64] In 2000, 4K enjoyed further electoral success, making sufficient gains in the senate to block constitutional change and delay ordinary legislation.[65] In November 1999 mass demonstrations against the perceived political stagnation brought about by the Opposition Agreement took place on the streets of Prague and other cities. In December 2001 similar mass protests and strikes by journalists took place against perceived political interference in the management of Czech Television by the two Opposition Agreement parties.[66] This suggested that the Quad-Coalition, whose leaders supported both protests and sought to collaborate with the civic initiatives that had organized them, might be able to form a wider societal coalition to articulate a powerful public mood for change.

However, almost from its inception, 4K was undermined by divisions of the type that plagued similar centre-right coalition groupings in Poland and Slovakia. These centred on rivalries between member parties, aggravated by their disproportionate size, and the weakness of coalition leadership structures to enforce decisions. Politicians in the four member parties were inconsistent and divided over the extent to which 4K should be integrated into a single party or bloc. In the case of 4K, it was the strongest coalition partner – namely the Christian Democrats (KDU-ČSL), whose mass membership, long party tradition and distinct electorate marked them out from other smaller, liberal and anti-communist coalition members – that became a source of instability. Rival factions within KDU-ČSL tended to use the coalition framework as an additional means of pursuing their own intra-party conflict.[67] More significantly, however, the Christian Democrats became increasingly unwilling and unable to meet the programmatic and political demands of 4K's smaller parties. Following the absorption in October 2001 of the Democratic Union (DEU) by the Freedom Union (US), creating US-DEU, the Christian Democrats intensified pressure on the smallest 4K member, the Civic Democratic Alliance, to resolve its long-running problems or merge with US-DEU. When ODA refused this perceived ultimatum and withdrew from 4K, the Quad-Coalition framework collapsed. Although replaced by a looser alliance between the Christian Democrats and the Freedom Union-Democratic Union ('the Coalition'), the potential for broad liberal-conservative bloc to rival ODS had dissipated. The June 2002 election results duly confirmed the position of the two 'Coalition' members as minor parties.[68]

Political Agents and Political Agency

The 'Klaus Phenomenon'

Many discussions of the Czech right, and Czech politics generally, tend to focus on Václav Klaus, often in juxtaposition to Václav Havel.[69] However, as Haughton suggests in previously published work, while overstressed empirically the role of charismatic individuals in post-communist politics is worryingly under-theorized.[70] Despite its democratic and representative mechanisms, which sometimes checked Klaus on internal matters, the Civic Democratic Party was from the outset dominated by the charismatic and forceful leadership of its founder. In April 1991, Miroslav Macek, an ODS deputy chairman, commented that 'it is a peculiarity of the party [ODS] that today it stands and falls with the personality of Václav Klaus',[71] 'the party Chairman is not selected. He simply exists . . . He is simply there and we all know it'.[72] Eleven years later, on the eve of Klaus's departure as leader, one of his colleagues conceded that Klaus's moustache and glasses were as much recognizable as a symbol of ODS, if not more so, as its official logo.[73] It has been widely observed that the self-confident, formal, well-dressed, tennis-playing Klaus personified (and was projected as personifying) the political optimism and impatience of the Czech centre-right of the early 1990s, as well as its belief in professionally administered market-led solutions. As optimism concerning transformation waned, such qualities were increasingly perceived negatively as the 'arrogance of power'.[74] Like Viktor Orbán in Hungary,

Klaus was also able to portray himself as an outsider challenging metropolitan intellectual elites disconnected from the concerns of ordinary people living in small town and provincial settings.[75]

However, perhaps the best clue to understanding the role of charisma in relation to centre-right party formation are Klaus's own comments after being elected OF Chairman in October 1990, that he wished to be 'the symbol of a programme not yet written'.[76] Charismatic leaderships provide a personal and immediate focus for identification by members and voters at a time when political programmes are likely to be underdeveloped, voters may still face cognitive difficulties choosing between parties and programmes, and loyalty to newly formed organizations is inevitably weak. It seems necessary, however, that charismatic leaders should be committed to developing party organization.

Ideological (Re-)construction: From Neo-Liberalism to National Interests

Communist regimes suppressed the public sphere and monopolized political discourse. In post-communist democracies the re-establishment of ideological discourses of left and right is an important means of creating the new political identities necessary to provide a meaningful framework for political action. The weaknesses of civil society and well-understood social interests also give ideological construction a particularly important role in orienting action in the early post-transition period. Politicians in early post-communist politics can therefore be seen not only as political entrepreneurs, but also as *ideological entrepreneurs.* In the Czech context, right-wing political entrepreneurs such as Klaus succeeded in framing a new discourse both of political organization and of post-communist transformation, which grounded imported Anglo-American New Right ideas in a Czech post-communist context. Both served to reinforce the support, cohesion and power of ODS and the centre-right and to de-legitimize opponents on the centre-left.[77]

The ideological discourse initially developed by ODS was an innovative synthesis of Hayekian neo-liberalism and aspects of Czech nationalism. It argued that the free market, political parties, ideologies of left and right and Western international institutions were 'tried and tested' and 'standard' forms of organization, which could and should be quickly re-established in the Czech lands. Opponents on the centre-left, who wanted a greater role for social movements and civil society in the political process or a greater role for the state in economic reform, were, it was argued, consciously or unconsciously seeking 'Third Ways' between Soviet-style communism and the West European mainstream. Such thinking, it was argued, echoed the failed reform communism of the 1960s. While arguing that it was ideologically conservative, the new Czech right-wing discourse was self-consciously radical, even 'revolutionary', both in its desire to break with the communist past and in its disdain for most pre-communist Czech thinkers and parties, viewed as too provincial or too collectivist.[78] Such neo-liberal conservatism stressed its links with the past, by suggesting in a non-specific way that affinity with the free market was rooted in the Czech national character and tradition.[79]

However, after losing office in 1997, Klaus's party underwent a significant degree of ideological reconstruction and realignment, which saw it rediscover a previously submerged traditional Czech nationalist paradigm. To a considerable extent, ODS's identity as an 'Anglo-Saxon' neo-liberal conservative party, rather than a Christian Democratic party on the German or Austrian model, was a conscious assertion of Czech national identity and independence against the dominance of Austro-German influences in Central Europe.[80] A veiled anti-German undercurrent can also be detected in many ODS statements on European integration during the early and mid-1990s. However, after 1997 ODS's ideological discourse shifted away from Western neo-liberalism as a point of reference, stressing instead the notion of defending Czech 'national interests' within an enlarging EU. In doing so it started to draw on traditional Czech nationalist paradigms.[81] Its April 2001 *Manifesto of Czech Eurorealism*, for example, attempted to align ODS's preferred neo-liberal model of European integration with the Czech national tradition, claiming that liberal-nationalist thinkers of the nineteenth century such as Havlíček, Palacký and Masaryk were 'strikingly close to Anglo-Saxon liberal-conservative thought'.[82]

As was the case with Hungary's Fidesz, a key element in ODS's political success appears to lie with its leaders' ability to frame a new ideological discourse of 'rightness' relating substantially to post-communist transformation. However, in challenging the consensual, anti-political 'ideology' of Civic Forum, ODS's ideology re-defined the *means* but not the ends of Czech post-communist transformation, rather than reacting against a transformation process seen as having fundamentally 'gone awry', as was the case with Hungary's Fidesz. There are, however, parallels between Fidesz's turn from the liberal camp to 'national revival' and ODS's post-1997 turn from neo-liberalism to 'national interests'. Both arguably reflected the limitations of liberalism as a durable ideology for a broad centre-right in Eastern and Central Europe. However, in the Czech case it was the waning of the big issues of post-communist transformation – and ODS's loss of credibility as vehicle for that transformation – that prompted ideological realignment, rather than competitive pressures on the liberal 'centre', as was the case in Hungary.

Conclusions

The Civic Democratic Party (ODS) is the most significant centre-right formation in modern Czech political history. The party's origins can be traced to the reactions of Czech counter-elites to the collapse of the reform communism in 1968 and the 1969–89 'normalization' period and subsequently – in combination with other groups – to the challenges of post-communist transformation. Late communism in Czechoslovakia – and the Czechoslovak mode of exit from communism that flowed from it – created a favourable opportunity structure for the early and successful formation of ODS as neo-liberal party championing socio-economic transformation. Key elements in this opportunity structure were the location of technocratic counter-elites, the ideological complexion of opposition groupings and the nature of Civic Forum as a transitional civic movement. Despite this, political strategy and contingent choices in the period 1990–92 can also be seen to have played an important role in translating opportunities into a strong, organizationally stable centre-right.

However, the circumstances that led to ODS's rapid formation and early dominance subsequently limited the concentration and consolidation of the centre-right in the Czech Republic. As well as being divided by ideological and cleavage differences from the small Christian Democratic right and the populist far right, the tightly organized, charismatically led Civic Democrats consistently failed to incorporate smaller centre-right liberal groups. To some extent, this failure of concentration was abetted by the incentives offered by the Czech electoral system. From the mid-1990s, an accumulation of policy failures enabled the rise of a strong centre-left opposition, which shared the same broad transformation goals of modernization and Europeanization, leading to the gradual displacement the centre-right from power.

The subsequent realignment of the Czech centre-right, resulting from the Opposition Agreement of 1998, allowed both Klaus and his opponents to share power in the short term but has further divided the Czech centre-right as a bloc. However, although it is the result of contingent choices in 1998, in many ways the pattern of left–right co-operation established in the Czech Republic – which appears exceptional in the region – should not surprise us. Despite its rhetoric of 'Third Ways', in the Czech context the regime–opposition divide ran not *between* centre-left and centre-right, as in Hungary and Poland, but *within* the left (dividing the Social Democrats from the Communists). Nevertheless, it remains to be seen whether the Czech centre-right will reunite and reassert itself, or whether it will remain within the confines of the pattern of limited success analysed in this study.

ACKNOWLEDGEMENTS

An earlier version of this article was presented at the European Consortium for Political Research General Conference, Marburg, Germany, 18–21 September 2003. The author would like to thank participants for their comments and to acknowledge the support of the British Academy in providing a travel grant that enabled him to attend the conference.

NOTES

1. In the 1990 election campaign the perception of collaboration was reinforced by the revelation that its then leader, Josef Bartončík, was listed as an informer in the records of the former communist secret police.
2. The Alliance thus failed to contest the 1998 parliamentary elections. In the June 2002 elections after leaving the Quad-Coalition, it ran an independent list, which received 0.50 per cent.
3. See S. Hanley, 'Europe and the Czech Parliamentary Elections of June 2002', Royal Institute of International Affairs/Opposing Europe Research Network Election Briefing No.5 (July 2002), at <http://www.riia.org> (accessed 7 March 2004).
4. See J. Urban, 'The Making of a Czech President', East European Perspectives, Vol.5, No.8 (16 April 2003), at <http://www.rferl.org/eepreport/2003/04/8–160403.html> (accessed 1 June 2003).
5. Reports suggested that Miroslav Topolánek was essentially seeking to balance out all major organizational and regional interests in ODS, rather than undertaking major new ideological initiatives; new ODS policy was said to be driven by individual ODS shadow ministers: see L. Bek, 'Topolánek nezvládl sjednotit ODS', Právo, 5 Sept. 2003, p.1.
6. See B. Pečinka, 'Komentář: ODS mezi stagnací a růstem', Proglas, No.2001/4 (2001) online edition, and 'Budoucnost české pravice', Proglas, No.8/2002 (2002), pp.11–13.
7. After the departure of Josef Lux in 1998, the Christian Democrats were led by Jan Kasal (1998–2001), Cyril Svoboda (2001–3) and Miroslav Kalousek (2003 to date). Since its foundation in 1998, the Freedom Union has been led by Jan Ruml (1998–2000), Karel Kühnl (2000–2001), Hana Marvanová (2001–2), Ivan Pilip (acting leader 2002–3) and Petr Mareš (2003 to date).
8. The most recent CVVM poll at the time of writing recorded the Freedom Union's electoral support at 2.5 per cent: 'CVVM: soc. dem spadl na 14 procent', Právo, 26 Feb. 2004, p.3.
9. The majority of KAN delegates rejected the merger agreement at a special conference, leading to a split in the organization.
10. Daniel Kroupa and Pavel Bratinka cite ideological differences and Klaus's indifference as the reason for the failure to merge: see D. Kroupa, Svoboda a řád (sváteční rozhovory) (Prague: Éós, 1996), pp.15–20, and M. Hamerský and P. Dimun (eds.), 10 let na straně svobody (kronika ODA z let 1989–1999) (Brno: Bachant, 1999), pp.24–5, 28. However, there is evidence that the Alliance's wish to enter Klaus's new party as a collective member was the real stumbling block: see comments by ODA representative Žegklitz at the Civic Forum Political Club, as reported in Infórum, No.54/91, 4 Jan. 1991. Klaus also cites his refusal to compromise on the principle of individual membership as the obstacle; see V. Klaus, První zpráva (Prague: Cartoonia, 1993), p.65.
11. The European Democrats won 18.3 per cent of the vote in Prague in the November 2002 local elections.
12. ODS's highest national vote was 33.9 per cent in the ballot to the lower house of the Czechoslovak Federal Assembly in 1992.
13. See M. Mareš, Pravicový extremismus a radikalismus v České republice (Brno: Barrister & Principal, 2003).
14. ODS's own figures suggest membership peaked at 23,269 in 1992, declining sharply to 16,289 after the party lost office in 1997, before recovering to 18,908 at the end of 2000: see L. Benešová, Kronika ODS: 10 let historie (Prague: ODS, 2001), published in electronic form at <http://www.ods.cz> (accessed 1 Feb. 2004).
15. The Christian Democrats at present have 9.58 per cent of elected communal and municipal councillors, marginally more than the Civic Democratic Party, although they typically represent smaller communes; the Freedom Union–Democratic Union, by comparison, has only 0.72 per cent of local councillors: see <http://www.volby.cz> (accessed 5 March 2004).

16. See, for example, L. Kopeček, 'Aplikace Rokkanovské theorie cleavages na české politické strany na počatku éry masové politiky', *Středoevropské politické studie*, Vol.4, Nos 2–3 (2002), published electronically at <http://www.iips.cz> (accessed 15 Sept. 2003). One peculiarity of the pre-1938 Czech party system was the presence of both a Catholic and an agrarian party.

17. The (re-)emergence of the Czechs as a political nation from the early nineteenth century largely excluded the aristocracy as a pro-Habsburg interest; similarly, the Catholic Church, although institutionally and numerically dominant in the Czech lands, was seen as ambivalent towards aspirations for national self-determination.

18. B. Garver, *The Young Czech Party 1874–1901 and the Emergence of a Multiparty System* (New Haven, CT and London: Yale University Press, 1978).

19. See G.M. Luebbert, *Liberalism, Fascism, or Social Democracy: Social Classes and the Political Origins of Regimes in Interwar Europe* (Cambridge: Cambridge University Press, 1991). A key difference with the Scandinavian context was the fragmentation of the Czech left, which reflected the divisive effect of the National Question and the strength of the Communist Party of Czechoslovakia.

20. See J. Rataj, *O autoritativní národní stát: ideologické proměny české politiky v Druhé republice 1938–1939* (Prague: Karolinium, 1997).

21. See G. Evans and S. Whitefield, 'The Structuring of Political Cleavages in Post-Communist Societies: The Case of the Czech Republic and Slovakia', *Political Studies*, Vol.46, No.1 (1998), pp.115–39; H. Kitschelt, Z. Manfeldová, R. Markowski and G. Toka, *Post-Communist Party Systems: Competition, Representation and Inter-party Collaboration* (Cambridge: Cambridge University Press, 1999); K. Vlachová, 'Levice a pravice v české republiky v letech 1996–2000', in Z. Manfeldová and M. Tuček, *Současná česká společnost* (Prague: Sociologickýústav, 2002) pp.254–70; K. Krause, 'Once More unto the Breach: The Politics of Cleavage in Slovakia and the Czech Republic', paper presented at the Annual Meeting of the American Political Science Association, Boston, MA, 29 Aug.–1 Sept. 2002.

22. See, for example, P. Matějů and B. Reháková, 'Turning Left or Class Realignment? Analysis of the Changing Relationship between Class and Party in the Czech Republic 1992–1996', *East European Politics and Societies*, Vol.11, No.3 (1997), pp.501–42, and B. Reháková, 'Social Stratification and Voting Behaviour', in Večerník and Matějů (eds.), *Ten Years of Rebuilding Capitalism: The Czech Republic after 1989* (Prague: Academia, 1999), pp.228–50; Krause.

23. See B. Abrams, 'Morality, Wisdom and Revision: The Czech Opposition of the 1970s and the Expulsion of the Sudeten Germans', *East European Politics and Societies*, Vol.9, No.2 (1995), pp.234–55.

24. Principally the writings of Petr Pithart and the *Střední Evropa* group: see P. Pithart, *Dějiny a politika* (Prague: Prostor, 1990); M. Laruelle, '*Střední Evropa': Une autre écriture de la nation?* (Prague: CEFRES Documents de travail, No.4, 1996).

25. See P. Oslzlý (ed.), *Podzemná univerzita* (Brno: Centrum pro studium demokracie a kultury, 1993); B. Day, *The Velvet Philosophers* (London: Claridge Press, 2001).

26. See S. Hanley, 'The New Right in the New Europe? Unravelling The Ideology of "Czech Thatcherism"', *Journal of Political Ideologies*, Vol.4, No.2 (1999), pp.163–89; G. Eyal, *The Origins of Postcommunist Elites: From Prague Spring to Breakup of Czechoslovakia* (Minneapolis, MN and London: University of Minnesota Press, 2003), pp.135–93.

27. Structural legacy arguments have difficulty explaining the failure of the 'Prague Spring', which appears to be a critical juncture when more than one path of political development was open, whose outcome was dependent on the contingent choices of political actors (including external actors in the USSR). In structural historical terms, arguably the same forces that generated 'bureaucratic authoritarian' opposition to reform also generated the powerful reform communist movement itself.

28. For example, A. Bozóki, 'The Ideology of Modernization and the Policy of Materialism: The Day After the Socialists', *Journal of Communist Studies and Transition Politics*, Vol.13, No.3 (1998), pp.56–102.

29. Much of the British politics literature of the 1980s on 'Thatcherism' does, however, suggests that, despite a conservative social policy agenda, the Conservative Party of Margaret Thatcher should be regarded primarily as an agent of market-led modernization; in this sense, the Czech New Right can be seen as paralleling its Western ideological models: see S. Hall and M. Jacques (eds.), *The Politics of Thatcherism* (London: Lawrence & Wishart, 1983); S. Hall, *The Hard Road to Renewal: Thatcherism and the Crisis of the Left* (London: Verso, 1988).
30. As one Charter 77 signatory wryly observed, 'all the other people in Civic Forum wear sweaters and call each other *ty*, but these gentlemen wear ties and say *vy*'; P. Uhl, 'The Fight For Socialist Democracy in Czechoslovakia', *New Left Review*, No.179 (1990), p.15.
31. 'Vážení přátele', *Bulletin ODS*, No.11, 15 May 1991.
32. See Article 2 of the first ODS Statutes on the function and role of the party: *Stanovy ODS* (Prague: ODS, 1991).
33. *Svoboda a prosperita* (Prague: ODS, 1992), p.2.
34. H. Appel, 'The Ideological Determinants of Liberal Economic Reform: The Case of Privatization', *World Politics*, Vol.52, No.4 (2000), pp.520–54.
35. P. Rutland, 'Thatcherism, Czech-style: Transition to Capitalism in the Czech Republic', *Telos*, No.94 (1992–93), pp.104–29; S. Holmes, 'The Politics of Economics in the Czech Republic', *East European Constitutional Review*, 1995, No.4, pp.52–5.
36. M. Dangerfield, 'Ideology and Czech Transformation: Neoliberal Rhetoric or Neoliberal Reality', *East European Politics and Societies*, Vol.11, No.3 (1997), pp.436–67.
37. M. Orenstein, *Out of the Red: Building Capitalism and Democracy in Postcommunist Europe* (Ann Arbor, MI: University of Michigan Press, 2001).
38. D. Stark and L. Bruszt, *Postsocialist Pathways: Transforming Politics and Property in East Central Europe* (Cambridge: Cambridge University Press, 1998).
39. On social democratic strategies for transformation, see P. Machonin, P. Štastnová, A. Kroupa and A. Glasová, *Strategie sociální transformace české společnosti* (Brno: Doplněk, 1996).
40. Kitschelt et al., pp.35–6, 157–96, 218–19.
41. Voters are able to cast a limited number of 'preference votes' for individual candidates on a list, which can have the effect of moving them to the top of the list.
42. For example, addressing his party's conference in December 1996 Klaus expressed satisfaction that the elections had 'made Czech politics more transparent . . . marginal and poorly defined parties have disappeared . . . there are two basic paths, two basic visions . . . represented, on one hand by ODS and, on the other by the Social Democrats': V. Klaus, *Obhajoba zapomenutých myšlenek* (Prague: Academia, 1997), p.116.
43. 'Smlouva ODS a ČSSD o výtvoření stabilního politického prostředí v zemi', *Lidové noviny*, 10 July 1998, p.2, Article VII, and 'Toleračni patent', Agreement No.2 at <http://www.ods.cz> (accessed 6 March 2004).
44. 'Zeman je skutečný politik, kterého odmítám podceňovat', *Lidové noviny*, 10 July 1998, p.5. ODS initially preferred a simple plurality system on British lines; however, under pressure from the Social Democrats and – following the November 2000 Senate elections – unable to command the necessary constitutional majority – the two parties agreed on a less proportional form of PR.
45. See T. Kostelecký, 'Navrhované zmeny volebního zákona vzeslé z dodatku "opoziční smlouvy" v roce 2000 a jejich možné dusledky', *Sociologický časopis*, Vol.36, No.3 (2000), pp.299–306.
46. The 1992 Czech Constitution specifies that proportional representation must be used for elections to the lower house of parliament: M. Klíma, *Kvalita demokracie v České republice a volební inženýrství* (Prague: Radix/Marshall, 2001), pp.108–22. A second electoral law reducing the proportionality of the previous system by increasing the number of electoral districts from six to 14 was passed in January 2002 and used for the June 2002 elections.
47. S. Saxonberg, 'The Influence of Presidential Systems', *Problems of Postcommunism*, Vol.50, No.5 (2003), pp.22–36.
48. See M. Shugart, 'The Inverse Relationship between Party Strength and Executive Strength: A Theory of Constitutional Choices', *British Journal of Political Science*, Vol.28, No.1 (1998), pp.1–29.

49. Moreover, the Constitution of the Czech Republic, whose presidency is weaker than that of post-communist Czechoslovakia, was agreed by major political parties in December 1992; the current weak Czech presidency is thus clearly the product of strong parties, not vice versa.

50. Y.M. Brudny, 'The Dynamics of "Democratic Russia", 1990–93', *Post-Soviet Affairs*, Vol.9 (1993), pp.141–70; T. Grabowski, 'The Party That Never Was: The Rise and Fall of the Solidarity Citizens' Committees in Poland', *East European Politics and Societies*, Vol.10, No.2 (1996), pp.214–45.

51. M. Hadjiisky, *La fin du Forum civique et la naissance du Parti démocratique civique (janvier 1990–avril 1991)* (Prague: Documents de travail du CEFRES, No.6, 1996).

52. See 'Daniel Kroupa: Meziparlamentní klub demokratické pravice', *Infórum*, No.44/90 (17 October 1990).

53. Hadjiisky.

54. P. Havlík, *Klaus & ti druzí: Osobní inventura Petra Havlíka* (Prague: Pallata, 1998), pp.25–6.

55. Here I follow Hopkin's synthesis of the literature on party institutionalization, adapting a rational choice framework: see J. Hopkin, *Party Formation and Democratic Transition in Spain* (Basingstoke: Macmillan, 1999); see also J.A. Aldrich, *Why Parties? The Origin and Transformation of Political Parties in America* (Chicago, IL: University of Chicago Press, 1995).

56. P. Fiala, M. Mareš and P. Pšeja, 'The Development of Political Parties and the Party System', in Večerník and Matějů, pp.273–4, and IVVM data cited at p.279.

57. See A. Innes, 'The Breakup of Czechoslovakia: The Impact of Party Development on the Separation of the State', *East European Politics and Societies*, Vol.11, No.3 (1997), pp.393–435.

58. 'Smlouva ODS a ČSSD' and 'Tolerační patent'.

59. V. Klaus, 'O politické odpovědnosti' and 'Pokus o interpretaci dnešní politické křižovatky', in V. Klaus, *Od opozičnÍ smlouvy k tolerančnímu patentu* (Prague: Votobia, 2000), pp.76–7, 82–4.

60. See, for example, J. Macháček, 'Země dvou Mečiarů', *Respekt*, No.29/98 (1998), p.2; J. Pehe, 'Mečiarismus najdeme i v Čechách', *Mladá fronta dnes*, 30 Sept. 1999.

61. See B. Pečinka, 'Luxova velká politická hra', *Lidové noviny*, 7 Dec. 1995; 'Pokus o zesvětštění strany', *Lidové noviny*, 18 May 1996; and 'Česká CDU se nekoná', *Respekt*, 1998, No.17 (20–26 April), p.3.

62. In addition to a governing Coalition Council established in September 1999, Quad-Coalition also sought to establish a common electoral list, an electoral programme, a 'Shadow Cabinet' and a prime minister-designate; the goals were formalized in an additional agreement in September 2000.

63. 'Svatováclavské čtyřkoaliční dohoda', in Hamerský and Dimun, p.227.

64. Interview in *Mladá fronta dnes*, 14 July 1998, cited in P. Dimun, 'Komentář: Taková byla Čytrkoalice', *Proglas*, No.2002/2 (2002), online edition.

65. One-third of the Czech Senate is re-elected every two years; after the November 2000 elections 39 of 81 senators represented the Quad-Coalition.

66. See V. Dvořáková, 'Civil Society in the Czech Republic', in P. Kopecký and C. Mudde (eds.) *Uncivil Society? Contentious Politics in Post-Communist Europe* (London: Routledge, 2002), pp.134–56.

67. Dimun.

68. The 'Coalition' received fewer votes than the total its two member party had received running separately in 1998: see Hanley, 'Europe and the Czech Parliamentary Elections of June 2002'.

69. See, for example, K. Williams, 'National Myths in the New Czech Liberalism', in G. Hosking and G. Schöpflin (eds.), *Myths and Nationhood* (London: Hurst, 1997), pp.132–40, or P. Bugge, *Czech Perceptions of the Perspective of EU Membership Havel vs. Klaus* (Florence: European University Institute Working Paper RSC No.2000/10, 2000), and S. Saxonberg, 'Václav Klaus: The Rise and Fall and Re-emergence of a Charismatic Leader', *East European Politics and Societies*, Vol.13, No.2 (1999), pp.391–418.

70. T. Haughton, 'Facilitator and Impeder: The Institutional Framework of Slovak Politics During the Premiership of Vladimír Mečiar', *Slavonic and East European Review*, Vol.81, No.2 (2002), pp.267–90.

71. D. Šrámek, 'Chceme vrátit lidem nzděje', *Fórum*, 1991, No.17, p.2.

72. 'One Man Party?', *Lidové noviny*, 22 April 1991.

73. Petr Nečas, 'Tvář's brýlemí je vedle ptáka cenným logem', *Právo*, 22 June 2002; the author was an ODS vice-chairman.
74. See Saxonberg, 'Václav Klaus'.
75. See also A. King, 'The Outsider as Political Leader: The Case of Margaret Thatcher', *British Journal of Political Science*, Vol.32, No.3 (2002), pp.435–54.
76. 'Václav Klaus: Jakou roli bude hrát?', *Infórum*, 1990, No.44 (17 Oct.), p. 8.
77. This paragraph summarizes arguments discussed at more length in Hanley, 'The New Right in the New Europe?'.
78. Klaus did, however, make sporadic attempts to incorporate traditional Czech national symbols and myths into ODS ideology in the early 1990s: see Williams.
79. Similarly, in stressing that political parties were not merely efficient, but were a 'standard' west European form of political organization, ODS co-opted arguments first used by small historic parties of the left, *indirectly* drawing on pre-communist traditions of 'partyness'.
80. For an example of this assertion see ODS's internal analysis of its prospects after the June 2002 elections, see M. Beneš, 'Volby PS PČR 2002 – analýza volební kampaně ODS materiál pro Výkonnou radu ODS', at <http://www.ods.cz> (accessed 1 Sept. 2003).
81. See S. Hanley, 'From Neo-Liberalism to National Interests: Ideology, Strategy and Party Development in the Euroscepticism of the Czech Right', *East European Politics and Societies*, Vol. 18, No. 3 (2004), pp.513–48.
82. Many scholars would find this parallel questionable: see J. Zahradil, P. Plecitý, P Adrian and M. Bednář, *Manifest českého eurorealismu* (ODS: Prague, April 2001); published electronically at <http://www.ods.cz> (accessed 4 March 2004)

The Polish Centre-Right's (Last?) Best Hope: The Rise and Fall of Solidarity Electoral Action

ALEKS SZCZERBIAK

As the introduction to this collection makes clear, explaining the varying fortunes of the centre-right formations in post-communist Eastern Europe remains a key a research issue for political scientists concerned with understanding party development in the region. Ostensibly, there are reasons for assuming that Poland should have been one of the most promising post-communist states for centre-right parties. With the formation of Solidarity in 1980, Poland was the only East European communist state with a mass democratic opposition movement. Solidarity, of course, played a pioneering role in bringing down East European communism after it won an overwhelming victory over its discredited communist opponent in the May–June 1989 'semi-free' elections. Poland also has a powerful Catholic Church, with over 90 per cent of Poles declaring themselves to be believers and over 50 per cent attending mass at least once a week. Given this, and the relatively independent and influential role that the Church played throughout the communist period, Poland potentially appears an excellent case for the development of a Christian democratic type of political formation based on conservative social values. However, this has not happened. Except for a brief period in the mid-1990s, centre-right parties have been weak and divided while facing a united, disciplined, well-organized and increasingly electorally successful opponent in the communist successor formation, the Democratic Left Alliance (Sojusz Lewicy Demokratycznej, SLD).

This study examines the fate of the centre-right in post-communist Poland by considering specifically the case of the Solidarity Electoral Action coalition (Akcja Wyborcza Solidarność, AWS). Solidarity Electoral Action appeared to break the cycle of disunity and incoherence on the Polish centre-right. It brought most of it together in a single electoral coalition that won the September 1997 election and headed a coalition government with the liberal Freedom Union (Unia Wolności, UW), another 'post-Solidarity' party. However, it then went on to disintegrate and face massive and humiliating electoral defeat at the hands of the Democratic Left Alliance in September 2001. In that sense, Solidarity Electoral Action is interesting because it appeared to represent the best (and perhaps last) hope of bringing together the disparate forces of the Polish centre-right into a single, united political formation.

This study, therefore, examines the rise and fall of Solidarity Electoral Action in the context of the development of the centre-right parties that emerged from the Polish democratic opposition movements. In doing so it considers the applicability of various analytical frameworks to the Polish case. It argues that it was Solidarity Electoral Action's structural weaknesses and the inadequacy of its leadership elites, rather than its ideological hetero-geneity or the weak performance of the Solidarity Electoral Action-led Buzek government, that lay at the root of its problems. While approaches that rely on analysing the structural legacy shed some light on understanding the Polish case (although not in the way predicted in the literature), as do those that emphasize critical junctures, macro-institutional factors such as electoral systems have much less explanatory power. The most convincing approaches appear to be micro-institutional ones that stress the importance of party origins together with those that emphasize the role of political leadership – or rather lack of it in Solidarity Electoral Action's case. Solidarity Electoral Action's key structural weakness was its failure to develop a strong institutional centre combined with (and caused by) the lack of organizational self-discipline among its leading elite. These leaders failed to fashion a structure and ideological profile that could hold together a fractious and eclectic group-ing in the long term. Only fear of electoral oblivion and cronyism held Solidarity Electoral Action together but, in the end, it was precisely this fissi-parous and clientelistic style of politics that served to drain away the party's electoral support and laid the basis for its disintegration.

The Rise and Fall of Solidarity

The Polish People's Republic was one of the most liberal East European communist regimes.[1] In his comparative typology, Kitschelt categorizes it, along with Hungary, as an example of the relatively open national-consensus communism that tolerated a certain level of dissent.[2] Linz and Stepan argue that, uniquely within the Soviet bloc, Poland never underwent a totalitarian experience even during the Stalin period.[3] Certainly, it always maintained a public sphere in which there were significant elements of autonomous social organization, most notably the Catholic Church with which the regime felt it necessary to negotiate and compromise.[4] It was also the only East European communist regime in which a mass democratic opposition movement emerged. The Solidarity trade union, led by the Gdańsk shipyard worker

Lech Wałęsa, co-existed uneasily with the communist regime from August 1980 until it was banned following the imposition of martial law in December 1981. In fact, Solidarity was always a much broader social movement that, at its height, embraced nearly ten million members including one-third of the communist party.[5]

The period of martial law repression was relatively short-lived and the communist leader General Wojciech Jaruzelski subsequently attempted to develop a broad social consensus in favour of the liberal reforms that were required to rescue Poland from economic catastrophe. This process accelerated in the late 1980s when Mikhail Gorbachev became general secretary of the Communist Party of the Soviet Union, with Jaruzelski one of the most enthusiastic advocates of his *glasnost'* and *perestroika* policies among East European communist leaders. At the same time, Solidarity continued to operate with a skeletal underground structure and, more importantly, acted as a 'mobilizing myth' for the democratic opposition. With Jaruzelski unable to secure public backing for his reforms in an unprecedented referendum held in October 1987, the communist regime – hegemonic but lacking authority – and the Solidarity movement – illegal but popularly credible – had fought each other to a standstill. Finally, following a wave of strikes in 1988 Jaruzelski agreed to re-legalize Solidarity in order to have a negotiating partner that enjoyed popular authority, and he held 'round table' talks with the democratic opposition and the Catholic Church. These culminated in the 'semi-free' elections held in May–June 1989 in which the communists and their allies (who soon proved unreliable) guaranteed themselves a parliamentary majority, but any lingering authority that they enjoyed collapsed when Solidarity won all but one of the 261 freely contested seats.[6] This was to lead to the rapid collapse of the communist system in Poland (and, subsequently, elsewhere in Eastern Europe) when, in August 1989, the Solidarity intellectual Tadeusz Mazowiecki was appointed prime minister in a government in which the communists were in a minority.[7]

Political parties that identified themselves as right-wing or centre-right began to develop in Poland primarily from the break-up of the Solidarity movement in 1989–91.[8] Some smaller parties were already beginning to emerge in 1989–90 even when the movement generally held together. These included the Christian National Union (Zjednoczenie Chrześcijańsko-Narodowe, ZChN) and the Liberal Democratic Congress (Kongres Liberalno-Demokratyczne, KLD) that were formed in 1989 by Solidarity deputies and activists of Catholic-nationalist and liberal hues respectively. There were also some centre-right and right-wing formations that emerged independently of the Solidarity movement, such as Leszek Moczulski's Confederation for an Independent Poland (Konfederacja Polski Niepodległej, KPN) which actually predated Solidarity, having existed as a small clandestine party since 1979.

The process of party formation gathered pace with the onset of the 'war at the top' between the rival supporters of Wałęsa and Mazowiecki, who formed two broad camps within the decomposing Solidarity Civic Committees.[9] The more conservative elements clustered around Wałęsa, for whom the idea of a more radical break with the past, based on the rather amorphous slogan 'acceleration', was a key one. Wałęsa's supporters were organized in the Centre Agreement (Porozumienie Centrum, PC), formed in May 1990 as a coalition of parties and groupings (including the Christian National Union and Liberal Democratic Congress) by a key Wałęsa aide (and subsequently enemy) Jarosław Kaczyński.[10] The more liberal elements clustered around the Mazowiecki government, more concerned with keeping the government's controversial economic reform programme introduced by its Finance Minister Leszek Balcerowicz on track.[11] Mazowiecki's supporters were initially organized primarily in the Citizens' Movement–Democratic Action (Ruch Obywatelski–Akcja Demokratyczna, ROAD) grouping formed in July 1990 in response to the formation of the Centre Agreement. It is interesting to note that, while Wałęsa's supporters seemed fairly comfortable with the 'right-wing' or 'centre-right' tag, the Mazowiecki camp, whose members objectively were probably more 'right-wing' in their approach to economic policy, eschewed it.[12] The struggle between the two camps culminated in the November–December 1990 presidential election which was won by Wałęsa with Mazowiecki finishing a humiliating third, beaten by an eccentric, unknown Polish–Canadian émigré businessman, Stanisław Tymiński. While Wałęsa proceed to cut himself off from Kaczyński and his erstwhile supporters in the Centre Agreement, Mazowiecki's supporters formed the new Democratic Union party (Unia Demokratyczna, UD) in December 1990.

As Table 1 shows, the first fully free parliamentary election, held in October 1991, produced a fragmented (almost atomized) parliament. The largest party, the Democratic Union, won only 12.31 per cent of the vote and 62 (out of 460) seats, while the eight largest parliamentary groupings won between 3.27 and 12.31 per cent of the votes and 16–62 seats. These included the main centre-right post-Solidarity groupings: the Centre Agreement, Christian National Union (as part of the Catholic Electoral Action coalition), Liberal Democratic Congress, the Solidarity trade union itself (under the leadership of Wałęsa's successor Marian Krzaklewski) and the Peasant Agreement (Porozumienie Ludowe, PL), together with the Confederation for an Independent Poland. This highly fragmented parliament was partly the result of the extremely proportional electoral system that was adopted, although arguably this served simply to *reflect* rather than create or exacerbate divisions within the post-Solidarity camp.[13]

The 1991–93 parliament sustained two weak centre-right coalition governments: the first, led by the Centre Agreement deputy Jan Olszewski,

TABLE 1

OCTOBER 1991 PARLIAMENTARY ELECTION RESULTS

Party	Votes	%	Seats
Democratic Union (UD)	1,382,051	12.31	62
Democratic Left Alliance (SLD)	1,344,820	11.98	60
Catholic Electoral Action (WAK)	980,304	8.73	49
Centre Agreement (PC)	977,344	8.71	44
Polish Peasant Party (PSL)	972,952	8.67	48
Confederation for an Independent Poland (KPN)	841,738	7.50	46
Liberal Democratic Congress (KLD)	839,978	7.48	37
Peasant Agreement (PL)	613,626	5.46	28
Solidarity (NSZZ'S')	566,553	5.05	27
Polish Beer Lovers' Party (PPPP)	367,106	3.27	16

Source: J. Raciborski, *Polskie Wybory: Zachowanie wyborczego społeczeństwa polskiego 1989–1995* (Warsaw: Wydawnictwo Naukowe 'Scholar', 1997), p.42.

lasted from December 1991 until June 1992 and the second, led by Democratic Union deputy Hannah Suchocka, from July 1992 to September 1993.[14] During this period the process of disintegration of the former Solidarity camp continued and intensified, with all the main centre-right parties and groupings suffering major splits and defections. For example, following his ousting as premier in June 1992 Olszewski took a significant number of Centre Agreement deputies with him to form a new party, the Movement for the Republic (Ruch dla Rzeczpospolitej, RdR).

All this culminated in the September 1993 parliamentary election which, as Table 2 shows, saw the Democratic Left Alliance and the successor to its one-time satellite the Polish Peasant Party (Polskie Stronnictwo Ludowe, PSL) returned to power with a huge majority. Virtually all the parties of the right and centre-right, representing around one-third of the electorate, were excluded from parliament. The partial exceptions were the Confederation for an Independent Poland and the rather amorphous, Wałęsa-inspired Non-Party Bloc for the Support of Reforms (Bezpartyjny Bloc na Wspierania Reform, BBWR), both of which proceeded to disintegrate rapidly. The right's virtual exclusion from the 1993–97 parliament was due to the provisions of the new electoral system. In particular, a five per cent threshold for parties to secure parliamentary representation (eight per cent for electoral coalitions) was introduced which punished the centre-right for failing to coalesce around a small number of electoral committees. The overwhelming victory of the former communists and their erstwhile allies (winning nearly two-thirds of the seats on the basis of only 36 per cent of the vote) was further exacerbated by other amendments to the electoral system that made it less proportional. These included an increase in the number of electoral districts (from 37 to 52), with fewer deputies elected per district, and the

TABLE 2
SEPTEMBER 1993 PARLIAMENTARY ELECTION RESULTS

Party	Votes	%	Seats
Above the threshold:			
Democratic Left Alliance (SLD)	2,815,169	20.41	171
Polish Peasant Party (PSL)	2,124,367	15.40	132
Democratic Union (UD)	1,460,957	10.59	74
Labour Union (UP)	1,005,004	7.28	41
Confederation for an Independent Poland (KPN)	795,487	5.77	22
Non-Party Bloc in Support of Reforms (BBWR)	746,653	5.41	16
Below the threshold:			
Catholic Electoral Committee 'Fatherland' (KKW'O')	878,445	6.37	
Solidarity	676,334	4.90	
Centre Agreement (PC)	609,973	4.42	
Liberal Democratic Congress (KLD)	550,578	3.99	
Union of Real Politics (UPR)	438,559	3.18	
Self-Defence	383,967	2.78	
Party X	377,480	2.74	
Coalition for the Republic (KdR)	371,923	2.70	
Polish Peasant Party–Peasant Agreement (PSL–PL)	327,085	2.37	

Source: S. Gebethner (ed.), *Wybory parlamentarne 1991 i 1993 a polska scena polityczna* (Warsaw: Wydawnictwo Sejmowe, 1995), p.10.

introduction of a 'national list' of seats reserved for parties that obtained at least seven per cent the vote, together with the less proportional d'Hondt counting method for apportioning seats.[15]

During this period, a number of distinctive features of the Polish right were becoming evident. First, it was not defined in terms of its approach to economic policy, as it was in many Western democracies, and encompassed elements highly critical of liberal reform as well as those supportive of them. In reality, there was little to divide the centre of gravity of the Polish centre-right and centre-left in terms of their approach to economic policy. Second, and consequently, de-communization and attitudes towards the past, together with moral and cultural issues, particularly religiosity and the role of the Church in public life, became critical in defining the right (and left and centre) in Poland. Economic issues formed a secondary axis around which competition revolved between liberal parties such as the Freedom Union (Unia Wolności, UW – formed in 1994 from a merger of Mazowiecki's Democratic Union and the Liberal Democratic Congress) and agrarian parties such as the Polish Peasant Party.[16] Third, in addition to more secular liberal-conservatives and those who drew their inspiration from Western Christian democracy, the Polish right also encompassed a strong (although very internally divided) Catholic nationalist element, sometimes drawing on the traditions of Roman Dmowski's pre-war National Democracy (the so-called *endecja*). Fourth, the Solidarity trade union remained a key political actor within parliamentary and party politics and was to do so right up until the September 2001 parliamentary election. Fifth, the right was characterized by weak party organizations with a lack of mass membership, social implantation or financial or organizational resources, combined with the lack of a culture of organizational self-discipline. This was in striking contrast to the communist successor Democratic Left Alliance.[17]

Finally, the role of personalities was, it may be argued, a very important factor in terms of explaining fragmentation on the Polish right. The large number of parties was due, in large part, to the inability of individual leaders to work with one another and created much more fragmentation than ideological or programmatic differences alone would have accounted for.[18] One explanation for this may be that it was the institutional framework, particularly the existence of a relatively strong presidency, that encouraged Wałęsa in particular to act as a divisive and polarizing figure by attempting to 'rise above' party politics and eschew the path of party development. Certainly, at various points Wałęsa undermined all the emerging centre-right parties including (perhaps in particular) the Centre Agreement that was formed to explicitly give him backing in 1990. This is an argument developed by Saxonberg in his comparative analysis of the different political strategies pursued by Wałęsa and Václav Klaus in the Czech Republic.[19] I shall return to this in the final section when I critically evaluate all the existing explanatory frameworks.

The Emergence of Solidarity Electoral Action

Following the shock of the 1993 parliamentary election, there followed two years of various attempts to try and create unity on the Polish centre-right. However, none of these succeeded in making any impact beyond the narrow circles of committed activists, and they all effectively disintegrated by the end of 1994.[20] Even the centre-right's qualified success in the June 1994 local elections was the result of locally brokered electoral coalitions and often despite, rather than thanks to, national leaders' efforts.[21] Indeed, it was only the shock of its defeat in the November 1995 presidential election by the Democratic Left Alliance leader at that time, Aleksander Kwaśniewski, that finally shook the centre-right out of its complacency. The five main centre-right and right-wing candidates who emerged to contest the first round (Lech Wałęsa, Jacek Kuroń, Jan Olszewski, Hanna Gronkiewicz-Waltz and Janusz Korwin-Mikke) expended as much energy on attacking each other as they did on Kwaśniewski. Having been snubbed by all the main right-wing parties, it was, in fact, the incumbent Wałęsa who unexpectedly emerged as the right's standard-bearer, winning 33.11 per cent in the first round (to Kwaśniewski's 35.11 per cent) and narrowly losing in the second by 48.28 to 51.72 per cent.[22]

However, in many ways Kwaśniewski's victory actually helped to create the conditions for the revival of the centre-right and emergence of Solidarity Electoral Action. The Wałęsa–Kwaśniewski presidential battle developed into a contest between the representatives of the two historic formations: 'post-Solidarity' and 'post-communist'. It thereby polarized the Polish political scene in relation to attitudes towards the past. The re-emergence of this 'historic' division, which had lain dormant but was never quite forgotten, was strengthened by the fact that control over all the main institutions of the state (presidency, government and parliament) now appeared to be concentrated in the hands of the ex-communists and their allies. This polarization was reinforced by the so-called 'Oleksy affair', in which the Democratic Left Alliance prime minister Józef Oleksy was forced to resign in January 1996, following (unproven) allegations by Wałęsa's outgoing interior minister that he had collaborated with the Soviet and then Russian security services. As people became more conscious of these 'old' divisions, attitudes towards the past (together with moral and cultural issues) rather than socio-economic policies became the key defining 'left–right' issue in Polish politics. The re-emergence of this 'historic' division provided the right with a clear rallying-point around which it could unite its electorate and define itself more clearly: it stood for 'anti-communism' and opposition to the Democratic Left Alliance. In the same way that fear of domination by the right had encouraged Poles who identified with the left to cluster around the Democratic Left Alliance in 1993, Kwaśniewski's victory closely followed by the 'Oleksy affair' created the conditions for a similar dynamic to develop among right-wing voters.

The shock of the 1995 presidential election defeat, therefore, led to the formation of Solidarity Electoral Action in June 1996 by 22 parties and other groupings spearheaded by the Solidarity trade union.[23] By the time of the September 1997 election it had expanded to encompass more than 30 such organizations. Although the union had become increasingly politicized since 1993 (for example, collecting two million signatures in support of its draft 'Citizens' Constitution' in 1994), it had also resisted attempts to be drawn too closely into any of the previous right-wing blocs. However, the 1995 débâcle convinced the union's leaders that only they were capable of uniting the right and creating an effective challenger to the Democratic Left Alliance.[24] Solidarity Electoral Action made an immediate impact in the opinion polls, running neck-and-neck with the ex-communists until, as Table 3 shows, it went on to a clear win in the September 1997 election, with 33.83 per cent of the vote and 201 seats, compared with the Democratic Left Alliance's 27.13 per cent and 164 seats.[25]

Why did Solidarity Electoral Action succeed where other centre-right political initiatives had failed? The single most important reason was its

TABLE 3
SEPTEMBER 1997 PARLIAMENTARY ELECTION RESULTS

	Votes	%	Seats
Above the threshold:			
Solidarity Electoral Action (AWS)	4,427,373	33.83	201
Democratic Left Alliance (SLD)	3,551,224	27.13	164
Freedom Union (UW)	1,749,518	13.37	60
Polish Peasant Party (PSL)	956,184	7.31	27
Movement for Poland's Reconstruction (ROP)	727,072	5.56	6
Below the threshold:			
Labour Union (UP)	620,611	4.74	
National Party of Retirees and Pensioners (KPEiR)	284,826	2.18	
Union of the Republic Right (UPR)	266,317	2.03	
National Agreement of Retirees and Pensioners (KPEiRRP)	212,826	1.63	
Christian Democratic–Bloc for Poland (ChD–BdP)	178,395	1.36	

Source: *Rzeczpospolita*, 2 October 1997.

ability to unite the various components of the previously deeply fragmented right and then to survive intact and reasonably coherent until polling day. By providing a clear focus for the anti-Democratic Left Alliance electorate at a time of polarization around historical divisions, Solidarity Electoral Action was able to mop up the wasted votes of those who had previously supported smaller right-wing parties that fell below the five per cent threshold. The main parties and groupings that went on to form Solidarity Electoral Action actually won 4,033,977 votes (29.24 per cent) in 1993, only slightly less than the 4,427,373 (33.83 per cent) secured by Solidarity Electoral Action in 1997. It was also considerably more than the Democratic Left Alliance's 1993 total of 2,815,169 (20.41 per cent). As noted above, it was only through a combination of their own disunity and fractiousness, and the effects of an electoral system that ruthlessly punished them for this, that the Polish right found themselves virtually excluded from the 1993–97 parliament. At the same time Solidarity Electoral Action obtained a 'premium' for unity by mobilizing those voters who had craved a united opposition but had been baffled by the shifting alignments in previous right-wing electoral blocs.

Moreover, by uniting the right, Solidarity Electoral Action was able to capture the symbolism of Solidarity movement and recreate a feeling of 'societal unity' from the 1980s. An important aspect of this was its successful attempt to identify itself with, and invoke the symbolism of, the original Solidarity opposition movement.[26] Indeed, this attempt to draw an analogy between the new spirit of right-wing 'political unity' represented by the formation of Solidarity Electoral Action and the 'societal unity' that had characterized Solidarity's previous anti-communist struggles in 1980–81 and 1989 was to become the outstanding overarching theme of Solidarity Electoral Action's entire 1997 election campaign.[27] One example of this strategy was the presentation of '21 programmatic tasks' on the anniversary of the signing of the August 1980 agreements when the communist authorities agreed to the striking coastal workers' '21 demands' that led to the formation of the original Solidarity. Such activities, together with other slogans that invoked the idea of 'finishing the Solidarity revolution', clearly struck an emotional chord with that section of a polarized electorate for whom the notion of 'settling accounts' with the communist past was still very important.[28]

However, this unity was possible – and this was the key difference between Solidarity Electoral Action and previous right-wing unity initiatives – only because it was explicitly not a partnership of equals. The small and medium-sized parties and groupings that constituted Solidarity Electoral Action, such as the Christian National Union, the Centre Agreement, the Confederation for an Independent Poland and the Conservative People's Party,[29] subordinated themselves to a clear hegemon in the shape of the Solidarity trade union. Solidarity's representatives were guaranteed 50 per cent of the votes (known as 'shares') in the Solidarity Electoral Action National Council, and the union's leader, Marian Krzaklewski, was automatically the grouping's unquestioned leader. Moreover, the union's hegemony was also guaranteed by two other factors: first, the fact that its organizational infrastructure dwarfed that of all other Solidarity Electoral Action members; second, and perhaps more importantly, the fact that, unlike the 'post-Solidarity' political parties, the trade union was the only grouping that could credibly claim a direct and unbroken organizational link to the 'heroic' pre-1989 Solidarity era. Consequently, Solidarity was the only organization capable of providing both a clear symbol and rallying-point for those opposed to the Democratic Left Alliance, in the same way that Wałęsa had for the anti-Kwaśniewski electorate in 1995. This made it very difficult for other party leaders to question Solidarity's authority and led some commentators to suggest that Krzaklewski played an almost 'dictatorial' role on the Polish right, thereby providing Solidarity Electoral Action with an organizational cohesion that previous right-wing blocs had lacked.[30] Once a hegemon around which they could unite emerged in the shape of the Solidarity trade union, it was then simply a question of surviving intact until polling day.

The main objective of Solidarity Electoral Action's election campaign, therefore, was to achieve the maximum possible mobilization of the existing right-wing electorate through a moral and ideological appeal focusing on 'values' associated with the family and the nation and by attempting to draw analogies with previous anti-communist struggles. However, it is also important to note that, as well as showing that they were capable of learning the lessons of previous defeats, the Solidarity Electoral Action campaign also demonstrated the right's ability to renew itself and present a youthful and forward-looking image to the electorate. In addition to re-building the old Solidarity coalition, then, Solidarity Electoral Action successfully presented the right's message with moderation and professionalism, portraying itself as a dynamic, modernizing force. At the same time, however, much of this was based on successful political communication rather than a well-thought-through attempt to develop a properly inclusive narrative that could provide the grouping with programmatic and ideological coherence beyond a single election.

The Decline and Fall of Solidarity Electoral Action

The September 1997 election result led to the formation of a coalition government based on the two 'post-Solidarity' groupings: Solidarity Electoral Action and the Freedom Union. Krzaklewski, the architect of its success, declined the office of prime minister in favour of the previously little-known Solidarity economic adviser Jerzy Buzek. Instead, he preferred to exercise 'behind the scenes' influence as Solidarity Electoral Action parliamentary club leader and to save himself for a presidential bid in 2000 (as Kwaśniewski had after the Democratic Left Alliance's 1993 victory).

However, Solidarity Electoral Action's September 1997 electoral triumph was to prove its high-water mark. During its first year in office, the introduction of a 'second wave' of four systemic reforms in the fields of local government, health, pensions and education gave the Buzek government a sense of purpose and momentum. This all contributed to Solidarity Electoral Action's relatively good results in the October 1998 local elections.[31] However, the new government was knocked off-balance by a wave of protests and labour disputes beginning with a series of illegal farmers' blockades in January 1999, and it never really recovered its authority. After that, the Buzek administration spent the next three years lurching from crisis to crisis and lacked any clear sense of direction. Buzek's calm and consensual style of government was originally seen as an asset. However, his tendency to compromise and avoid confrontation also created the impression of dithering and incompetence at a time when the electorate wanted a stronger and more decisive leadership style. As the parliament progressed, the government's flagship reforms became increasingly unpopular and exacerbated tensions between and within the coalition parties. The economic policy pursued by the liberal finance minister and Freedom Union party leader Leszek Balcerowicz provided a particular source of conflict with the more economically interventionist elements within Solidarity Electoral Action. The coalition finally broke up acrimoniously in June 2000, leaving Buzek at the head of a minority government.

From the beginning of 1999, therefore, Solidarity Electoral Action began to slump in the opinion polls. At the next major electoral test, the October 2000 presidential poll, Kwaśniewski won a landslide victory, securing over 50 per cent of the vote in the first round, while Krzaklewski finished a humiliating third with only 15.57 per cent, behind the independent liberal-conservative Andrzej Olechowski who won 17.3 per cent.[32] Krzaklewski's defeat brought to a head simmering tensions within Solidarity Electoral Action over policy, strategy and leadership, which culminated in the September 2001 election catastrophe when its rump failed to secure election to parliament. When, with extreme reluctance, Krzaklewski relinquished the Solidarity Electoral Action leadership to Buzek in December 2000 and its main constituent groupings negotiated a Christmas truce, the crisis briefly appeared to have been resolved. However, this was to prove the calm before the storm. Sejm Marshal Maciej Płażyński had been promoted as an alternative Solidarity Electoral Action presidential candidate by its anti-Krzaklewski liberal–conservative faction clustered around the Conservative People's Party. It soon emerged that he was dissatisfied with the agreement that would have seen him become Solidarity Electoral Action vice-chairman and election campaign organizer. Consequently, in January 2001 Olechowski, Płażyński and the deputy marshal of the Senate (and recently defeated leadership candidate) Freedom Union's Donald Tusk (known collectively as 'the three tenors') decided to form a new political grouping, the Civic Platform (Platforma Obywatelska, PO).

Initially it appeared that it would be the Freedom Union that would be hardest hit by the Civic Platform's formation and that Solidarity Electoral Action would not suffer any significant defections other than Płażyński. However, in March 2001, following a couple of months of prevarication and internal debate, the Conservative People's Party eventually decided to leave Solidarity Electoral Action and contest the election under the Civic Platform banner. This party's defection was followed quickly in April 2001 by the decision of the justice minister Lech Kaczyński (nominated by Solidarity Electoral Action but politically independent) to support the formation of the new Law and Justice (Prawo i Sprawiedliwość, PiS) party led by his twin brother Jarosław. Since joining the Solidarity Electoral Action government (by then a minority administration) in June 2000, Lech Kaczyński had carved out a niche for himself as an uncompromising enemy of corruption and crime. His tough rhetoric helped to him to gain huge popularity, increasing his approval rating from 31 per cent in June 2000 to 71 per cent in June 2001, second only to Kwaśniewski among Polish politicians.[33] However, this was very much a personal base of support and did nothing to broaden the government's wider appeal.

In retrospect, the Conservative People's Party's defection and the formation of Law and Justice sealed Solidarity Electoral Action's fate. When, in May 2001, Solidarity Electoral Action rejected the Kaczyński brothers' terms for a joint electoral list, it was clear that there would be at least two right-wing blocs competing for what remained of the Solidarity Electoral Action electorate. On the one hand, the rump Solidarity Electoral Action parties were joined (for a few weeks at least) by the remnants of Olszewski's Movement for the Republic (Ruch Odbudowy Polski, ROP) party to form Solidarity Electoral Action of the Right (Akja Wyborcza Solidarność Prawicy, AWSP).[34] The latter was formally backed by Solidarity but, after the union finally decided to withdraw from party politics in May 2001, it kept very much at arms' length and did not provide the kind of organizational support that had proved crucial to Solidarity Electoral Action's 1997 success. On the other hand, there was the Law and Justice electoral bloc that comprised two main elements: the Law and Justice party itself, swiftly cobbled together by individuals who had once been members of the Centre Agreement party,[35] and the Right-wing Agreement (Przymierze Prawicy, PP) party.[36]

A number of other ex-Solidarity Electoral Action politicians went on to form smaller right-wing groupings and coalitions, the most significant of which was to prove the radical right-wing League of Polish Families (Liga Polskich Rodzin, LPR). This was important because the League was able to prise the 'religious right' electorate clustered around the fundamentalist Catholic–nationalist broadcaster Radio Maryja away from Solidarity Electoral Action.[37] Led by its charismatic director, Father Tadeusz Rydzyk, Radio Maryja is a specifically Polish phenomenon that has struck a deep chord with the most traditionalist elements of Polish society and demonstrated an ability to mobilize a limited but not insignificant bloc of several hundred thousand voters. Solidarity Electoral Action was the main beneficiary of Radio Maryja's mobilizing power in previous elections. In September 1997, for example, the broadcaster was able to secure the election of a sizeable faction of its supporters from the Solidarity Electoral Action electoral lists. Even though Solidarity Electoral Action was a broad centre-right coalition in which the Catholic–nationalist wing was in a clear minority, Father Ryzdzyk continued to back it throughout the 1997–2001 parliament. In the October 2000 presidential election, for example, he supported Krzaklewski against the radical right anti-EU candidate Jan Łopuszański, who had at one time been closely aligned with Radio Maryja. However, in the September 2001 parliamentary election Radio Maryja decided not to back Solidarity Electoral Action, the key moment here being the decision, little noticed at the time, of Sejm deputy Anna Sobecka (who was very closely associated with Father Rydzyk) to defect from Solidarity Electoral Action to the League. This decision was a key factor in ensuring that an important segment of the core right-wing electorate voted for the League rather than for Solidarity Electoral Action.

A final 'own goal' was the decision to register Solidarity Electoral Action of the Right as an electoral coalition rather than as a single party (as, for example, Law and Justice and the League of Polish Families had done by simply adding candidates from other parties to one party list). This meant that that they had to secure a higher threshold of votes for both parliamentary representation (eight instead of five per cent) and state party funding (six instead of three per cent). In fact, had it registered as a single party then Solidarity Electoral Action of the Right would have crossed the threshold for both. In the event, as Table 4 shows, it suffered a catastrophic defeat, winning 5.6 per cent of the vote and holding on to only 14.8 per cent of 1997 Solidarity Electoral Action voters.[38]

Why Did Solidarity Electoral Action Fail?

Why did Solidarity Electoral Action fail so spectacularly? Some commentators have argued that it was its poor record in government, and in particular the deep unpopularity of its four flagship reforms. Certainly, most Polish voters considered these reforms to be poorly conceived, hastily introduced and incompetently managed, and they clearly contributed towards making Buzek's government the most unpopular since 1989. A July 2001 CBOS poll, for example, found that 74 per cent of respondents felt that the health service had deteriorated as a result of the reforms (only nine per cent that it had improved); 49 per cent said that they had a negative impact on the education system (13 per cent positive), 38 per cent on the pension system (17 per cent positive) and 32 per cent on local government (20 per cent positive).[39] However, Solidarity Electoral Action's momentous September 2001 defeat was as much a verdict on the quality and style of the Buzek governments as on their specific policies, and the grouping actually faced more fundamental

TABLE 4
SEPTEMBER 2001 PARLIAMENTARY ELECTION RESULTS

	Votes	%	Seats
Above the threshold:			
Democratic Left Alliance–Labour Union (SLD–UP)	5,342,519	41.04	216
Civic Platform (PO)	1,651,099	12.68	65
Self-Defence (Samoobrona)	1,327,624	10.20	53
Law and Justice (PiS)	1,237,624	9.50	44
Polish Peasant Party (PSL)	1,168,659	8.98	42
League of Polish Families (LPR)	1,025,148	7.87	38
Below the threshold:			
Solidarity Electoral Action of the Right (AWSP)	729,297	5.60	
Freedom Union (UW)	404,074	3.10	

Source: *Rzeczpospolita*, 19 October 2001, and Polish State Electoral Commission.

problems. A June 2001 OBOP poll, for example, found that the four reforms were cited as only the fourth most important reason why Solidarity Electoral Action had lost support (17 per cent). The two most important by far were the linked issue of Solidarity Electoral Action's internal difficulties (43 per cent) and the fact that it was perceived to have placed its own interests ahead of those of the country as a whole (30 per cent).[40]

As noted above, from the outset Solidarity Electoral Action was an ideologically eclectic and heterogeneous political construct encompassing socially conservative trade unionists, Christian democrats, Catholic nationalists (both economically interventionist and more liberal), and relatively secular liberal–conservatives. There was always a danger that centrifugal tendencies would emerge in an organization encompassing such a wide spectrum of apparently contradictory views. However, Solidarity Electoral Action was not necessarily any more ideologically eclectic than many other successful centre-right coalitions in other states, and the problems associated with this heterogeneity were by no means insurmountable. So why was Solidarity Electoral Action unable to overcome these difficulties? This was due partly to its disparate internal structure, which significantly exacerbated these problems. As noted above, Solidarity Electoral Action was formed as a conglomerate of more than 30 right-wing and centre-right parties and political groupings under the hegemony of the Solidarity trade union. These groupings originally agreed to subordinate themselves to, and vest enormous power in, the Solidarity leader Krzaklewski in order to guarantee a certain amount of discipline and cohesion. But Solidarity Electoral Action remained an amorphous political conglomerate and failed to develop a strong institutional centre. Krzaklewski's original idea, that all the existing parties should dissolve themselves and Solidarity Electoral Action transform itself into a single, unitary political party even before the 1997 election, met with a negative response from the leaders of the most influential parties. They feared losing their identity and influence within the new, larger grouping that would inevitably be dominated by former Solidarity trade union leaders.[41]

The best, and perhaps only, time to have driven this proposal through was in the run-up to the 1997 election when Krzaklewski and Solidarity still held all the cards. At this stage, they still had a credible threat against the leaders of the smaller parties who could have undermined his plans: exclusion from the Solidarity Electoral Action candidate lists, and therefore potential electoral oblivion. This was the real 'critical juncture' for Solidarity Electoral Action. Krzaklewski's hegemonic power disappeared once the smaller parties that made up the coalition achieved parliamentary representation, and thereby obtained blackmail power by threatening the Solidarity Electoral Action leadership with the sanction of refusing to support the government; in this way it threatened its majority in parliament.[42] Given the smaller parties' potential for blackmail, Krzaklewski's proposal was modified gradually so that Solidarity Electoral Action remained a political conglomerate clustered round five main constituent elements. A new union-sponsored political party, the Solidarity Electoral Action Social Movement (Ruch Społeczny Akcji Wyborczej Solidarność, RS AWS) led by Buzek was set up in November 1997 to take over the union's political functions as it gradually withdrew from politics. However, the Solidarity trade union continued to retain a key role as it remained Krzaklewski's power base. It simply agreed to share some power with the Social Movement and three other parties with which most of the other groupings had merged: the Christian National Union, the Conservative People's Party and the Polish Agreement of Christian Democrats. All that this particular model of partial organizational consolidation round five more or less equal constituent elements succeeded in doing was transforming a situation where Krzaklewski could impose his will on a large number of weak parties into one where he had to deal with a smaller number of medium-sized parties on a more equal basis. It thereby actually weakened rather than strengthened the Solidarity Electoral Action organizational centre.

The fact that all the main Solidarity Electoral Action partners strongly underlined their distinctive identity and could potentially threaten the government's majority also meant that the government constantly had to square off these various partisan interests. This, in turn, made an already fractious and ideologically eclectic political grouping even more organizationally unstable, and inevitably led to gridlock and political cronyism.[43] It also fed the perception of an immobile and helpless government. Indeed, while the government was probably the one power centre round which Solidarity Electoral Action could have been integrated, this proved impossible because its leader Krzaklewski chose to remain outside it. Moreover, he also prevented Buzek from exercising effective leadership by ensuring that all key decisions and conflicts had to be negotiated with and resolved by him personally.[44]

However, quite apart from its formal structural difficulties, Solidarity Electoral Action's most serious weakness was the lack of even elementary organizational self-discipline among most of its members. Indeed, very often supposed ideological, programmatic or strategic differences were used as a pretext to justify the intense personal rivalry that existed between the various sub-group leaders. It soon became clear that all that held Solidarity Electoral Action's various strands together was their common desire to defeat the Democratic Left Alliance and the subsequent fear that leaving Solidarity Electoral Action would consign them to electoral oblivion. The key to Solidarity Electoral Action's survival was, therefore, always going to be the performance of the Buzek government. If this were a success, Solidarity Electoral Action's various constituent elements would want to remain part of it; if it failed then there was always a danger that they would begin to peel off to find more successful or ideologically more comfortable alternatives. The 1998 local elections and opinion polling evidence taken until the beginning of 2001 appeared to indicate that none of the individual parties that constituted Solidarity Electoral Action was capable of independent electoral success.[45] However, as Solidarity Electoral Action's poll ratings slumped and it became increasingly clear that life outside of it did not necessarily lead to electoral oblivion (or, at least, no more so than remaining within it) centrifugal tendencies began to emerge. This process moved up a gear as large numbers of individuals (and even whole parties) started to jump ship following Krzaklewski's heavy electoral defeat. As it became increasingly clear that Solidarity Electoral Action was not necessarily the best vehicle for the various individuals and groupings that comprised the organization to maintain their parliamentary presence, they began to seek other alternatives. The end of the 1997–2001 parliament had reduced the Solidarity Electoral Action fraction from 201 Sejm deputies to only 134.[46] The fear of electoral defeat that prompted these defections became, in turn, a self-fulfilling prophecy. Ironically, this was exacerbated by a 2001 amendment to the electoral law to make it more favourable to medium-sized parties[47] such as Solidarity Electoral Action supported when it began to lose support.

Moreover, the fact that each of Solidarity Electoral Action's constituent elements was constantly determined to secure the most advantageous position for itself not only made it difficult for the Buzek government to exercise firm leadership by, for example, initiating a major re-shuffle: it also meant that the Solidarity Electoral Action leadership was constantly having to square off these interests and pacify dissent through the use of patronage. This led Solidarity Electoral Action to adopt an increasingly clientelistic style of politics in order to keep the grouping together, and this, in turn, contributed to the image of a government that was corrupt and engaged in the 'partification' of the state. Certainly, the previous Democratic Left Alliance–Polish Peasant Party coalition had also been closely associated with the practice of placing party supporters in key areas of the economy, particularly the management and supervisory boards of state or 'para-state' institutions such as Treasury-owned companies. Introducing a 'cleaner' and more ethical style of government – and therefore implicitly breaking with this practice of what became known as 'political capitalism' – was one of Solidarity Electoral Action's key election pledges in 1997. Solidarity Electoral Action voters, therefore, had high expectations of a grouping that was committed to 'cleaning up' government. In this sense, the Solidarity Electoral Action government was always going to be judged by much more rigorous ethical standards than the previous coalition, whose voters tended to evaluate its performance in more pragmatic terms. So it came as a shock to its supporters when it became clear that, far from leading to the hoped-for 'de-partification' of the state and de-politicization of the economy, the Solidarity Electoral Action-led government proved as adept, if not more so (and certainly much less subtle), at placing party appointees in key positions.[48] A June 2001 PBS poll, for example, found that the largest number of respondents (33 per cent) cited Solidarity Electoral Action as the most corrupt Polish party (compared with ten per cent who named the Democratic Left Alliance).[49]

Explaining Solidarity Electoral Action's Failure

So which of the explanatory frameworks outlined in the introduction to this collection best explain Solidarity Electoral Action's failure?

Approaches based on structural legacy have only very limited explanatory power, and not in the way envisaged in the literature. The legacy of the communist period that produced the only mass opposition movement in the Soviet bloc, together with the existence of a strong and independent Catholic Church and relatively religious citizenry, ought to have produced fertile ground for a cohesive and successful Polish centre-right grouping. In fact, as discussed above, this has not been the case. Moreover, the fact that throughout much of the 1990s the Solidarity trade union movement constituted an indispensable component of any successful centre-right (indeed, at one point a necessary condition for this) created its own problems. A trade union movement whose membership was based in declining, publicly owned industries, likely to be most affected negatively by economic reform, was always going to have a problematic relationship with the more liberal elements of the centre-right. However, successful centre-right political formations in modern democracies (Solidarity Electoral Action included) have tended to combine some kind of alliance between social conservatism and economic liberalism, and Solidarity's pivotal role in Solidarity Electoral Action was, therefore, always going to make this problematic. Clearly, the kind of assets required to develop a successful mass democratic opposition movement against a communist dictatorship were very different from those necessary to fashion a successful centre-right party in a post-communist democratic context.

The actions of leaders and the importance of decisions taken during the early transition period also offer little help in terms of explaining Solidarity Electoral Action's failure. As the discussion above shows, 1989–91 was certainly an extremely divisive period for the Polish right. However, the formation of Solidarity Electoral Action in 1996 appeared to demonstrate that these divisions could be overcome. Lessons appeared to have been learned, and the decisions taken in the wake of the 1995 presidential election defeat showed that previous mistakes could be rectified to create a united centre-right formation. It is possible to argue that the depth and bitterness of the divisions that emerged in the early transition period were to continue to blight the centre-right even when they started to draw conclusions from their electoral defeats. In other words, they made it impossible to do anything other than put together a very loose and fragile construct based on a temporary hegemon.[50] But, arguably, the real critical juncture was the 1996–97 period, when Krzaklewski could perhaps have used his brief period of hegemony to fashion a more coherent and robust political organization with a stronger institutional centre, able to ride out political crises and ensure longer-term survival.

In terms of macro-institutional explanations, there are clearly moments when the electoral system appeared to provide incentives for the centre-right both to unite and to divide. The highly proportional 1991 system may well have encouraged fragmentation. The bitter experience of exclusion from parliament in 1993 as a result of the new, less proportional voting system may have been one of the factors that eventually spurred the formation of Solidarity Electoral Action. Its 2001 amendment to the electoral law to make it more favourable to medium-sized groups may also have accelerated the grouping's own decomposition by making the option of 'exit' more attractive to some of its members. However, it is difficult in these cases to distinguish cause from effect as it was the centre-right political elites themselves who were at least in part responsible for drafting these laws and they may simply have *reflected* divisions rather than *created* them. Moreover, these approaches do not really explain why the communist successor left – who, after all, had to operate within the same kind of electoral system – was able to develop a much more cohesive and unified political party.

At the same time, as Saxonberg suggests, the existence of a semi-presidential system in Poland may have encouraged Wałęsa to avoid a party-building strategy – indeed, actually to frustrate attempts to develop a unified and coherent right-wing formation. It is clear that at certain points the distribution of power within the executive did create some incentives for Wałęsa to do this and these may have interacted with his personality to foster fragmentation of the Polish centre-right. However, this may have been more to do with his pre-existing anti-party sentiments rather than the degree of incentive provided by a semi-presidential system. Moreover, and perhaps most significantly, while it may offer insights into the fragmentation and weakness of the Polish centre-right during the early 1990s, Saxonberg's framework of institutional incentives does not really offer an adequate explanation for the rise (and subsequent fall) of Solidarity Electoral Action during the second half of the decade. Indeed, it can be argued that the 1995 presidential election played a polarizing role that actually facilitated Solidarity Electoral Action's formation in mid-1996.[51] Implicitly, Saxonberg argues that

Krzaklewski's defeat in the 2000 presidential election played a critical role in the break-up of Solidarity Electoral Action, and therefore appears to fit into his broad framework. However, as noted above, while it certainly provided the catalyst for the grouping's final break-up, the 2000 election simply exacerbated Solidarity Electoral Action's existing deep structural weaknesses. These were, in particular, its unstable institutional configuration (particularly the blackmail power exercised by its constituent elements) and the failure of its leaders (especially Krzaklewski) to overcome this through skilful political crafting. Indeed, had Solidarity Electoral Action possessed a stronger candidate in 2000, then the presidential election could actually have played an integrative function for the grouping.

Saxonberg's account of why the Polish communist successor left was able to overcome the difficulties of operating within the same institutional framework is also not entirely convincing. Saxonberg argues that the Democratic Left Alliance had 'no charismatic "hero" who could hope to gain power by placing themselves above party politics', and therefore had no choice but to pursue a party-building strategy. Saxonberg describes Kwaśniewski as a 'former apparatchik who owed his career to the party and remained dependent on its endorsement to have any chance at becoming president'.[52] However, in so far as this was true in 1995, it does not account for why Kwaśniewski did not fragment (or even significantly weaken) the Democratic Left Alliance once he actually secured his position as president. Having become Poland's most popular politician, with approval ratings consistently above 70 per cent by the late 1990s, he would have been well placed to adopt a political strategy that sought to place him 'above party politics'. On the other hand, Kwaśniewski actually played an important role in *uniting* the left by laying the groundwork for the 2001 electoral alliance between the Democratic Left Alliance and the only other significant party on the Polish centre-left, the Labour Union (Unia Pracy, UP). Admittedly, there was much speculation from 2003 of Kwaśniewski using this enormous personal popularity to launch a new 'centre' party. However, this is highly speculative, and at the time of writing (January 2004) it remains to be seen whether Kwaśniewski will play a more divisive role on the centre-left in the future.

Micro-institutional explanations, on the other hand, do appear to have some explanatory power. External sponsors created Solidarity Electoral Action and most of the key actors within it continued to maintain allegiance to these constituent elements rather than the organization as a whole, so that it developed as a weak confederal structure rather than one based on a strong institutional centre. This helps to explain why Solidarity Electoral Action's constituent parts owed the organization so little residual organizational loyalty that could see it through periods of crisis. It also explains why clientelism, which was so damaging to a grouping that had fought on the basis of having a 'clean' image and bringing high moral virtues back to politics, became so important to holding the Solidarity Electoral Action coalition together.

Finally, the role of agency and political entrepreneurship (notably its failure) also appears to have played a critical role in Solidarity Electoral Action's demise. While ideological divisions clearly existed within Solidarity Electoral Action, there is no necessary reason why these could not have been overcome if the key leaders had not lacked the organizational self-discipline and other political skills that their former communist opponents so clearly possessed. The Solidarity Electoral Action leadership needed to find a political formula for its long-term survival that would provide it with organization and coherence when the initial basis on which its constituent elements had come together (anti-communism and, specifically, a desire to defeat the Democratic Left Alliance in the 1997 election) began to wane. Indeed, there is evidence that the both of the factors that defined the Solidarity Electoral Action electorate – anti-communism and the church–state divide – have diminished as the basis for political divisions and remain important for structuring politics primarily on the far left and right flanks.[53] Krzaklewski, in particular, proved to be an ineffective and uncharismatic leader who was really capable only of negotiating the backroom deals necessary to establish Solidarity Electoral Action and hold it together up to the September 1997 election, when it was on an upward curve anyway. He was not up to the more difficult task of fashioning Solidarity Electoral Action into a more durable political formation. As noted above, he probably wasted his best opportunity to transform Solidarity Electoral Action into a more cohesive political grouping with better long-term prospects in the run-up to the September 1997 election.

Conclusion

Although at one stage it appeared that Solidarity Electoral Action could have provided the basis for a unified and coherent Polish centre-right grouping, it failed to use its four years in office to build on its 1997 victory. The Buzek government, led by Solidarity Electoral Action, was associated with dithering and incompetence and its four flagship social reforms were widely perceived to have been badly designed and poorly implemented. It also found it extremely difficult to overcome its ideological breadth and heterogeneity. But it was as much the quality and style of the Solidarity Electoral Action government that led to its deep unpopularity, and the breadth of opinions that the grouping encompassed were not necessarily greater than those that co-exist within more coherent and electorally successful centre-right groupings in other countries. Solidarity Electoral Action's key structural weaknesses were its failure to develop a strong institutional centre combined with, and caused by, the lack of organizational self-discipline among its leaders. Fear of electoral oblivion and cronyism rather any overarching organizational loyalty were what held Solidarity Electoral Action together. As soon as it became clear that alternative structures might be more electorally promising, and that with the prospect of imminent electoral defeat the sources of this patronage might dry up, it was bound to break up. This fissiparous and clientelistic style of politics, in turn, further drained away the party's remaining electoral support, creating a vicious circle. Solidarity Electoral Action appears to have passed into history following its catastrophic election defeat of September 2001.

The experience of the Polish case, and particularly the story of the rise and fall of Solidarity Electoral Action, the most successful attempt to date to develop a united and cohesive centre-right formation in post-1989 Poland, leads one to a number of tentative comparative conclusions. Structural-legacy approaches (although not in the way outlined in the literature) and critical-juncture or formative-moment approaches provide only partial explanations for Solidarity Electoral Action's failure. Explanations based on the electoral system, on the other hand, do not really explain why the communist successor left has been able to develop organizational coherence while centre-right formations such as Solidarity Electoral Action have not. They also do not really explain whether the electoral system created and exacerbated or simply reflected existing divisions. Poland's semi-presidential system may offer some insights into the fragmentation of the Polish centre-right in the 1990s, but it is difficult to determine how much of this was due to the institutional incentives to which it gave rise and how much to the personality of Wałęsa. Moreover, it does not really account for the rise and fall of Solidarity Electoral Action, whose formation was actually prompted by the 1995 presidential election and whose demise can be accounted for only in part by the role of Krzaklewski's defeat in the 2000 poll. Micro-institutional approaches that point to the importance of party origins, particularly whether this led them to develop as a loose federation with a weak institutional centre, appear on the other hand to have more explanatory power. Moreover, the role of agency, notably the inadequacy of its political leadership, also appears to be a critical factor in explaining Solidarity Electoral Action's failure. Its leaders, especially Krzaklewski, singularly failed to overcome its possibly surmountable ideological and personality differences and develop a programmatic coherence that could provide the basis for ideological renewal once its original anti-communist appeal began to decline in electoral salience. In particular, they failed to use key opportunities such as the run-up to the September 1997 election to create a more cohesive and durable organizational structure and ideological profile.

NOTES

1. On communist Poland see, for example, G. Kolankiewicz and P.G. Lewis, *Poland: Politics, Economics and Society* (London and New York: Pinter, 1988).
2. See H. Kitschelt, *Post-Communist Party Systems: Competition, Representation and Interparty Collaboration* (Cambridge: Cambridge University Press, 1999), p.40.
3. See J. Linz and A. Stepan, *Problems of Democratic Transition and Consolidation: Southern Europe, South America and Post-Communist Europe* (Baltimore, MD and London: Johns Hopkins University Press, 1996), p.255.
4. See B. Szajkowski, *Next to God...Poland* (London: Pinter, 1993).
5. On Solidarity see, for example, T. Garton Ash, *The Polish Revolution* (London: Cape, 1983); D. Ost. *Solidarity and the Politics of Anti-Politics: Opposition and Reform in Poland Since 1968* (Philadelphia, PA: Temple University Press, 1990); G. Sanford, *Polish Communism in Crisis* (London: Croom Helm, 1993); J. Staniszkis, *Poland's Self-Limiting Revolution* (Princeton, NJ: Princeton University Press, 1983); A. Touraine, F. Dubet, M. Wieviorka and J. Strzelecki, *Solidarity: The Analysis of a Social Movement: Poland, 1980–1981* (Cambridge: Cambridge University Press, 1983).
6. 99 out of the 100 seats in the newly created senate and all of the 161 contested seats (there were 460 in total) in the more powerful Sejm: see P.G. Lewis, 'Non-competitive Elections and Regime Change: Poland 1989', *Parliamentary Affairs*, Vol.43, No.1 (1990), pp.90–107.
7. On the Polish transition to democracy see W. Connor and P. Płozajski (eds.), *Escape from Socialism: The Polish Route* (Armonk, NY: Sharpe, 1992); G. Sanford (ed.), *Democratization in Poland, 1988–90: Polish Voices* (Basingstoke: Macmillan, 1992).
8. For the best account of party development in Poland during the first phase of post-communist politics see F. Millard, 'The Shaping of the Polish Party System, 1989–93', *East European Politics and Societies*, Vol.8, No.3 (1994), pp.467–94.
9. See T. Grabowski, 'The Party That Never Was: The Rise and Fall of the Solidarity Citizens' Committees in Poland', *East European Politics and Societies*, Vol.10, No.2 (1996), pp.214–55.
10. In 1991 the Centre Agreement went on to transform itself into a single, unitary party.
11. This is an over-simplification. As noted above, Wałęsa's camp at this time included liberals such as the Liberal Democratic Congress, while Mazowiecki's supporters also numbered more conservative politicians such as those clustered around the Forum of the Democratic Right grouping (Forum Prawicy Demokratycznej, FPD).
12. One of the leaders of the Citizens' Movement–Democratic Action, Władysław Frasyniuk, referred to their politics as 'to the west of centre'; see L. Vinton, 'Solidarity's Rival Offspring: Center Alliance and Democratic Action', *RFE/RL Report on Eastern Europe*, 21 Sept. (1990), p.22.
13. On the 1991 election see F. Millard, 'The Polish Parliamentary Elections of October 1991', *Soviet Studies*, Vol.44, No.5 (1992), pp.837–55.
14. There was also a very short-lived government in May 1992, led by Waldemar Pawlak, the leader of the ex-communist satellite Polish Peasant Party.
15. On the 1993 election see F. Millard, 'The Polish Parliamentary Election of September, 1993, *Communist and Post-Communist Studies*, Vol.27, No.3 (1994), pp.295–313.
16. See A. Szczerbiak, 'Interests and Values: Polish Parties and their Electorates', *Europe–Asia Studies*, Vol.51, No.8 (1999), pp.1401–32; T. Szawiel, 'Zróznicowania lewicowo prawicowe i jego korelaty', in R. Markowski (ed.), *Wybory Parlamentarne 1997: System partyjny, postawy polityczne, zachowanie wyborce* (Warsaw: ISP PAN, 1999); K. Jasiewicz, 'Portfel czy rózaniec? Ekonomiczne i aksjologiczne determinanty zachowań wyborczych', in Markowski, pp.149–68.
17. See A. Szczerbiak, *Poles Together? The Emergence and Development of Political Parties in Post-Communist Poland* (Budapest: Central European University Press, 2001).
18. For an attempt to account for this using a historical-cultural framework that focuses on the role of Polish intellectuals see T. Szawiel, 'Prawica a kultura. Dlaczego prawica w Polsce po 1989

r. jest słaba i skłócona?', in M. Grabowska and S. Mocka, *Pierwsza sześciolatka 1989–1995: Próba bilansu polityki* (Warsaw: ISP PAN, 1997), pp.129–49. Unfortunately, the relatively weak position of Polish conservative elites that Szawiel identifies is equally applicable to other post-communist states where more successful and cohesive centre-right formations have emerged.

19. See S. Saxonberg, 'The Influence of Presidential Systems: Why the Right Is So Weak in Conservative Poland and So Strong in the Egalitarian Czech Republic', *Problems of Post-Communism*, Vol.50, No.5 (2003), pp.22–36. For a similar macro-institutional approach that focuses on the role of the presidency see K. Jasiewicz. 'Wybory prezydenckie 1995 roku a kształtowanie się polskiego systemu partyjnego, *Studia Polityczne*, 1996, No.5, pp.7–16.

20. For a good account of the activities of the Polish right during this period see A. Domoswalski, 'W Okopach Św. Katarzyny', *Gazeta Wyborcza*, 10 Sept. 1997.

21. See A. Sabbat-Swidlicka, 'Local Elections Redress Political Balance in Poland', *RFE/RL Research Report*, Vol.3, No.27 (1994), pp.1–8.

22. See F. Millard, 'The 1995 Presidential Election', *Journal of Communist Studies and Transition Politics*, Vol.12, No.1 (1996), pp.101–9.

23. For an early analysis of Solidarity Electoral Action, see A. Szczerbiak, 'Harmonising the Discordant Right', *Transition*, Vol.3, No.6 (1997), pp.44–7.

24. See *Czas na Akcję: Marian Krzaklewski w rozmowie z Maciejem Lętowskim i Piotrem Zarembą* (Warsaw: Tysol, 1997), p.220.

25. See A. Szczerbiak, 'Electoral Politics in Poland: The Parliamentary Elections of 1997', *Journal of Communist Studies and Transition Politics*, Vol.14, No.3 (1998), pp.58–83.

26. See M. Wenzel, 'Solidarity and Akcja Wyborcza Solidarność: An Attempt at Reviving the Legend', *Communist and Post-Communist Studies*, Vol.31, No.2 (1998), pp.139–56.

27. See, for example, 'Jedność, rodzina i wolne soboty', *Rzeczpospolita*, 30 June 1997.

28. See, for example, '21 zadań dla Polski', *Rzeczpospolita*, 1 Sept. 1997; 'Wielke Obietnice', *Gazeta Wyborcza*, 1 Sept. 1997; M. Krzaklewski, '21 punktów w XXI wiek', *Gazeta Wyborcza*, 10 Sept. 1997.

29. Formed by the merger of a number of small liberal–conservative parties and right-wing defectors from the Freedom Union in January 1997.

30. See K. Grabowski, 'Dyktator', *Wprost*, 27 October 1996.

31. See A. Szczerbiak, 'The Impact of the 1998 Local Elections on the Emerging Polish Party System', *Journal of Communist Studies and Transition Politics*, Vol.15, No.3 (1999), pp.80–100.

32. See A. Szczerbiak, 'Explaining Kwaśniewski's Landslide: The October 2000 Polish Presidential Election', *Journal of Communist Studies and Transition Politics*, Vol.17, No.4 (2001), pp.78–107.

33. See M. Subotić and A. Stankiewicz, 'Drugi po prezydencie', *Rzeczpospolita.* 5 July 2001.

34. The Movement for Poland's Reconstruction was formed by Olszewski's supporters following his relatively good result in the 1995 presidential election; the party won 5.56 per cent of the vote in 1997 but obtained only six deputies; it was severely weakened by subsequent splits and remained in opposition throughout the 1997–2001 parliament.

35. The Centre Agreement had formally merged with a small Christian Democratic grouping in September 1999 to form the Polish Agreement of Christian Democrats (Polskie Porozumienie Chrześcijańskich Demokratów, PPChD) but Jarosław Kaczyński and his most loyal supporters refused to recognize this and continued to operate a separate independent party.

36. The Polish Agreement was formed in March 2001 by the Conservative People's Party minority that refused to accept the decision to support the Civic Platform and a faction within the Christian National Union that had been narrowly defeated at the party's May 2000 Congress; they were joined by a number of other well-known right-wing politicians, particularly from the radical anti-communist youth organization, the Republican League (Liga Republikańska, LR).

37. See M.D. Zdort, 'Świadectwo eurosceptyków', *Rzeczpospolita*, 25 Sept. 2001; W. Załuska, 'To jest partia ojca Rydzyka', *Gazeta Wyborcza*, 25 Sept. 2001.

38. See A. Szczerbiak, 'Poland's Unexpected Political Earthquake: The September 2001 Parliamentary Election', *Journal of Communist Studies and Transition Politics*, Vol.18, No.3 (2002), pp.483–5.
39. See 'Coraz krytycznej o reformach', *Rzeczpospolita*. 31 July 2001.
40. See J. Paradowska, 'Wszyscy do szalup', *Polityka*, 7 July 2001.
41. See M.D. Zdort, 'AWS trudno do zintegrowania', *Rzeczpospolita*, 3 June 1997.
42. See M. Łętowski, 'Prawicy grzechy główne', *Rzeczpospolita*, 2 Oct. 2001.
43. For a good analysis see T. Żukowski, 'Zabrakło czasu i woli', *Rzeczpospolita*, 27 April 2001.
44. See R. Ziemkewicz, 'Samozagłada', *Rzeczpospolita*, 8 May 2001; B. Wildstein. 'Koalicja konfliktów', *Rzeczpospolita*, 21 June 2001.
45. See, for example, M.D. Zdort, 'Premia za nazwę AWS', *Rzeczpospolita*, 3 Feb. 2000.
46. See J. Pilczyński. 'Wielke tasowanie', *Rzeczpospolita*, 21 Sept. 2001.
47. By changing the counting system to the modified Sainte Lague, increasing district magnitude and abolishing the national top-up list for larger parties winning more than seven per cent of the vote: see F. Millard, 'Elections in Poland 2001: Electoral Manipulation and Party Upheaval', *Communist and Post-Communist Studies*, Vol.36, No.1 (2003), pp.69–86.
48. For more on this see M.D. Zdort, 'Prawica nie potrafiła pokazać wyborcom, dlaczego rządzi', *Rzeczpospolita*, 3 Jan. 2001; A. Hall. 'Niewykorzystana szansa', *Rzeczpospolita*, 8 Jan. 2001; B. Wildstein, 'Koalicja konfliktów', *Rzeczpospolita*, 21 June 2001; J. Paradowska, 'Wzyszczy do szalup', *Polityka*, 7 July 2001.
49. See 'Nie ma partii czystych rąk', *Rzeczpospolita*, 16 July 2001.
50. I am grateful to Paul Lewis for drawing my attention to this argument.
51. I am grateful to Seán Hanley for drawing my attention to this argument.
52. See Saxonberg, 'The Influence of Presidential Systems', p.30.
53. See A. Szczerbiak. 'Old and New Divisions in Polish Politics: Polish Parties' Electoral Strategies and Bases of Support', *Europe–Asia Studies*, Vol.55, No.5 (2003), pp.729–46.

Concentrated Orange: Fidesz and the Remaking of the Hungarian Centre-Right, 1994–2002

BRIGID FOWLER

The story of the Hungarian centre-right between 1994 and 2002 is one of progressive electoral and organizational concentration in a single party, Fidesz.[1] This study addresses the reasons for this outcome, as suggested by the four-way typology of explanations for post-communist party and party system developments presented by Hanley and Szczerbiak in their introduction to this collection. 'Electoral concentration' is understood as a process in which one continuously existing party gains a larger share of the vote over time, while the vote shares of other parties shrink, sometimes to effective non-existence. Table 1 presents the electoral results that display this process in the Hungarian case. The term 'organizational concentration' is used to refer to the process whereby, rather than simply 'stealing' votes in competition with the other centre-right parties, Fidesz also engaged in various forms of institutional co-operation with them, or at least groups of their elites. As a result, by 2002 these other parties – or key figures from them – were all formally integrated to varying degrees into Fidesz or the Fidesz-led bloc.

This process of concentration spanned periods of both opposition and government for the centre-right. Inter-party co-operation began after the centre-right had been ejected from office in the second post-communist parliamentary elections in 1994. Electoral co-operation allowed the centre-right to return to power in the next elections, in 1998, and electoral and organizational concentration continued while the centre-right was in office in 1998–2002. However, the process did not prevent the centre-right from losing power again in 2002, in the fourth post-communist polls.

Despite being in opposition, Fidesz was, as of early 2004, the largest centre-right party in the new EU member states of Eastern and Central Europe, as a result of the process of electoral concentration. Fidesz was also one of the oldest parties in the region, having been founded in March 1988 and continuously represented in the first four post-communist parliaments. In the context of this collection of studies, therefore, Fidesz counts as a

TABLE 1
PARLIAMENTARY ELECTION RESULTS OF RIGHT-WING PARTIES, 1994–2002

	1994 (68.92% turnout)		1998 (56.26% turnout)		2002 (70.53% turnout)	
	List vote %	Seats (%)	List vote %	Seats (%)	List vote %	Seats (%)
Centre-right						
Fidesz	7.02	20 (5.18)	29.48	148 (38.34)		164 (42.49)
Fidesz/MDF					41.07	
MDF	11.74	38 (9.84)	2.80	17 (4.40)		24 (6.22)
FKGP	8.82	26 (6.74)	13.15	48 (12.44)	0.75	
KDNP	7.03	22 (5.70)	2.31			
Extreme right						
MIÉP	1.59		5.47	14 (3.63)	4.37	
Centre-right						
In parliament	34.61	106 (27.46)	45.43	213 (55.18)	41.07	188 (48.71)
Total	34.61		47.74		41.82	
Right						
In parliament	34.61	106 (27.46)	50.90	227 (58.81)	41.07	188 (48.71)
Total	36.20		53.21		46.19	
1998–2002 government (Fidesz + FKGP + MDF)			45.43	213 (55.18)		

Note: Total seats: 386. Turnout shown is for the first round. Results are shown for right-wing parties winning parliamentary representation in at least one of the elections. MDF – Hungarian Democratic Forum; FKGP – Independent Smallholders' Party; KDNP – Christian Democratic People's Party; MIÉP – Party of Hungarian Justice and Life.

Source: Publications of the National Election Office.

centre-right success. However, electoral and organizational concentration involved the partial or wholesale failure of the other three parties that for the purposes of this article are regarded as part of the Hungarian centre-right.[2] The Hungarian Democratic Forum survived as a parliamentary party after 1998 only thanks to electoral co-operation with Fidesz; the Christian Democratic People's Party disintegrated in 1997 and failed to enter the 1998 parliament; and the Independent Smallholders' Party repeated this performance in 2001–2. These three parties had formed the first post-communist administration in 1990. In this light, a key feature of the Hungarian case is that its centre-right success, Fidesz, moved to this part of the political spectrum from an originally liberal position, in opposition to the first centre-right government. It therefore represents a major case of party identity change.[3] Fidesz is also notable as the only party in Europe that originated as a generational youth party but has become a major political player.

Individual party performances, and the factors behind them, played a major role in Hungarian centre-right concentration, and will therefore be encompassed to some extent by this study.[4] However, rather than individual party success or failure, the focus is on the process of concentration across the centre-right as a whole.[5] The main question that the study seeks to answer is: why did a single centre-right electoral force emerge out of these four parties, under Fidesz leadership, between 1994 and 2002? This provides greater purchase on the development of the Hungarian party system as a whole. The process of centre-right concentration in Hungary is inextricable from the development, by the 2002 elections, of one of the most organization-ally concentrated, and organizationally and electorally stable, bipolar party systems in the region.

The concentration of the Hungarian centre-right up to 2002, and the nature of the resulting party system, provide a particular contrast with their counter-parts in Poland. In both countries, centre-right parties were in opposition in the mid-1990s and developed greater organizational cohesion, which saw them returned to office in 1997–98. However, as Szczerbiak discusses in his contri-bution to this collection, the Polish centre-right government coalition, and its main component, Solidarity Electoral Action, then fell apart in office; none of its constituent elements was returned to parliament in 2001; and after 2001 the Polish centre-right was being refashioned by new parties. In Hungary, by con-trast, the Fidesz-led bloc only narrowly lost office in 2002, and Fidesz remained united, the largest centre-right party and a serious electoral chal-lenge to the new left-liberal administration.

Given that Poland and Hungary are often regarded as having the two 'most similar' post-communist party systems and patterns of electoral politics, this divergence demands explanation. Among the types of explanation listed by Hanley and Szczerbiak, those based on communist-era 'legacies' are confronted by a particular problem as regards Polish–Hungarian centre-right divergence, since such accounts predict similarity in the Polish and Hungarian cases.[6] To be sure, such approaches have not sought to account for individual party performances or precise party-system formats, such as those involved in the divergent trajectories of the centre-right in Poland and Hungary. Other factors among the four identified by Hanley and Szczerbiak made for the key difference between the two cases, most importantly elite action and institutional features. However, 'legacies' from the pre-communist as well as communist periods may also have played a role – but to the extent that Polish and Hungarian 'legacies' were different, in ways more fine-grained than are often highlighted in the literature.

We first sketch the state of the Hungarian centre-right in 1994, and the process of centre-right concentration that took place between that date and 2002, to identify key features of the way in which concentration took place.[7] We then discuss in turn the ways in which factors suggested by Hanley and Szczerbiak's typology may help to account for this result, considering a range of factors: macro-institutional provisions; 'legacies' in the sphere of elite ideologies; 'critical junctures' in party system development, in the shape of coalition choices; elite action, in the form of ideological construction in the mid-1990s; and micro-institutional features of Fidesz and of the centre-right in office in 1998–2002.

The State of the Centre-Right in 1994

Following the second post-communist parliamentary elections in 1994, the Hungarian centre-right was in shock and disarray, like its Polish counterpart. The centre-right government had been ejected from office and the reformed communist successor Socialist Party returned by a landslide, only four years after being removed from power in the founding election. The Socialists had won an outright parliamentary majority, but formed a coalition government with the liberal Alliance of Free Democrats, based on former dissidents, who had previously been in electoral alliance with Fidesz. The new administration commanded the two-thirds parliamentary super-majority needed to amend the constitution and certain key laws.

Facing this new left-liberal super-majority, the centre-right was fragmented. Divergent responses to the failing (and then failed) Democratic Forum-led governments of 1990–94, primarily that led by the Democratic Forum chief József Antall until his death in December 1993, were a major source of centre-right fracturing. In all cases, although at different times and to different degrees, this fracturing was to occur within as well as between the centre-right parties. With groups peeling off in several directions from both the failing administration and the main governing party, the fate of the Hungarian centre-right in the early 1990s foreshadowed that of its Polish counterpart in 2000–2001, but contrasted with the performance of the later Fidesz-led government.

Two Hungarian centre-right parties had remained loyal to the Antall administration, and in 1994 therefore constituted a 'core' centre-right – the Democratic Forum and the Christian Democrats. Flanking them on their radical side were the Independent Smallholders. The Smallholders had split in 1991 into a pro-administration faction consisting of government ministers and most Smallholder MPs, and a more radical party proper under József Torgyán, comprising most of the party bureaucracy and membership, but only a minority of its MPs.[8] Torgyán had taken the Smallholders out of the governing coalition in 1992, primarily because of the administration's failure to deliver full land reprivatization, but also because Antall had made clear that Torgyán would not obtain ministerial office. Owing to his earlier unstable behaviour, by 1994 Torgyán was regarded by Antallites in the 'core' centre-right as at best unreliable, politically harmful and effectively an unacceptable coalition partner – negative sentiments that were entirely reciprocated by Torgyán. Flanking the 'core' centre-right parties on their liberal side was Fidesz, which had formed part of the liberal opposition to the Antall administration, but which had opened up to the moderate centre-right from autumn 1992 when faced with the prospect of a Socialist- and Free Democrat-dominated coalition as the only apparent alternative.[9]

At the individual level, the centre-right parties differed in two particular respects: leadership and electoral position (see also Table 2).

TABLE 2
CENTRE-RIGHT PARTIES IN 1994

	Fidesz	Democratic Forum	Christian Democrats	Independent Smallholders
Unchallenged leadership?	Yes	No	No	Yes
Relatively large membership and/or developed local organization?	No	Yes	Yes	Yes
Relatively clear ideological profile?	No	No	Yes/No	Yes
Socio-economically distinct electoral base?	No	No	Yes	Yes

Notes: On membership and organization, see also I. van Biezen, *Political Parties in New Democracies* (Basingstoke: Palgrave, 2003), ch.5; J. Toole, 'Straddling the East–West Divide: Party Organization and Communist Legacies in East Central Europe', *Europe–Asia Studies*, Vol.55, No.1 (2003) pp.101–18.

Leadership

Fidesz and the Smallholders stood out from the two 'core' centre-right parties by having secure leaderships. The 1994 elections had effectively secured Torgyán's leadership of the Smallholders, since none of the splinter Small-holder parties formed by anti-Torgyánites had been returned to the new legis-lature. In Fidesz, meanwhile, the opening to the centre-right had contributed to a party split in 1993 which saw the party's popular liberal figurehead, Gábor Fodor, leave while the leadership group around party president Viktor Orbán was left in unchallenged control.

The Democratic Forum had also split in 1993, when Antall finally abandoned his efforts to contain the most prominent 'national liberal' and 'populist-national' figures in a single party. Purged of at least its most extreme 'populist-national' elements, the Forum after 1993 was a somewhat less problematic potential partner.[10] However, in contrast to the split within Fidesz, the Forum's rupture did not fully resolve underlying ideological, organ-izational and personal differences. Antall's death then left these to be faced by a weak and divided successor leadership. Finally, the leader of the Christian Democrats was, to a large extent, 'Antall's man', vulnerable to those who wished to develop a more independent Christian Democratic profile by distan-cing the party from the Democratic Forum and the Antall legacy.[11]

Electoral Position

The four centre-right parties were also aligned differently in terms of their electoral positions. The Christian Democrats and Smallholders had distinct socio-economic voting bases, in the shape of elderly, regular (primarily Catholic) churchgoers in the case of the former, and elderly, poorly educated, rural residents linked to private agriculture in the case of the latter. Potentially, this gave these parties some electoral security, but it also probably limited the extent to which they could expand their electo-rates. The Democratic Forum and Fidesz had a greater 'catch-all' potential, as suggested by the Forum's 1990 election win, and Fidesz's high opinion poll rating of over 30 per cent before 1994 (before the party's opening to the centre-right and subsequent split). However, by 1994 its association with the post-1990 governments had electorally compromised the Forum, probably irreparably and even under a more appealing leadership than Antall's immediate successors.

Overall, the challenges facing the centre-right parties in 1994 were several: to find an effective response to the Socialist–liberal administration; to organize their mutual relations (especially so as to deal with Fidesz's arrival, Democratic Forum–Smallholder hostility, and the potential for rivalry created by the ending of Democratic Forum dominance); and to develop a way of dealing retrospectively with the Antall legacy so as to further both of the other processes.

The Electoral and Organizational Concentration of the Centre-Right, 1994–2002

The concentration of the four centre-right parties into the single Fidesz-led electoral bloc took place in two overlapping phases, which spanned the periods of centre-right opposition and government:

Fidesz and the 'Core' Centre-Right

In this phase, Fidesz was integrated into, and emerged to lead, a moderate centre-right force consisting of itself and elements of the old 'core' centre-right: a rump Democratic Forum and the more moderate elements of the Christian Democrats. Debates about the precise organizational form of this grouping continued while the centre-right was in office in 1998–2002 (and subsequently), but it was basically in place by the end of 1997.

During the phase up to late-1997, the centre-right was marked by competition between the two parties on its flanks, Fidesz and the Independent Smallholders, for leadership of the opposition and the allegiance of the two 'core' centre-right parties. Having gone into the post-1994 period without secure leaderships, as sketched above, these two 'core' centre-right parties were split by this competition.

The Fidesz leader Orbán set out to create a moderate centre-right formation of some sort with the Democratic Forum and Christian Democrats from the start of the 1994–98 parliament. His conception was shared by the leaderships that were initially in place in these two parties. Following successful electoral co-operation in the December 1994 local elections, Fidesz and the Democratic Forum announced a 'Civic Alliance' (*Polgári Szövetség*)[12] in January 1995 and opened talks on future co-operation that extended to the Christian Democrats.

However, the Smallholders were gaining in popularity on the back of the Socialist-led government's economic austerity measures, encapsulated in the 'Bokros package' of March 1995 (see Table 3). The Smallholders' rise strengthened resistance to the 'Civic Alliance' project, which had already existed within the Forum and Christian Democrats. Objections to the 'Civic Alliance' were that it appeared too closely associated with the Antall legacy, and was mistaken in its exclusion of the Smallholders, when a pan-rightist front (possibly also extending to Justice and Life) might be required to unseat the Socialist-led government. The Smallholders' leader Torgyán signalled his wish to gather the Democratic Forum and Christian Democrats under his leadership by launching a 'National Alliance' in 1995, as an explicit rival to Fidesz's 'Civic Alliance'.

TABLE 3
PARTY OPINION POLL STANDINGS, 1994–98 TERM

	Fidesz	MDF	FKGP	KDNP	SZDSZ	MSZP
1994						
Jun	5	5	6	3	19	31
Jul	5	4	5	4	19	32
Aug	5	7	5	5	13	31
Sep	6	7	4	4	12	29
Oct	6	4	6	4	14	27
Nov	6	8	7	5	14	22
Dec	5	6	10	4	15	27
1995						
Jan	4	5	9	5	11	21
Feb	5	5	8	5	15	19
Mar	8	6	11	5	11	17
Apr	7	7	11	5	12	16
May	7	6	12	5	10	16
Jun	6	5	15	5	10	15
Jul	8	8	12	5	9	14
Aug	8	6	16	5	9	14
Sep	8	7	13	4	11	15
Oct	9	6	14	5	10	14
Nov	7	5	17	5	9	13
Dec	7	5	15	4	10	14
1996						
Jan	8	6	16	5	8	15
Feb	8	5	15	6	8	16
Mar	8	3	16	4	8	16
Apr	6	4	11	4	9	23
May	10	4	11	6	10	19
Jun	8	5	13	5	8	18
Jul	10	3	12	4	9	19
Aug	10	5	12	4	8	16
Sep	12	3	13	4	8	16
Oct	15	5	14	5	7	15
Nov	15	3	15	5	8	15
Dec	16	2	13	4	8	16
1997						
Jan	17	2	14	4	6	12
Feb	17	3	16	3	6	12
Mar	17	4	15	4	6	12
Apr	16	3	15	4	5	14
May	15	4	13	2	6	16
Jun	15	3	14	2	5	17
Jul	15	3	14	3	5	17
Aug	14	3	13	3	5	17
Sep	14	3	13	2	5	18
Oct	14	3	13	2	5	20
Nov	15	2	13	2	5	19
Dec	14	2	12	2	6	21

(Continued)

TABLE 3   *CONTINUED*

	Fidesz	MDF	FKGP	KDNP	SZDSZ	MSZP
1998						
Jan	14	3	11	–	5	22
Feb	16	2	9	–	5	21
Mar	17	2	10	–	5	21
Apr	16	3	11	–	6	21

Notes: Figures are per cent naming relevant party among all respondents to the question: 'If the parliamentary elections were this Sunday, which party would you vote for?'. MDF – Hungarian Democratic Forum; FKGP – Independent Smallholders' Party; KDNP – Christian Democratic People's Party; SZDSZ – Alliance of Free Democrats; MSZP – Hungarian Socialist Party

Source: Szonda Ipsos data in successive editions of S. Kurtán, P. Sándor and L. Vass (eds.), *Magyarország politikai évkönyve* (Budapest: Demokrácia Kutatások Magyar Központja Alapítvány, annual publication).

More pro-Smallholder, 'pan-rightist' views gained ground in both the 'core' centre-right parties. This led to leadership change in the Christian Democrats in January 1995, and in the Forum in March 1996, when the party's 'founding father', the 'populist-national' poet Sándor Lezsák, defeated the Antallite Ivan Szabó for the party presidency. However, neither of the new leaderships succeeded in uniting their respective party. The Christian Democrats were convulsed by internal conflict for two and a half years, while the Szabó group departed from the Forum immediately in March 1996 to found the Hungarian Democratic People's Party. However, in the rump Forum, Lezsák reversed his alliance policy, and in May 1996 made an offer of co-operation to Fidesz, which was accepted. This was a key signal of Fidesz's willingness to work with partners further to the right than it had originally intended, if this appeared to offer institutional or electoral gain. Owing to Lezsák's refusal to work with the former Democratic Forum rebels, Szabó's new party, which Orbán had encouraged to break away but which made little electoral or institutional impact, was effectively cut out of future co-operation between Fidesz and the Lezsák-led Forum.[13] In December 1997, Fidesz and the Forum finally agreed an electoral pact under which they would run joint or unopposed candidates in 85 constituencies in the 1998 parliamentary elections, and withdraw the less well-placed of their candidates from the run-offs in all the rest. However, the Democratic Forum would not run on a joint party list, assuming that it would pass the five per cent threshold for independent list-based parliamentary representation.[14] For their part, the Christian Democrats finally disintegrated in July 1997. While the party proper under its more radical leader was offered electoral co-operation by

Torgyán, its more moderate leading figures, formed into a Christian Democratic Alliance that was too small to sustain a parliamentary group, joined the Fidesz parliamentary group and then went on to run as Fidesz candidates in 1998.[15]

The moderate Christian Democrats' accession to Fidesz in autumn 1997 encapsulated two interrelated developments. First, it exemplified the way in which centre-right concentration was coming to take place. At elite level, rather than an alliance of separate parties, as in the original 'Civic Alliance' conception, the centre-right was developing around a single party, with institutionalized pluralism internally and satellite parties externally. As regards the electorate, the difficulties encountered by the 'Civic Alliance' project, and the sinking of support for its other two parties below the five per cent threshold, encouraged the Fidesz leader Orbán to shift from exclusive reliance on 'uniting' the moderate centre-right, as a means of aggregating its vote, to an attempt to 'occupy' it.[16] In other words, if Orbán could not rely on the 'core' centre-right party elites to deliver their electorates, or retain significant electorates at all, he would seek to attract their voters himself.

Second, the balance of power had shifted not only among the moderate centre-right parties but also across the centre-right as a whole. Fidesz had already pulled away from the Independent Smallholders as the most popular opposition party by the end of 1996 (Table 3). By autumn 1997, with its new Christian Democratic Alliance MPs, Fidesz also became the largest parliamentary opposition party (see Table 4).

TABLE 4
PARLIAMENTARY SEATS OF CENTRE-RIGHT PARTIES AND INDEPENDENTS,
1994–98 TERM

	June 1994	Dec 1995	Apr 1996	Dec 1996	Sep 1997	Dec 1997	Mar 1998
Democratic Forum	38 (9.84)	37	19	19	19	20	20 (5.18)
Independent Smallholders	26 (6.74)	25	25	24	25	24	22 (5.70)
Christian Democrats	22 (5.70)	22	23	23			
Fidesz	20 (5.18)	20	20	21	33	32	32 (8.29)
Democratic People's Party			15	15	15	15	15 (3.90)
Independents	1 (0.26)	4	6	6	19	21	23 (5.97)

Note: Seat distributions are shown for the opening and closing sessions of the parliament, the end of each of its middle years, and immediately after the two main centre-right party splits. Percentages in parentheses. Figures do not tally exactly because the Independents also took MPs from, and lost them to, the Socialists and Free Democrats.

Source: Compiled from successive editions of S. Kurtán, P. Sándor and L. Vass (eds.), *Magyarország politikai évkönyve* (Budapest: Demokrácia Kutatások Magyar Központja Alapítvány, annual publication).

Bringing the Smallholders (Back) In

During this phase, having established itself as the leading centre-right force, Fidesz came together with the Independent Smallholders, first co-operating with them for electoral and governmental purposes, and then integrating leading members as the smaller party disintegrated. This phase began in autumn 1997 and was concluded by the end of 2001.

The divergent trajectories of the Christian Democrats' two wings in the summer and autumn of 1997 seemed to confirm a continuing division between a more moderate Fidesz-led centre-right and a more radical Smallholder-centred strand. However, this division was superseded almost immediately. The specific issue on which the two centre-right strands came together was land ownership. In response to government plans to amend the Democratic Forum-led administration's 1994 land law, in a way that would have allowed corporate and foreign land ownership, the Forum launched a campaign for a referendum on the issue, to which both Fidesz and the Smallholders acceded, and which Fidesz came to lead. The message of the land-ownership campaign was that common antipathy to the Socialist–liberal administration could be the basis for an opposition front. The Smallholders found themselves defending legislation passed by the Democratic Forum-led government, which they would normally have despised; for its part, Fidesz signalled to the Smallholders that its wish to damage the Socialist-led administration now stretched to adopting Smallholder policy on the issue that was definitive for the Smallholders.

Reassured on the policy front, the Smallholders began to pursue electoral co-operation with Fidesz, effectively acknowledging that they had lost the competition for leadership of the opposition and the centre-right. The Smallholders' leader, Torgyán, abandoned the radical rump Christian Democrats, who were failing electorally, and expelled the most prominent Smallholder figure who continued to urge the more radical, anti-Fidesz, 'National Alliance' strategy.[17] Fidesz did not respond to Torgyán's overtures, aware of popular antipathy to the Smallholder leader outside his core electorate, and hoping to unseat the government without him. However, in the constituency run-offs in 1998, the two parties, together with the Democratic Forum, made mutually beneficial candidate withdrawals that allowed the centre-right to win the election.

The Centre-Right in Government, 1998–2002

The integration of the Democratic Forum and the Independent Smallholders into a single Fidesz-led electoral force continued while the three parties were together in government in 1998–2002. It was in this respect that Hungarian developments diverged from those in Poland, where, as we have seen, the centre-right fragmented again once in office. Continued centre-right concentration in Hungary reflected the fact that, unlike both the Democratic Forum in Hungary in 1990–94 and Solidarity Electoral Action in Poland after 1997, Fidesz remained a reasonable bet for re-election throughout its term – and certainly the only prospect for electoral success on the centre-right.

As regards the Democratic Forum, the issue was whether the party should try again to pass the five per cent threshold without Fidesz. The Forum's new leader, elected in January 1999, wanted to pursue this goal by gathering up the extra-parliamentary Democratic Forum splinter, the Democratic People's Party, and other mini-parties in a second moderate centre-right mini-bloc. Lezsák's ouster as Forum leader had removed the obstacle to Forum–People's Party co-operation. However, Fidesz rejected this concept. It continued to urge organizational concentration – or at least the closest electoral co-operation possible – on the moderate centre-right. The argument was played out in parliamentary by-elections in 2000, in which the Forum ran separate candidates against joint Fidesz–Smallholder competitors.[18] However, the results seemed to show that the Forum still ultimately depended on Fidesz for constituency wins, and the Forum's general popular standing remained stuck (see Table 5). In an April 2001 by-election, the Forum fell into line behind the Fidesz–Smallholder candidate, and in August 2001 finally agreed to an electoral pact with Fidesz for the 2002 elections under which the two parties would run not only joint candidates in all constituencies but also, for the first time in Hungary's post-communist electoral history, joint party lists.[19]

In contrast to its attitude to the Democratic Forum, Fidesz appeared content for the Independent Smallholders to remain a co-operative but basically independent electoral force, leaving them to continue to deliver their distinct electorate for the centre-right. However, in autumn 2000, a series of corruption scandals destroyed Torgyán's always vulnerable credibility and pushed Smallholder support below five per cent (Table 5). This triggered a revolt against Torgyán among senior Smallholder MPs for which the ground had long been laid by grievances about his style of leadership. The party effectively spent 2001 where it had been a decade earlier: divided into pro- and anti-Torgyán factions and spawning multiple Smallholder mini-parties – only this time at lower support levels. The Fidesz leadership decided that Torgyán and his party had become a liability, and effectively cut them loose, by suspending talks on electoral co-operation and soliciting Torgyán's resignation from the government. However, in December 2001, with two former Smallholder MPs having already joined its parliamentary group, Fidesz reached agreement with one of the main anti-Torgyán Smallholder groupings, which included the other Smallholder ministers, to run 11 of their figures as Fidesz candidates in 2002.[20] In this way, anti-Torgyán Smallholder MPs, who had effectively lost their party, preserved their careers in a way not achieved by their counterparts in 1994.

TABLE 5
PARTY OPINION POLL STANDINGS, 1998–2002 TERM

	Fidesz	MDF	FKGP	SZDSZ	MSZP
1998					
Jun	35	2	6	3	22
Jul	39	2	7	2	18
Aug	37	1	4	3	21
Sep	32	1	6	2	21
Oct	33	1	5	2	21
Nov	31	1	6	4	24
Dec	29	1	4	3	25
1999					
Jan	30	2	4	2	24
Feb	30	1	6	3	25
Mar	27	1	5	4	25
Apr	28	1	5	3	25
May	26	1	5	3	25
Jun	26	1	5	4	25
Jul	27	1	4	3	27
Aug	23	2	4	3	23
Sep	22	1	4	3	26
Oct	22	2	5	3	27
Nov	19	2	6	3	28
Dec	20	2	6	4	28
2000					
Jan	19	3	5	3	27
Feb	20	3	6	3	26
Mar	21	3	5	3	25
Apr	20	3	5	3	27
May	20	2	5	4	25
Jun	20	3	4	4	25
Jul	19	3	3	4	26
Aug	18	2	3	3	24
Sep	20	2	4	4	23
Oct	21	1	3	2	23
Nov	19	1	2	4	24
Dec	17	1	3	5	26
2001					
Jan	19	3	3	4	25
Feb	21	3	3	4	24
Mar	23	2	2	4	23
Apr	24	2	2	3	25
May	24	2	2	3	25
Jun	24	2	2	2	26
Jul	23	2	1	3	25
Aug	22	2	2	4	25
Sep	23	2	1	3	25
Oct	25	–	1	2	24
Nov	26	–	2	3	24
Dec	27	–	2	3	25

(Continued)

TABLE 5 *CONTINUED*

	Fidesz	MDF	FKGP	SZDSZ	MSZP
2002					
Jan	22	–	2	3	25
Feb	25	–	1	4	28
Mar	26	–	1	5	26

Note: Figures are per cent naming relevant party among all respondents to the question: 'If the parliamentary elections were this Sunday, which party would you vote for?' Fidesz and the MDF are counted together from October 2001. MDF – Hungarian Democratic Forum; FKGP – Independent Smallholders' Party; SZDSZ – Alliance of Free Democrats; MSZP – Hungarian Socialist Party.

Source: Szonda Ipsos data in successive editions of S. Kurtán, P. Sándor and L. Vass (eds.), *Magyarország politikai évkönyve* (Budapest: Demokrácia Kutatások Magyar Központja Alapítvány, annual publication).

From August and especially December 2001, therefore, it became clear that Fidesz would contest the 2002 elections at the head of a single electoral conglomerate. Three features are notable about the process of Hungarian centre-right concentration. First, it took place among a given group of parties, operating within a part of the political spectrum that was already delineated, not by means of change in the underlying structure of party competition. Second, it took place around the party that started the period as the most liberal among the centre-right forces, progressively co-operating with parties further to the right. Third, concentration took place around the party that was new to the centre-right, and that had not been part of the 1990–94 centre-right governments.

More specifically, this single Fidesz-led force had come into being since 1994 along two mutually reinforcing tracks, elite and mass, corresponding to the organizational and electoral forms of concentration. In the three failed parties, falling public support helped to trigger leadership conflict which then exacerbated the problem, and pushed parties or their elites towards electoral co-operation with Fidesz. At Fidesz, by contrast, there was a virtuous circle: stronger electoral prospects made Fidesz an attractive potential partner, but the party also proved able institutionally to integrate elites from failing parties. This further enhanced Fidesz's electoral appeal, contrasting with the conflicts in other parties, and encouraging vote switching by non-Fidesz centre-right voters. In accounting for the emergence of the Fidesz-led bloc, therefore, in comparison with the divergent developments in Poland, we need to address Fidesz's electoral appeal, and its ability to manage relationships with centre-right partners, including while in office. The rest of this study explores possible explanations for this process, as suggested by Hanley and Szczerbiak's introductory typology.

Macro-institutional Explanations and their Limits

The most readily available explanation is a macro-institutional one, in the shape of the electoral system. Hungary has a mixed electoral system in which majoritarian effects dominate proportional ones – that is, the conditions for the running of party lists and (more importantly) the formulae for converting votes into seats advantage large parties and penalize small ones. The system combines three elements: two-round single-member constituency contests; multi-member regional constituencies, where seats are distributed proportionally on the basis of voting for closed party lists; and top-up seats awarded proportionally to closed national lists on the basis of votes 'wasted' in both the first single-member constituency rounds and the regional list voting. The national lists thus link the single-member constituency and list-based regional elements. The award of both regional and national list seats is subject to a threshold of five per cent of the total regional list vote.

From the parties' perspective, this system has two 'all or nothing' elements that shape electoral tactics. For large parties, with hopes of leading an administration, the key element is the single-member constituency contests. For such parties, the aim in these campaigns must be to aggregate votes against a single rival, by defining a favourable bipolar contest and encouraging vote switching, by *inter alia* avoiding competing candidacies. The single-member contests thus encourage inter-party electoral co-operation and bipolarism, if not constituency bipartism.

For small parties, the key issue is crossing the five per cent threshold. Below this, parties can win seats only in the single-member constituencies, but this is unlikely with support below five per cent nationally. Moreover, the gains that accrue from running even unsuccessful constituency candidates (namely qualification to run party lists, and the accumulation of 'wasted' constituency votes) convert into seats only if parties also pass five per cent. Once a party cannot be sure of passing five per cent, in other words, from the narrowest seat-seeking perspective the electoral system discourages it from running both lists and constituency candidates, and thus from continuing as an independent electoral force. This reduces the capacity of the two-round constituency system to sustain the smallest parties, and means that party bipolarism is more likely to be converted into electoral bipartism.[21] The tyranny of the five per cent barrier is intensified if parties are concerned for the seats won by a group of parties, rather than only their own, since votes given to a party which misses five per cent are lost to the bloc as a whole.[22]

Alongside its constraints, the electoral system endows parties with resources, in the shape of the list seats. Effectively, any party certain of passing five per cent has at least 15 or so seats in the next parliament in its gift. As party lists are closed (that is, voters cannot express preferences among candidates, who receive seats in the order determined by their parties), parties can effectively promise seats in advance to particular individuals with a degree of security, through the ordering of candidates on their lists.[23] For seat-seeking politicians of parties at risk of missing the five per cent target, therefore, the best option – if it is available – is to bail into a safe-looking place on the list of a party sure of passing it.

The electoral system offers an inherently plausible explanation of the post-1994 concentration of the Hungarian centre-right. It is the right kind of explanation for this kind of party-system change. An explanation based on the electoral system also fits with the timing of Hungarian–Polish centre-right divergence, since electoral-system effects are likely to become evident only after several electoral rounds. In addition, whereas Szczerbiak points out that differences between the left and right in Poland undermine the explanatory power of the electoral system (and other macro-institutional factors) there, Hungary has seen electoral co-operation and concentration in the left–liberal camp as well as on the centre-right.[24] Most importantly, Hungary is the only country considered in this collection that uses a predominantly majoritarian, not proportional, electoral system. It is therefore tempting to 'read off' Hungary's more concentrated centre-right, and its more concentrated party system as a whole, simply on the basis of its electoral system.

Hungary's centre-right parties were clearly responding to electoral system incentives in coming to form a single electoral bloc after 1994. Orbán argued from the outset in 1994 that the centre-right's problem was its split vote. Following their parties' splits, moderate Christian Democrats and some anti-Torgyán Smallholders realized that any new party they might form would probably miss the five per cent threshold, and thus not secure their seats. They therefore decided to run under the Fidesz banner. With a lower electoral threshold, the Democratic Forum would also probably have avoided being integrated so comprehensively into the Fidesz-led electoral bloc. Meanwhile, Fidesz used its prospective control of a large number of list seats both before and after 1998 to attract key figures from failing centre-right parties, preventing them from running separate lists – possibly below the five per cent threshold – and thus 'wasting' centre-right votes. At the same time, Fidesz sought to avoid multiple – vote-splitting – centre-right candidates in the single-member constituencies, via a range of electoral co-operation mechanisms.

However, electoral system effects do not 'just happen'. They depend on parties (and their voters) responding appropriately to the incentives facing them. In this respect, Hungary's centre-right parties seem to have had a relatively sophisticated understanding of the electoral system and its implications in relation to their electoral strengths, in a way that contrasts with, for example, the suicidal decision of Solidarity Electoral Action prior to Poland's 2001 elections to register as a coalition, not a party, thereby raising its own electoral threshold. Hungarian parties' understanding of the electoral system was facilitated by the system's stability. In contrast to the several reforms made in Poland, only one major change has been made to Hungary's electoral system since 1990 (the raising of the threshold from four to five per cent before the 1994 elections). However, Hungarian centre-right elites also seem to have engaged in more learning than their Polish colleagues. For example, they consciously used elections other than parliamentary polls – local elections and by-elections – to test voters' responses to different electoral line-ups, thus gaining further information relevant to their parliamentary election tactics.[25] Hungarian elites also seem to have drawn lessons from the failure of all post-1990 new parties but one (Justice and Life) to cross the five per cent barrier. Following what proved to be, for some, a career-ending exit from the Democratic Forum to form the Democratic People's Party in 1996, at least some Christian Democrat and Smallholder politicians joined Fidesz when their parties split, rather than launching new electoral vehicles.

As well as understanding the system, parties need to be able to follow its dictates. Two general aspects of Hungarian centre-right behaviour are notable in this respect. First, at least some centre-right elites were prepared to work with figures with whom they might have preferred not to deal, and to cut out possibly more congenial partners, or those to whom they had already made commitments. This is evident in Orbán's dealings with the Lezsák and Szabó wings of the Democratic Forum in the mid-1990s and later with Torgyán, as well as in Torgyán's abandonment of the radical rump Christian Democrats before the 1998 elections. Second, driven partly by the electoral system to find partners, Fidesz and the Independent Smallholders were able to adjust their appeals to secure such partners without splitting internally over such ideological and strategic issues. Both features suggest what might be called a relatively high degree of 'party-ness', understood as two dimensions: clarity about the fact that the organization's minimal goals are seats and office, and willingness to subordinate individual considerations to the pursuit of these goals. In general, the picture in Hungary is of at least some relatively well-institutionalized centre-right parties, operating in a comparatively well-developed elite electoral marketplace, with party poll ratings as the universally accepted measure of value.

According to Saxonberg, such relatively well-institutionalized parties – in the case of the Czech Republic, in his study – result from an indirectly elected presidency. He contended that Poland's weak centre-right parties were the result of the incentives facing that country's directly elected head of state.[26] This explanation appears also to fit with Hungary, which like the Czech Republic has an indirectly elected presidency. However, even apart from the question of how widely applicable Saxonberg's hypothesis is, there is a chicken-and-egg problem as regards Hungary and Poland. Hungary possesses

an indirectly elected presidency only because of the actions of multiple opposition parties, successfully pursuing their diverse political interests, in forcing
and then winning the November 1989 referendum on the issue.[27] In Poland, on
the other hand, the fact that Lech Wałęsa contested the presidency against
rivals from Solidarity, whose proto-parties he proceeded to undermine,
speaks of pre-existing problems with Solidarity as a centre-right party; it
may also reflect weak norms of 'party-ness' as such. In other words, presidential politics may reflect, not cause, party characteristics.[28]

There are two not necessarily exclusive alternative possible explanations
for the apparent 'party-ness' of centre-right parties in Hungary. One might
be norms among the political elite that draw on a historical awareness
(rather than direct experience) of the pre-communist period. This is especially
plausible in the case of centre-right elites, who – unlike their Socialist and
liberal counterparts – sometimes look back positively to aspects of Hungary's
interwar and pre-1914 politics.[29] Among the types of explanation outlined by
Hanley and Szczerbiak, this would be a 'legacy', but a pre-communist one.
Second, there is the nature of opposition party formation in the late communist
period. This occurred early, meaning that by the mid-1990s the Hungarian
centre-right elites had enjoyed a longer period of learning about party
discipline and management than their Polish counterparts.[30] Opposition
parties in Hungary also formed as parties, not as other types of social organizations, and typically did so on the basis of relatively well-established, extra-
parliamentary elite networks, not mass movements or non-party organizations
such as trade unions. This meant that they were relatively clear from a
comparatively early stage that their goals were 'party-like' ones (votes,
seats, policy, office), rather than any less 'party-like' alternatives. Compared
with Poland's Solidarity, their origins also gave Hungarian parties less
unwieldy, more conventional and more strongly elite-dominated organizational structures that, it may be argued, better provided the flexibility
demanded by seat- and office-seeking electoral tactics. These features of opposition party formation reflected in part the reformism of Hungary's late communist regime, which allowed parties to form without the creation of a united
mass opposition movement ever coming on to the agenda.[31] In this sense,
these features might also be classed as 'legacies'. However, they also
became lasting micro-institutional features of the centre-right parties.

The electoral system therefore figured largely in the concentration of the
Hungarian centre-right, but its impact depended partly on the 'party-ness'
of Hungarian centre-right parties. Hungarian 'party-ness' may in turn have
reflected communist and pre-communist 'legacies'. However, even this
'macro-institutionalist-plus' approach cannot account for two aspects of the
Hungarian centre-right story. First, it cannot explain why Fidesz, rather
than any other party, emerged as the centre-right hegemon. Second, if

centre-right parties were willing and able to pursue seats and office, why did they seek co-operation only with one another before 1998, not with the Socialists? Despite their periods of unpopularity, the Socialists were expected to win re-election for most of the 1994–98 term, principally because of the apparent incoherence on the centre-right.[32] Moreover, the Socialists' coalition with the Free Democrats was troubled, meaning that the larger party might well have sought alternative or additional partners. This second question effectively concerns the contours of the Hungarian centre-right.

Elite Conceptions of the Right as 'Legacies'

The Hungarian political elite went into the post-communist era with a relatively clear ideological framework and notion of the right within it. Crucially, this framework was not coterminous with the 'regime divide' between former ruling and opposition forces that was so prominent in Poland. Compared with the 'post-oppositional' right generated by Poland's stronger regime divide, the version generated by Hungary's alternative framework was more ideologically cohesive, and thus a more promising basis for the development of a lasting centre-right bloc.

Kitschelt and his collaborators identified four possible divides around which post-communist elite politics might be organized. As well as the regime divide, these were: an economic–distributive divide, comprising attitudes to the free market versus state intervention; a national–cosmopolitan divide, comprising attitudes to national particularism versus internationalization; and a socio-cultural divide, comprising attitudes towards traditional social institutions versus individualism and libertarianism.[33] Political identities and alignments in the Hungarian elite were defined in terms of the last two. That is, right-wing parties were those that placed greater emphasis on the cultural nation and were more socially and culturally traditionalist, embracing a more favourable attitude to Christianity and a greater concern for provincial and rural Hungary. This understanding of the right was defined most clearly against another post-oppositional political strand, namely the 'cosmopolitan' or 'universalist' liberalism identified mainly with the Budapest-based, former dissident Alliance of Free Democrats.

Parties' positions on Kitschelt's other two divides – the regime divide and the economic divide – tended to be more contingent, and to derive from the dominant two.

Regime Divide

The dominant conception of the right, asserted most importantly by Antall, defined it also against communism and the communist successor party. However, there had been some scope for flexibility in the late 1980s regarding the extent to which a 'national', socially conservative position required non-cooperation with the communist party and its successor. This reflected the extent to which the ruling party had itself deviated from purely 'universalist', materialist and effectively individualist leftist positions towards 'national-populist' ones. The degree and certainly the content of right-wing opposition to communist successor forces could therefore depend to at least some degree on the latter's stance vis-à-vis the 'national' and socio-cultural divides, as well as on the nature of the leadership on the right. In this context, from late 1989 the 'national' element in the communist successor force appeared progressively to lose prominence.

Economic Divide

In the pre-Second World War period, the ruling centre-right was characterized by its inegalitarianism and its support for large-scale private property, as opposed to the egalitarianism of the 'universalist' left, whether this was of the pro-nationalization, social democratic, communist or radical liberal variety, or the agrarian variety that favoured redistribution of private land. In the post-communist era, however, the 'universalist' economic ideology is market liberalism. In Hungary, this challenged both its predecessor – the remnants of state socialism – and the right. In comparison with free market liberalism, the post-communist right supported a 'social market' economy on matters of regulation and welfare, drawing on Christian Socialist and Christian Democratic traditions, and was more cautious about privatization of major state assets; but it was a strong supporter of small-scale private ownership in property, business and land, in a way that contrasted with orthodox communism.

By 1990, therefore, the right was already defined in contrast with both the 'universalist' liberals and the increasingly 'universalist' communist successor left. With the liberals and the communist successor Socialists themselves divided by the regime and economic divides, this generated the tripolar political arrangement characteristic of the early post-communist period.

The right generated in Hungary by the relatively strong national and socio-cultural divides still encompassed highly diverse strands.[34] However, compared with the post-oppositional right generated in Poland by that country's relatively stronger 'regime divide', the Hungarian version was more cohesive, in particular because it clearly excluded one political strand and included another. Excluded, as will be clear, were the 'universalist' liberals. This removed one source of ideological conflict that bedevilled post-oppositionist formations in Poland, where liberals found themselves allied with trade unionists and nationalists under the same post-Solidarity banner. Included in the Hungarian right, on the other hand, were the Independent Smallholders. This contrasted with the position of the Polish Peasant Party, which is identified as a 'centrist' force.[35] Although small-scale private land ownership was the defining issue of the Hungarian party, and the Smallholders gained their greatest electoral support on the basis of economic populism in the mid-1990s, the party defined itself in less exclusively economic terms than its Polish counterpart: the Hungarian party consistently stressed also its Christian and 'national' identity. This made it a more clearly right-wing force. The land-ownership issue in any case placed the Smallholders squarely on the right in the post-communist context. In contrast to the well-known Polish case, the Hungarian communist regime allowed little private land ownership, instead collectivizing or nationalizing the smallholdings created by the 1945 land reform. The Hungarian communist regime also did not co-opt the Small-holders as a satellite party, as its Polish counterpart did with the Peasant Party, instead subjecting the Smallholders to the same 'salami tactics' as other rivals. The Hungarian Smallholders' Party therefore emerged into the post-communist era as clearly a former opposition and right-wing formation. As well as contributing to the more unidimensional pattern of party competition in Hungary, this placed an important electoral constituency in the right-wing camp.

Kitschelt and his associates suggested that, if the regime and economic divides were relatively weaker in Hungary than in Poland, and the national and socio-cultural divides relatively stronger, this was due to the longer time-span since the major incident of violent communist repression in Hungary (in 1956), and the greater economic and political reformism of Hungary's late communist regime and communist successor party.[36] In that case, the more ideologically cohesive right generated in Hungary by the relatively stronger national and socio-cultural divides would be a 'legacy' of the late communist regime.

However, the example of the Smallholders suggests that Hungary's more coherent right may also derive from historical legacies extending back beyond the late communist period. In the case of the Smallholders, the key period was the early communist one, when the land nationalization and collectivization that came to distinguish Hungary from Poland got under way. However, the strength of the national and socio-cultural divides in Hungary may also reflect experiences that differed from those of Poland in the pre-communist period. These might include a longer history of statehood and pluralist politics, allowing the development of clearer ideological alternatives and a stronger right-wing governing tradition along 'national', socially conservative lines; the starkness and violence of the lurch from communist revolution to right-wing counter-revolution in 1919, which helped to encourage continuing right-wing conservatism, and a tendency to construe politics in terms of potentially extreme and non-negotiable polar opposites; the existence of the Hungarian minorities outside Hungary, following the border changes made under the 1920 Treaty of Trianon, which maintained the centrality of the 'national' question; Hungary's wartime record, eventually as an ally of Nazi Germany, which did likewise; and the survival of at least some of Budapest's Jewish population, which furnished the personal background for prominent figures in both the communist regime and the communist-era liberal dissident movement. The micro-mechanism that would allow such historical 'legacies' to impinge on the ideological conceptions of the post-communist elite would be the elite's own awareness of Hungary's history – a history that is consistently interpreted in terms of a tension (at least latent) between more particularist, nationalist, pro-independence tendencies and more universalist, internationalist, pro-integrationist ones, whatever their specific content.[37] The availability in Hungary of historical references reaching back beyond the anti-communist struggle was nicely illustrated in the run-up to the 1998 elections: whereas Szczerbiak reports Poland's Solidarity leader presenting a policy programme in 1997 on the anniversary of the August 1980 agreement between Solidarity and the communist authorities, the Fidesz leader Orbán presented an equivalent statement, his 'Opposition Manifesto', in June 1997 on the 150th anniversary of the launch of the 'Opposition Manifesto' that preceded the outbreak of revolution in 1848.

1990 and 1994: Coalition Choices as 'Critical Junctures' in Party System Development

The dominance of the national and socio-cultural divides, and the nature of the political right that they generated, were confirmed and reinforced in two steps, via coalition decisions following the 1990 and 1994 parliamentary elections. In the process, Kitschelt's remaining two elite divides, the regime divide and the economic divide, came to coincide with the already dominant national and socio-cultural divides, generating a powerful unidimensional pattern.

1990

After the founding election, the Democratic Forum leader, Jozsef Antall, formed a government with the other two parliamentary parties of the 'national', socio-culturally–based right, the Christian Democrats and the Independent Smallholders. In doing so, Antall may have rejected the urgings of no less a figure for the moderate Hungarian centre-right than German Chancellor Helmut Kohl to include some holdover Socialist ministers; and he certainly rejected including the other main former opposition party, the liberal Free Democrats, so as to have a broader-based government (with the two-thirds super-majority).[38] Although Antall may have been motivated partly by a wish to govern only with much smaller parties, his decision was seen as driven primarily by considerations of ideological proximity.

Given the way in which the centre-right was concentrated after 1994 – namely, by a party new to that part of the political spectrum – the importance of the 1990–94 government lay partly in its role as a source of information for Fidesz. The formation of the exclusively right-wing government seemed to suggest that its member parties were policy-seeking. When Fidesz began to espouse centre-right policies, these parties could not fail to respond without jeopardizing their ideological reputations. The formation of the Antall administration also confirmed that Hungarian 'right-ness' excluded co-operation with both the Free Democrats and the Socialists. In this respect, when Fidesz in 1994 rejected overtures from the Socialists suggesting that it too might join them and the Free Democrats in the new government, it was already putting down a key marker of right-wing identity and credibility. Equally, the ideological reputations of the 1990–94 governing parties meant that they could not seek co-operation with the Socialists after 1994.[39] Once the government was up and running, its experience established a repertoire of specific right-wing language and policy which Fidesz could appropriate and deploy in targeted fashion to make itself a credible right-wing force for right-wing elites and voters, both before and after 1998.[40] Even the defection of Torgyán's Smallholders from the governing coalition established the land-ownership issue as definitive for that party's choice of political alignments, providing the informational basis for the autumn 1997 Fidesz–Smallholder *rapprochement*. It can be argued that Fidesz could have gleaned this information with a different government in place, but the picture might have been more confused. Finally, the experience of the post-1990 government established attitudes to Antall as a key to centre-right positioning. Precisely because the first post-communist prime minister came to be so widely rejected, embracing him retrospectively was a means by which Orbán could build solidarity at least with the 'core' centre-right elites who had remained loyal to his administration. Such an embrace appeared to be offered when Orbán invited one of Antall's sons to join his group of advisers from summer 1994.[41]

1994

Given the elite ideological framework sketched above, the decision of the liberal former dissident Free Democrats to go into a coalition with the reform communist successor party, the Socialists, in 1994 was the key point in the development of Hungary's post-communist party system. It brought together both of the political strands against which the post-communist right had defined itself – the 'universalist' liberals and the communist successor left – in a single administration. In forming the coalition, and especially in the policies then pursued, the Socialists confirmed the continuing rise of their own 'universalist', liberal elements. Crucially, this applied not only in the socio-cultural sphere but also in economic policy. The Socialist-led government implemented one of the most radical neo-liberal economic programmes in the post-communist region, encapsulated in the 1995 'Bokros package', and the cash privatization of major economic sectors, mostly to foreign investors. The Socialists and Free Democrats thus seemed to overcome the economic divide that had run between them, bringing it into line with the national and socio-cultural ones that already brought them together, and establishing the left as more economically liberal and internationalist than the right.

As regards the 'regime divide', the formation of the Socialist–Free Democrat coalition did not so much bury it as potentially infuse it with substantive post-communist political content. The Free Democrats' decision to join the coalition did not simply reflect the absolute weakness of the 'regime divide', since this could not account for Fidesz's opposite choice.[42] Rather, for both of what were now two political camps, the decision appeared to fit with the national and socio-cultural divides, and therefore further strengthened them. For the right, the Free Democrats' alliance with the Socialists confirmed what was claimed to be the latent affinity between broadly leftist, 'internationalist' forces. Rather than a divide reflecting historical origins, the 'regime divide' thus became one comprising contemporary coalition choices, which themselves seemed to reflect 'national' and socio-cultural ideological commitments. Under this political line-up, with 'universalist', rights-based anti-communism compromised, anti-communism could be increasingly monopolized by its more 'national' and socio-culturally conservative right-wing version. Equally, the right became more strongly associated with anti-communism, since it no longer comprised only some of the political forces rejecting co-operation with the communist successor party, but all of them.[43]

By the mid-1990s, therefore, all four of Kitschelt's possible party divides coincided. This created a potentially powerful ideological basis for a right-wing opposition front against the left–liberal administration, on the basis of more 'national', socially conservative and anti-communist, and less economically liberal, positions.

The political constellation also encouraged solidarity on the right, since there was a shared sense of being 'losers' from the 1994 elections, and, crucially, of facing a powerful common 'enemy'. As noted above, the Socialist–liberal government commanded a super-majority; and the president, Árpád Göncz, was also already seen by the right as part of the left–liberal bloc. The Hungarian right in the mid-1990s therefore perceived the same power monopoly dominated by the communist successor party as did its counterpart in Poland, with the same galvanizing effect. For example, the moderate centre-right parties were especially keen to co-operate in the December 1994 local elections in order to defy the new administration, which had used its super-majority to amend the local electoral law in a way that discouraged joint candidacies. However, the political constellation that encouraged right-wing cohesion was already in place in Hungary by the summer of 1994, whereas in Poland it came into being only after the presidential election in 1995. As well as a stronger ideological basis, Hungary's potential right-wing bloc thus had more time than its Polish counterpart, with four years rather than two to go before the next parliamentary elections.

Elite Action: Ideological Construction in the Mid-1990s

The preceding three sections suggested that the Hungarian centre-right elites might have inherited behavioural norms, organizational structures and ideological conceptions that were more promising for the development of a centre-right bloc than their counterparts in Poland. The political constellation in place by summer 1994 also appeared more helpful. However, Hungarian conditions were arguably not sufficiently different from those in Poland to account for the divergence evident on the centre-right in the two states by 2001–2002, and they did not determine the emergence of the Fidesz-led bloc.

One key step in Hungary was the construction of an ideology that converted the potential of the 'national' and socio-culturally–based right into the source of at least some policies that were relatively popular with the electorate in the circumstances of the late 1990s. The normal translations (also used by Fidesz) of the ideology's key concepts are 'civic' (*polgári*) and 'citizen' (*polgár*), but 'bourgeois' is a legitimate and perhaps more helpful rendering, with the associated social process translated as 'bourgeoisification'. The *polgári* concepts had two sets of historical associations: the political and socio-economic developments of the nineteenth century, and the communist designation of the Western capitalist states as the '*polgári* [that is, 'bourgeois'] democracies'. The *polgári* ideology was associated specifically with Fidesz, which sponsored the relevant process of ideological construction from 1994, and incorporated the term *polgári* into its name in 1995. By helping to keep Fidesz relatively popular while in office, the ideology and its associated policies helped to sustain the process of centre-right concentration around the party after 1998, in a way that contrasted with the splintering of the Polish centre-right coalition in government after 1997.

The *polgári* ideology located the post-1994 Socialist–liberal administration in a sweeping critique of the Hungarian transition, which itself formed part of a longer historical narrative. The ideology was an anti-elitist one, identifying an elite that had been expropriating and exploiting national property since the early communist period. The ideology was also a rejection of neo-liberal economics, which it saw as serving the interests of the Hungarian elite and its foreign sponsors, and as part of the reason why the expected benefits of transition had not been more widely felt. However, the *polgári* ideologues argued that policy should favour the 'sinking middle', rather than all those who might consider themselves 'transition losers'. This was partly because the state was seen as having a greater duty to help those apparently willing and able to help themselves, and partly because the struggling middle groups were seen as carriers of moral and cultural values, such as respect for work and the family, which the *polgári* thinkers wished to promote as goods in themselves.

Compared with Szczerbiak's account of the appeal of Poland's Solidarity Electoral Action, two related features of this ideology are striking. First, it responded to phenomena identified as post-communist, rather than simply harking back to the anti-communist struggle. Indeed, the ideology of bourgeoisification depended on the communist successor party's practice of neo-liberal economics. Second, the ideology stood in a wholly different relationship to 'transition', offering itself as a critique and promise of change, rather than a commitment to complete an existing process.[44] In both respects, given the aggregate position of public opinion, the ideology was more electorally promising.

More specifically, the *polgári* ideology carried advantages along both tracks of the Hungarian centre-right concentration process: mass and elite.

Mass

Three features of the ideology were notable in the electoral context. First, at least in the version presented to the electorate, and at least until the latter stages of the 1998–2002 administration, it appeared to entail a greater focus on voters' concrete socio-economic concerns than had the policies and ideology of either the Antall or the Socialist–liberal government (although, as ever, not sufficiently to satisfy voters). Fidesz's focus on individual and family-level effects was part of a revolution in presentational politics strongly associated with the *polgári* phenomenon. Second, at least compared with the 'Bokros package', some of the policies generated by the *polgári* ideology were electorally popular among those seeking greater welfare provision and protection (although, again, not to a sufficient extent);[45] but the *polgári* ideology also initially promised tax cuts to support the 'sinking middle', and in general carried a more aspirational message than a straightforward appeal to the archetypal 'transition loser'. Third, because the *polgári* concept had not previously had strong associations with the post-communist right, it helped Fidesz to reassure voters that the party was not offering a reversion to the Antall administration, and to continue to appeal in a liberal direction, at least for a time.[46] Moreover, since the term *polgári* had previously had no special prominence in post-communist electoral politics, it underlined a key element in Fidesz's appeal: that, thanks to the age of its leaders and its lack of governing record, the party represented something new and different.

Centre-Right Elites

While it appeared to voters to offer something new, the *polgári* ideology simultaneously encompassed long-standing centre-right elite positions as established in 1990–94. This was achieved through three mechanisms. First, there was substantial overlap between core positions generated by the *polgári* ideology and longstanding right-wing ones, such as social and cultural conservatism, support for a state role in economic regulation and social welfare, and, most importantly, support for small-scale private property as the basis for a Hungarian middle class. The full name of the Smallholders, for example, had always been the Independent Smallholder, Land-worker and *Polgári* Party. Second, the central stable element of the *polgári* concept was its exclusion of the Socialists, making it highly appropriate as the key term for a front aimed primarily against the Socialist-led bloc. Third, the concept proved highly plastic, allowing it to be applied to the antithesis of almost any phenomenon identified as communist or communist-successor in origin. In its vagueness, as well as its ability to unite disparate forces, the concept was the functional equivalent for the centre-right of 'modernization' for the left–liberal camp.[47]

Finally, the *polgári* ideology facilitated organizational concentration of the centre-right because of the way it was developed. It emerged from a milieu of discussion circles and intellectual societies that were initiated or mobilized after 1994 by Fidesz and leading figures associated with other moderate centre-right parties who wished to promote the coming together of moderate centre-right forces. These bodies and their activities constituted a key mechanism by which Fidesz was integrated into 'core' centre-right elite circles, and through which the party gained access to, and credibility from, contacts with personnel who had gained government experience in 1990–94. According to László Kövér, one of Orbán's chief lieutenants and later Fidesz leader, 'co-operation between the intellectuals and expert bases of Fidesz and the [Democratic Forum] and Fidesz and the [Christian Democratic Alliance] in the period 1994–98 became so close that party affiliations in more than one case ran together and lost their significance'.[48]

Among the challenges facing the centre-right parties in 1994, identified above, the *polgári* ideology therefore represented the response to the Socialist–liberal coalition. The ideology also constituted a means of dealing intellectually with the Antall administration, by portraying it almost as the victim of long-term socio-economic processes that it was barely able to comprehend, let alone counter. This diverted the attention of centre-right anti-Antallites from their grievances against him, at least to some extent, while chiming with a tendency among pro-Antallites to see, retrospectively, many of the weaknesses of his legacy as the consequence of his illness, rather than a result of political error.

Micro-Management: The Pecularity of Fidesz

In comparison with the Polish case, two sets of micro-institutional factors seem to have facilitated the concentration of the centre-right in Hungary under Fidesz leadership. One concerned Fidesz as a party, and the other the management of relations within the governing coalition after 1998. As with the *polgári* ideology, both sets of factors impinged upon both tracks of the process of centre-right concentration, elite and mass, facilitating Fidesz's emergence as the centre-right hegemon.

It was suggested above that there might have been more 'party-ness' on the Hungarian centre-right in general, in comparison with Poland. This was understood as clarity about the organizational goals of seats and office, and a willingness among party elites to subordinate personal considerations in pursuit of them. These norms translate into relatively high party unity. Fidesz possessed these characteristics to a high degree even compared with other Hungarian parties. For example, there has been only one contested presidential election in Fidesz, in 1994; even then, in the aftermath of the party's election disaster, none of the party's other major figures stood against Orbán. The leadership remained with Orbán unchallenged in 1995, 1997 and 1999, and passed to Kövér in 2000 and Zoltán Pokorni in 2001 (and back to Orbán in 2002) also without contest. Fidesz's internal unity seemed to extend from the leadership to a relatively quiescent membership: there was, for example, no turnover in the party presidium, elected by congress delegates, between 1995 and 2001. Compared with the conflicts at the other moderate centre-right parties in the mid-1990s, Fidesz's internal unity was electorally attractive. Fidesz's 'party-ness' was also a key resource facilitating centre-right organizational concentration around the party, in two ways. First, internal unity allowed the Fidesz leadership to make the shifts in ideological appeal and political partnerships involved in its emergence to head the centre-right bloc. As we have seen, neither the Democratic Forum nor the Christian Democrats managed to make equivalent decisions without splitting. Second, the willingness of Fidesz leaders to give 'incomers' elected and ex officio party leadership positions, and 'safe' places on party electoral lists, triggered a key mechanism by which Fidesz integrated elites from other centre-right parties.[49]

Fidesz's 'party-ness' exceeded even that of the Smallholders, the other party which went into the post-1994 period with a secure leadership. This is suggested by the difference between the ways in which Orbán and Torgyán were replaced as leaders in 2000 and 2001–2 respectively. In both parties, the perceived problem was at least partly the same, namely that the party was suffering because the leader was too engaged by his government duties. In Fidesz, the solution was thrashed out behind closed doors before being approved by the party congress. Orbán stood aside, Kövér was elected unopposed and the party statutes were simply changed so that any serving Fidesz prime minister would be in the presidium ex officio. In the Smallholders, despite the electoral damage that his continued leadership was inflicting, Torgyán could not be removed without an internal revolt. Both the greater nature of the problem in the Smallholders, and the way in which the issue was resolved in the two parties, highlighted another difference between their leaderships: Torgyán's leadership of the Smallholders was highly individualistic; in Fidesz, by contrast, for all Orbán's dominance, decisions seem to have been made among the core leadership group, rather than by him alone.

There might be two types of explanation for Fidesz's 'party-ness', although neither explains why Orbán and the group around him appear to have had strong notions of 'party-ness' from the outset. One explanation would be sociological. The Fidesz leadership group was highly uniform in socio-demographic characteristics and life experiences. For example, of the ten party presidium members in the period 1995–2001, all were men; they were born within seven years of one another (1959–65); seven grew up in the provinces; six had been members of one of the live-in 'disciplinary colleges' of Budapest's two elite universities, the network that formed the immediate intellectual, institutional and personal cradle for Fidesz from the early 1980s; and five had been founder members of the party in 1988, with another two joining the same year.[50] All these features were shared by Orbán's rival Gábor Fodor, so did not determine leadership unity. However, once the Orbánites had established their supremacy in 1993, this shared history eased informal internal decision making and provided a powerful sense of group identity. Moreover, because most of the leadership group had been heavily involved with Fidesz from such a young age, they may have been exposed to fewer alternative organizational cultures than the leaderships of more sociologically conventional parties. They also possessed an intense sense of institutional ownership and loyalty that, on Szczerbiak's account, seems to have been conspicuously lacking in Poland's Solidarity Electoral Action.

The second explanation would point to elite norms, conflict and learning. The major internal conflict that Fidesz did experience, culminating in the 1993 split, was at least in part precisely about the party's 'party-ness'. The group around Fodor was more interested in encouraging cultural and intellectual activities, rather than focusing only on 'party-like' goals, and was more resistant than the Orbánites to the establishment of a single 'party line'. The immediate trigger for the split was Orbán's rejection of an offer from Fodor that represented an explicit attempt to institutionalize internal diversity.

Fodor wanted to take unopposed the chairmanship of the party body immediately below the presidium, as a retrospective quid pro quo for having allowed Orbán to take the presidency unchallenged.[51] When Fodor lost the chairmanship to the Orbánite candidate and left the party, the Orbánites could feel that their political victory was also a victory for their notion of 'party-ness'. This may have affected in turn the behaviour of members who remained in the party after 1993. No leadership group in the Democratic Forum ever secured such an absolute victory. However, the Orbánites in Fidesz also seemed to draw stronger lessons from the electoral damage inflicted by party infighting before 1994 than did elites in the Forum, who – as we have seen – suffered a second split in 1996. In Fidesz, after 1993 and certainly after 1995, such leadership differences as existed were not aired in public.

Antall's less complete command of the Forum contributed to there being, in Debreczeni's words, 'always a bit of tension' between the government and the Forum as a party after 1990. By contrast, conflict between the various 'faces of party' was avoided in Fidesz after 1998 because such 'faces' barely existed. 'In political terms, [Fidesz central office] did not exist; with Fidesz, there [was] no separate party, government and parliamentary group – they dissolved into one, with a single elite at their head'.[52] For example, of the ten party presidium members during 1995–2001, all were MPs after 1998, seven were in government for at least some of Fidesz's term, one was the parliamentary speaker, and one led the Fidesz parliamentary group. As well as helping to avoid internal conflict, this high degree of personnel overlap sustained Fidesz leaders' awareness of the needs of government. In both respects, the situation contrasted with that in Poland after 1997, when the leader of Solidarity Electoral Action remained outside 'its' administration.

Fidesz's management of the 1998–2002 governing coalition had two strands. On the one hand, Fidesz built consultations between the three governing parties and their leaders into the routine business of government. This represented learning from the Socialist–Free Democrat administration. Principally because the Free Democrat leader had not taken a government post, party-to-party contacts between the 1994–98 coalition partners took place in a dedicated body outside normal government structures. However, the convening of this body tended only to draw attention to the fact that there was a coalition dispute. In this respect, by having Smallholder leader Torgyán in his government, in a move rejected by the more fastidious Antall, Orbán eased at least one potential problem of political management. Inasmuch as coalition coordination was a function of a strengthened prime minister's office after 1998, the Fidesz government also learned from the Antall administration. The development of a stronger institution at the centre of government was the key proposal of a research project commissioned by Fidesz in the autumn of 1996, in the course of which members of the Antall administration were quizzed on their experiences of government. There was considerable overlap between the personnel involved in the research project (both researchers and informants) and those developing the *polgári* ideology.[53]

For public consumption and strategic purposes, however, coalition management in 1998–2002 was marked by the absence of many signs of a coalition. For example, there was no deputy prime minister from a junior party; and there was not a single coalition agreement signed by all the governing parties. Instead, Fidesz operated a 'hub-and-spoke' model of coalition management. That is, it dealt separately with its two coalition partners, each of which had to come through Fidesz for influence. There were two bilateral coalition agreements, signed between Fidesz and the Smallholders, and Fidesz and the Democratic Forum.[54] This mode of coalition management carried a number of advantages that facilitated Fidesz supremacy. It allowed Fidesz to manage still uneasy relations between the Smallholders and the Democratic Forum, and eventually to integrate the two parties or leading figures from them separately into the Fidesz-led bloc, without having to resolve their mutual grievances, and while being able to play the two off against each other as long as the Smallholders existed. For electoral purposes, meanwhile, 'hub-and-spoke' coalition management maintained a degree of distance between Fidesz and the Smallholders in particular, protecting the former's popular standing from the disapproval that came to accompany Torgyán and his party.

Conclusion

Compared with the Polish case, the electoral and organizational concentration of the Hungarian centre-right under Fidesz leadership after 1994 looks overdetermined. As regards all four of Hanley and Szczerbiak's types of explanatory factor, there were differences between Hungary and Poland that favoured the emergence of a single centre-right bloc in the former case. Hungarian centre-right parties faced more powerful electoral incentives to co-operate, they shared greater ideological cohesion, and they had more time before facing parliamentary elections following the emergence of political conditions that favoured their formation into a single front. These conditions did not make the emergence of the Fidesz-led bloc inevitable; but at the micro-institutional level, Hungarian centre-right parties were also found to be more 'party-like' than their Polish counterparts, in ways that facilitated concentration; elite action also played an important role, via the construction of a unifying post-communist ideology of the right that was relatively popular electorally. It is commonly argued that 'legacies' are a source of similarities between Hungary and Poland. However, Polish and Hungarian 'legacies' in fact differed in ways that contributed to the greater ideological cohesiveness and 'party-ness' of parties that are evident on the Hungarian right. This applies especially if pre-communist as well as communist-era legacies are taken into account. However, these national features alone cannot account for Fidesz's emergence as the centre-right hegemon. The Hungarian centre-right also benefited from an extremely unusual case: the arrival of a party that was new to this part of the political spectrum, following major identity change. This allowed the centre-right to overcome the electoral legacy of the first post-communist governments. However, the 'new force' also had as much experience of post-communist party politics as any other; and its peculiar micro-institutional norms and make-up, moreover, inclined it especially strongly to learning and strategic action.

ACKNOWLEDGEMENTS

The author would like to thank her co-contributors to this collection for the many exchanges that helped shape this article.

NOTES

1. Pronounced *FID*-ESS. The party changed its name during the period considered here, from *Fiatal Demokraták Szövetség* (Federation of Young Democrats, Fidesz) until 1995 to *Fidesz–Magyar Polgári Párt* (Fidesz–Hungarian Civic Party, Fidesz–MPP) subsequently. Here, 'Fidesz' is used throughout for simplicity. *Polgári* is translated as 'civic' to follow the party's own practice; the term is discussed below.
2. The label is applied on the basis of parties' relationship to the central institutional development addressed, not ideological analysis. These four parties – or key figures from them, where parties split – were all formally integrated to some degree into Fidesz or the Fidesz-led bloc by 2002. As such, they were distinct from the extremist Party of Hungarian Justice and Life. 'Right' refers to the centre-right plus Justice and Life. 'Moderate' and 'radical' are used purely relatively, to distinguish tendencies within centre-right parties and party groupings.
3. See Cs. Kiss, 'From Liberalism to Conservatism: The Federation of Young Democrats in Post-Communist Hungary', *East European Politics and Societies*, Vol.16, No.3 (2003), pp.739–63.
4. Although by no means fully. In particular, this article does not attempt a full account of Fidesz's electoral performance. Fidesz in the electorate is considered in Zs. Enyedi, 'Cleavage Formation in Hungary: The Role of Agency', paper prepared for the ECPR Joint Sessions of Workshops, Edinburgh, 2003.
5. For this reason, Hanley and Szczerbiak's four types of explanation are interpreted in terms more of the party system than of individual parties – although, as already indicated, the two levels are intertwined.
6. H. Kitschelt, Z. Mansfeleova, R. Markowski and G. Tóka, *Post-Communist Party Systems* (Cambridge: Cambridge University Press, 1999); M. Vachudova, 'Right-Wing Parties and Political Outcomes in Eastern Europe', paper prepared for the American Political Science Association Annual Convention, San Francisco, 2001.
7. This article draws on a more detailed study of Hungarian centre-right developments that forms part of the author's PhD thesis. The support of the Economic and Social Research Council is gratefully acknowledged.
8. For the distinction between the party in public office, the party in central office and the party in the country, see R.S. Katz and P. Mair, 'The Evolution of Party Organizations in Europe: The

Three Faces of Party Organization', *American Review of Politics*, Vol.14 (1993), pp.593–617.

 9. The opposed choices of Fidesz and its liberal partner, the Free Democrats, when faced with the apparent choice between the right and the communist successor party after 1992, spelled the end of the liberal ex-opposition pole in the party system and the victory of bipolarism along left-liberal and right-wing lines. The sources and wisdom of these critical liberal party decisions remain bitterly contested, among both politicians and commentators. The importance of the formation of the Socialist–Free Democrat coalition is touched on below; but for the purposes of this study, Fidesz's position on the centre-right is taken as given.

10. The extreme 'populist–national' group under István Csurka founded the Party of Hungarian Justice and Life. Three of the Forum's 'national liberal' MPs, meanwhile, joined the Fidesz parliamentary group. In retrospect, the start of centre-right organizational concentration around Fidesz might therefore be dated to autumn 1993.

11. In 1990, Antall had appointed László Surján to what was then the only Christian Democrat-held ministerial post in his government, over the head of the Christian Democrat leader (whom Antall did not regard as ministerial material). Antall then (intentionally) further facilitated Surján's elevation to the Christian Democrat leadership by despatching the incumbent as Hungary's ambassador to the Vatican: see J. Debreczeni, *A Miniszterelnök. Antall József és a rendszerváltozás* (Budapest: Osiris, 1998), p.101; on the Christian Democrats more generally, see E. Pék, 'Koalíciós függésben – KDNP', in A. Böhm and Gy. Szoboszlai (eds.), *Parlamenti választások 1994* (Budapest: MTA Politikai Tudományok Intézete, 1995), pp.165–75.

12. The career of this term encapsulates the post-1994 development of the Hungarian centre-right. In May 2003, after the period discussed here, Fidesz changed its name again, from *Fidesz-Magyar Polgári Párt* to *Fidesz–Magyar Polgári Szövetség*. This was partly in recognition of the ways in which the organization had already altered, and partly to signal the further changes in organizational form and strategy it was making in response to its 2002 election defeat. Whereas in 1994–95 Fidesz had wanted to be part of an alliance, therefore, by 2003 it had become one.

13. This sketch draws especially on J. Debreczeni, *Orbán Viktor*, 2nd edn. (Budapest: Osiris, 2002), also cited elsewhere. Debreczeni was one of the 'national liberals' expelled from the Democratic Forum in 1993. He sat out the term as an independent and did not return to electoral politics. He was an adviser to Orbán from 1994 to 1996, when he broke with the Fidesz leader over Orbán's treatment of the Szabó group. As a political commentator, Debreczeni has published sympathetic, but in the latter case also more scholarly and critical, biographies of Antall and Orbán.

14. See *Népszabadság*, 4 Dec. 1997. The electoral system is discussed below.

15. In September 2000, Fidesz and the Christian Democratic Alliance signed a co-operation agreement that allowed the latter to nominate members to Fidesz's National Board, and each partner to have non-voting representation in the other's presidium; this was supplemented in May 2001 with an electoral pact for the 2002 parliamentary polls.

16. The terms are Debreczeni's: *Orbán Viktor*, pp.290, 308–12.

17. See T. Kovács, 'FKGP: A népi-nemzeti-keresztény politizálástól a polgári összefogásig', in A. Böhm, F. Gazsó, I. Stumpf and Gy. Szoboszlai (eds.), *Parlamenti választások 1998* (Budapest: Századvég/MTA Politikai Tudományok Intézete, 2000), pp.144–51.

18. For the by-elections, see the reports by Á. Sándor in the 2000 (pp.631–44), 2001 (pp.643–59) and 2002 (pp.932–44) editions of the *Hungarian Political Yearbook*: S. Kurtán, P. Sándor and L. Vass (eds.), *Magyarország politikai évkönyve* (Budapest: Demokrácia Kutatások Magyar Központja Alapítvány, annual publication), hereafter *MPÉK*. For the Democratic Forum initiative generally, see G. Kuglics, 'A Békejobb 2000', *Politikatudományi Szemle*, 2001, No.4, pp.77–95.

19. Reprinted in *MPÉK 2002*, pp.1162–3.

20. See *Népszabadság*, 20 Dec. 2001.

21. See M. Duverger, *Political Parties*, 3rd edn. (London: Methuen, 1964), pp.216–28; and K. Benoit, 'Evaluating Hungary's Mixed-Member Electoral System', in M. Shugart and

M. Wattenberg (eds.), *Mixed-Member Electoral Systems: The Best of Both Worlds?* (Oxford: Oxford University Press, 2001), pp.477–93.

22. This cuts both ways, however: before the 2002 elections, the Democratic Forum needed Fidesz's help to get into parliament at all; but Fidesz needed the Forum not to run separate – and potentially unsuccessful – lists, in order to avoid losing a potentially crucial two or three per cent of the vote for the centre-right camp.

23. The effect is strengthened because candidates can run on a regional and the national list, giving them two chances to take a list seat.

24. B. Fowler, 'The Parliamentary Elections in Hungary, April 2002', *Electoral Studies*, Vol.22, No.4 (2003), pp.799–807.

25. As this article went to press, the Democratic Forum was running independently in the June 2004 European Parliament elections. This falls into the same pattern of behaviour, representing yet another attempt by the party to break the five per cent barrier as the basis for running separately in the 2006 parliamentary polls.

26. S. Saxonberg, 'The Influence of Presidential Systems: Why the Right is So Weak in Conservative Poland and So Strong in the Egalitarian Czech Republic', *Problems of Post-Communism*, Vol.50, No.5 (2003), pp.22–36.

27. Strictly speaking, the referendum was on the timing, not the mode, of presidential election, but its proxy character was well understood, at least at elite level.

28. Similarly, the stability of the Hungarian electoral system arguably reflects party interests and behaviour, as well as shaping them: see Benoit. S. Birch, F. Millard, M. Popescu and K. Williams, *Embodying Democracy: Electoral System Design in Post-Communist Europe* (Basingstoke: Palgrave, 2002), ch.3.

29. This is not to say that the Socialists and Free Democrats necessarily lack their own sources of 'party-like' elite norms – not least, in the case of the Socialists, the communist period.

30. Although we might ask why Polish centre-right elites do not seem to have done more 'catching-up' by the late 1990s.

31. See R.L. Tőkés, *Hungary's Negotiated Revolution* (Cambridge: Cambridge University Press, 1996).

32. In April 1998, the month before the elections, only 21 per cent of respondents expected Fidesz to win, against 59 per cent for the Socialists: Századvég/TÁRKI data in *MPÉK 1999*, p.693.

33. Kitschelt et al., pp.64–7.

34. As will be clear from the fact that this section discusses the 'right' rather than the 'centre-right', the broad conception of the right generated by the national and socio-cultural divides cannot, for example, in itself distinguish between more moderate and more radical varieties.

35. See A. Szczerbiak, 'The Polish Peasant Party: A Mass Party in Postcommunist Eastern Europe?', *East European Politics and Societies*, Vol.15, No.3 (2002), pp.554–88.

36. Kitschelt et al., pp.69–92.

37. On these issues, see especially A. Körösényi, 'Revival of the Past or New Beginning? The Nature of Post-Communist Politics', *Political Quarterly*, Vol.62, No.1 (1991), pp.52–74.

38. Kohl would, with an equal lack of success, advise Orbán eight years later to form a 'grand coalition' with the Socialists: see Debreczeni, *Orbán Viktor*, p.356.

39. We might ask why, if the parties of the 1990–94 administrations were subsequently constrained by considerations of reputation, Fidesz was clearly not. The most likely answer would be that pre-1994, Fidesz had not made an ideological appeal, instead basing its popularity on its generational identity and its focus on practical issues; this later gave it more room for manoeuvre: see Kiss.

40. For one example, concerning the constitutional and symbolic spheres, see B. Fowler, 'Nation, State, Europe and National Revival in Hungarian Party Politics: The Case of the Millennial Commemorations', *Europe–Asia Studies*, Vol.56, No.1 (2004), pp.57–83. Other policy examples include a tougher stance on lustration, greater support for the traditional churches, and a higher priority for support for the Hungarian minorities outside Hungary.

41. In accepting, György Antall seemed to confer his late father's approval on Orbán; rumours abounded in the mid-1990s that there had been some kind of deathbed 'passing of the mantle' from Antall to Orbán; according to Debreczeni, whose source was Antall's son, there

was no such meeting, but Antall did telephone Orbán during his final hospitalization and urge him to remember who they had fought against together at the Round Table: Debreczeni, *A Miniszterelnök*, p.370; *Orbán Viktor*, pp.284–5. Like Debreczeni, Antall's son broke with Orbán in 1996 over the latter's abandonment of Szabó's moderate Democratic Forum wing.

42. For the argument on the regime divide, see A. Grzymala-Busse, 'Coalition Formation and the Regime Divide in New Democracies', *Comparative Politics*, Vol.34, No.1 (2001), pp.85–103. Grzymala-Busse tests whether all the members of an administration come from the post-opposition or post-regime camps, not whether all the members of the post-opposition or post-regime camps join an administration.

43. Including those Free Democrat elites and voters who would not cross the regime divide, and instead left the party.

44. One of the most important collections of *polgári* writings was entitled 'Janus-faced Transition': M. Schmidt and L.Gy. Tóth (eds.), *Janus-arcú rendszerváltozás* (Budapest: Kairosz, 1998), available in English as *Transition with Contradictions* (Budapest: Kairosz, 1999) or *From Totalitarian to Democratic Hungary* (Boulder, CO: Atlantic Research and Publications, 2000). A second Hungarian-language collection was published as Zs. Körmendy (ed.), *Jobbközéparányok. Janus-arcú rendszerváltozás II* (Budapest: Kairosz, 2002). The taster of the *polgári* ideology presented here also draws on L. Bogár, 'Csapdában', in *MPÉK 1995*, pp.245–50; *A Polgári Magyarországért* (Budapest: Fidesz, 1996); Gy. Tellér, 'A rendszerváltozás két útja', in *MPÉK 1999*, pp.17–28; and Gy. Tellér, *Hatalomgyakorlás az MSZP-SZDSZ koalíció idején* (Budapest: Kairosz, 1999).

45. According to one 2000 poll, the Fidesz-led government's most popular policies were promising to raise the minimum wage, stopping large price rises, and increasing state support for large families: Medián data in *MPÉK 2001*, p.800.

46. In a March 1998 poll, over a third of respondents identified with *polgári* from a choice of ten alternatives: Századvég data in *MPÉK 1999*, p. 662. In a December 1999 poll, asked to choose four terms to describe their political views, 40 per cent of respondents included *polgári*, against 27 for 'Christian', 9 for 'right-wing' and 7 for 'conservative': Marketing Centrum data in *MPÉK 2000*, p.760.

47. See A. Bozóki, 'The Ideology of Modernization and the Policy of Materialism: The Day After for the Socialists', *Journal of Communist Studies and Transition Politics*, Vol.13, No.3 (1997), pp.56–102.

48. L. Kövér, 'A Fidesz-Magyar Polgári Párt és a Független Kisgazdapárt koalíciós megállapodása 1998-ban', in *MPÉK 1999*, pp.336–46. On these bodies, see also Debreczeni, *Orbán Viktor*, pp.275–6, 282–3, 291–4, 326, 353–4. On a similar process of centre-right ideological construction in the Czech Republic, see S. Hanley, 'The New Right in the New Europe? Unravelling the Ideology of "Czech Thatcherism" ', *Journal of Political Ideologies*, Vol.4, No.2 (1999), pp.163–89.

49. This phenomenon was seen most drastically in the party's 2003 reorganization, after the period considered here, in which several long-standing senior Fidesz figures were effectively demoted, in the interests of the party's further transformation into an electoral conglomerate: see Zs. Enyedi, 'Cleavage Formation in Hungary'.

50. Members of Fidesz leadership bodies to 1999 are listed in Cs. Machos, *A magyar parlamenti pártok szervezeti felépítése (1990–1999)* (Budapest: Rejtjel, 2000), pp.107–8; later data are at <http://www.fidesz.hu>. Personal data were taken from various parliamentary almanacs.

51. For the 1993 Fodor–Orbán conflict, see Debreczeni, *Orbán Viktor*, pp.227–43; for Fodor's account, Gy. Petőcz, *Csak a narancs volt* (Budapest: Irodalom, 2001), pp.307–21. On the party's 1993 organizational changes more generally, see M. Balázs and Zs. Enyedi, 'Hungarian Case Studies: The Alliance of Free Democrats and the Alliance of Young Democrats', in P.G. Lewis (ed.), *Party Structure and Organization in Eastern and Central Europe* (Cheltenham: Edward Elgar, 1996), pp.43–65; and I. van Biezen, *Political Parties in New Democracies* (Basingstoke: Palgrave, 2003), ch.5.

52. Debreczeni, *Orbán Viktor*, p. 487.

53. See I. Stumpf, 'Kormányzásváltás 1998-ban', in *MPÉK 1999*, pp.324–35.

54. Reprinted in *MPÉK 1999*, pp.893–900.

All Right Now? Explaining the Successes and Failures of the Slovak Centre-Right

TIM HAUGHTON and MAREK RYBÁŘ

The forces of the centre-right in Slovakia were the clear winners of the September 2002 parliamentary elections. Within days of the polling stations closing, a four-party centre-right coalition consisting of Prime Minister Mikuláš Dzurinda's Slovak Democratic and Christian Union, the Christian Democratic Movement, the Alliance of the New Citizen and the Party of the Hungarian Coalition had been formed. There were notable aspects of continuity with the previous (1998–2002) administration, including the continuation of Dzurinda as prime minister, but there were also changes. The most significant of these was the ejection not only from the government, but also from parliament, of the leftist Party of the Democratic Left and also the removal from the legislature of the radical–nationalist Slovak National Party. It could be argued, therefore, that the re-election of the centre-right in the 2002 elections highlighted its strength and vitality. We argue, by contrast, that the electoral achievements of the four centre-right parties in 2002 can be explained only by reference to the weakness of the centre-right in the 1990s and the divisions that overshadowed left–right competition throughout the decade.

In terms of defining the centre-right, we follow Hanley's conceptualization in this volume, which categorizes centre-right parties as those seeking 'electoral support for programmes fusing elements of (neo-)liberalism and conservatism, which balance the demands of post-communist social transformations, modernization and Europeanization with older historical identities and ideologies'.

There has been a veritable alphabet soup of parties in Slovakia since 1989 that could be labelled centre-right. Most of these groupings have been of little relevance to the overall shape of party politics in Slovakia. This study will focus on the two most important centre-right parties since 1989: the Christian Democratic Movement (KDH) and the Slovak Democratic and Christian Union (SDKÚ). None the less, several points need to be made about the other two parties in the governing coalition. First, on the basis of its economic and social agenda the Party of the Hungarian Coalition cannot be labelled unequivocally a centre-right party, despite its membership of the centre-right grouping the European People's Party–European Democrats. Indeed, its primary appeal is as the party representing the interests of the ethnic Hungarians who live in Slovakia. In its various incarnations since 1989, the party has mopped up some 90 per cent of the votes of ethnic Hungarians, although those ethnic Hungarians who do not vote for the party are self-ascribed leftist voters.[1] Second, many of the programmatic appeals of the party call for more state subsides and more redistribution in favour of rural and less-developed areas, where most of its electorate resides. Hence, the economic orientation of the party is more *leftist* than the other members of the current Slovak government,[2] even though the party stands for rather traditional conservative values such as family, tradition and nation.

A degree of caution is also needed in analysing the Alliance of the New Citizen. Even though it projects itself as a centre-right liberal party, it was founded and created primarily as a 'personal vehicle' party by the media magnate Pavol Rusko.[3] A sizeable chunk of its appeal lay not in its position on the left–right scale, but in its novelty, a party unencumbered by the battles of party politics in the 1990s. As the dispute between two members of the government nominated by the party – Nemcsics and Opaterný – and Rusko demonstrated,[4] it is still more of a one-man show grouping than a consolidated centre-right party. None the less, the acrimonious dispute between KDH and Rusko's party over the role Catholic values should play in Slovak life, particularly regarding the issue of abortion, which plagued the coalition in the summer of 2003,[5] demonstrates the clash inherent in many centre-right groupings between liberals and conservatives. Both the Party of the Hungarian Coalition's ability to capture the bulk of the ethnic Hungarian vote and the Alliance of the New Citizen's appeal to novelty highlight the salience in Slovak politics of issues that are not usual on the left–right scale.

This study grapples with one central and two subsidiary questions. What explains the overall level of performance, in electoral terms, of KDH and SDKÚ from 1989 to 2002? Why has the centre-right remained rather marginal for most of that period? Why in spite of that weakness has the centre-right been the leading force in government since 1998? Although we argue that structural–legacy approaches may help to explain why the conservative Catholic KDH emerged as the main centre-right party in the early 1990s and we suggest that the early transition period particularly Czechoslovakia's constitutional imbroglio and the painful policies of economic reform harmed KDH at the ballot box, we maintain that arguments stressing the role of legacy and the dynamics of the transition do not per se provide a sufficient explanation. Indeed, they are of limited value in explaining SDKÚ's fortunes largely because the party only emerged on to the scene a decade after the 1989 revolution. Institutional factors, particularly the electoral system, are more helpful in explaining SDKÚ's unexpected success in the 2002 elections. Above all, however, we argue that political crafting and decisions by political actors at critical moments are central to explaining the electoral performance of KDH and SDKÚ. (For figures on the electoral performance of different parties, see Table 1.)

The Movement for a Democratic Slovakia and the Polarization of Party Politics in Slovakia in the 1990s

The classic left–right divide has always existed in post-communist Slovakia, but until recently its salience was overshadowed by other issues. During 1989–93 the future of Czechoslovakia, albeit at times muddied with other issues, was central to political debate. After the federal state's 'divorce' and until as late as the 2002 elections, the dominant conflict revolved round the liberal aspects of democracy and the isolation or integration of Slovakia into international bodies, especially the EU and NATO.

TABLE 1
PARLIAMENTARY ELECTION RESULTS (% OF THE POPULAR VOTE) OF KDH, SDKÚ
AND THEIR RIVALS

Party/Movement	1992	1994	1998	2002
KDH (Christian Democratic Movement)	8.89	10.08	–[a]	8.25
SDK (Slovak Democratic Coalition)	–	–	26.33[a]	–
SDKÚ (Slovak Democratic and Christian Union)	–	–	–	15.09
Other notable right-leaning parties				
DS (Democratic Party)	3.31	3.43	–[a]	–[c]
ODÚ (Civic Democratic Union)	4.04	–	–	–
SNS (Slovak National Party)	7.93	5.4	9.07	3.33[d]
PSNS (Real Slovak National Party)	–	–	–	3.65[d]
SKDH–KSÚ (Slovak Christian Democratic Movement–Christian Social Union)	3.05	2.06	–	–
ANO (Alliance of the New Citizen)	–	–	–	8.01
DÚ (Democratic Union)	–	8.57	–[a]	–
Slovakia's most popular party				
HZDS (Movement for a Democratic Slovakia)	37.26	34.96[b]	27.00	19.50

[a]In 1998 KDH, DÚ and DS together with two minor parties supported SDK and provided SDK with their own candidates; however, they themselves did not take part in the elections.
[b]In 1994 HZDS formed an electoral coalition with the small Agrarian Party of Slovakia.
[c]In 2002 DS withdrew its party list and supported SDKÚ.
[d]In 2002 SNS broke up into SNS and PSNS, which contested elections separately.

Source: Slovak Statistical Office, at <http://www.statistics.sk>.

Central to both these phases is the distorting role played by the party created and led by the three-time prime minister, Vladimír Mečiar: the Movement for a Democratic Slovakia (HZDS). Founded in March 1991, it tried initially to project itself as the true heir of the anti-communist umbrella organization, Public Against Violence. HZDS built its appeal on a programme of managed economic reform, a rhetoric and concern for those who suffered from the process of marketization, and the charisma and personality of Mečiar – all articulated in a national accent.[6] Although campaigning on a policy of greater autonomy, after winning the 1992 elections in their respective parts of the common state, Mečiar and his counterpart in the Czech lands, Václav Klaus, negotiated Czechoslovakia out of existence. From late 1992 onwards Mečiar liked to portray himself as the father of the nation and his political opponents as enemies of the Slovak nation.[7] Such rhetoric, plus the policies of the 1994–98 HZDS-led government, 'when it played fast and loose with constitutional niceties and democratic norms', helped foster a dichotomized Slovak polity.[8] Moreover, on Mečiar's watch both NATO and the EU refused to open accession negotiations with Slovakia. The increasing international isolation and the tendency towards authoritarianism was central to the creation of the Slovak Democratic Coalition (see below), which became the main party after the 1998 election. In response to its removal from power, HZDS re-branded itself as a Christian Democratic party of the West European type at its congress in Trnava in March 2000.

The HZDS phenomenon raises a number of questions relating to the centre-right in Slovakia, the most pertinent of which are: why did HZDS and not KDH become the dominant party in 1991–92, and how did HZDS manage to hold on to its pre-eminent position until the 1998 election?

Party Purity Versus a Broad Church

In 1990 the Christian Democratic Movement (KDH) appeared to stand an excellent chance of becoming one of the most prominent political parties in Slovakia. The party had much going for it including its roots in the dissident past and its Roman Catholicism in a country where a majority of citizens declare themselves to be Catholic.[9] The party's initial levels of support indicated the potential support for KDH,[10] but for most of the post-1989 period the party managed to muster a mere ten per cent. Much of the blame for the party's relatively poor showing lies with decisions made by the party's leaders.

KDH owed its initial strength to networks of Catholics established during communist times. The 'normalization' following the Prague Spring is often thought of as a period of repression, but the regime was less punitive in the Slovak part of the federation, and this more relaxed attitude had important consequences. Linked to the greater religiosity in the Slovak lands was the salience of opposition groups based on Catholicism rather than on human or civic rights. The most significant demonstrations, such as the candlelight processions in Bratislava in 1988 and the pilgrimages to Levoča and Šaštín in the same year, were all driven by religion.[11] The leading figures in the Catholic dissident movement, especially Ján Čarnogurský, became the driving-forces behind the creation of KDH soon after the 1989 revolution. Moreover, it was KDH that emerged as the strongest potential rival to the anti-regime umbrella grouping, Public Against Violence. An explanatory approach such as that of Vachudová, stressing the type and strength of organized opposition during the late communist period and the nature of the post-communist right, therefore seems to bear fruit in the Slovak case.[12]

Religion was central to KDH when it was formed and has remained so ever since. 'Most of the party's initial members were Catholic, anti-communist lay people and activist priests who operated a "secret church" during the 1970s and 1980s'.[13] At the party's founding congress in February 1990, Čarnogurský's speech to the assembled mass was permeated with references to religion. The party leader's ecumenism, however, extended only to other Christian faiths rather than to non-believers as well.[14] Since 1990 the party's statutes have at times tried to stress that the party brings together citizens 'without regard to their ethnicity [národnost'] and religious beliefs';[15] but, as the very name of the party suggests, Christianity pervades KDH. Čarnogurský described Christianity as 'the source of our internal stability, the inspiration for our decisions and the source [zásobarnou] of our supporters'.[16] Indeed, on one occasion he declared that 'Christian politics in Slovakia is KDH and KDH is Christian politics in Slovakia'.[17] None the less, at other times he has been keen to stress that his party was a political, not a Christian, movement.[18] Despite the reference to all Christian faiths in some KDH statements, the party did little to reach out to non-Catholics. Its strong Catholicism has harmed the party at the ballot box, particularly among the small, but not statistically insignificant, evangelicals,[19] and is in stark contrast to other Christian Democratic parties such as the German CDU.

In a country with a large proportion of self-declared Catholics, albeit fewer than in Poland, it might be expected that a party with an explicit appeal to Catholic values would be successful. There is evidence to suggest that KDH has indeed been relatively successful in garnering support from Catholics and relatively unsuccessful in persuading non-believers to support the party.[20] What has harmed KDH has not so much been its Catholicism, despite concerns articulated by Čarnogurský,[21] but rather the legacy of Catholic dissent and the strategic errors of its own leadership in contrast to the adept leadership and political crafting of opponents.

KDH was established from the bottom up, although it could have been created from the top down. (There had been Christian democratic deputies in the parliament before the 1990 elections thanks to co-optations, although it is worth stressing these deputies became MPs only after November 1989; that is, they were not members of the communist assemblies.) The party's founding congress was attended by some 1,200 delegates who belonged to the *Christian democratic clubs* that had been created in November 1989 following the call by several prominent individuals of Christian Democratic persuasion at that time. The delegates constituted a broad church of opinion, linked only by the appeal of some sort of Christian Democracy (to some the *Christian* was more important than the *democratic*, and vice versa).

Three broad streams of opinion within the party emerged and crystallized. First, the conservative Catholics revolved around the party's founder and leader for the first decade, Ján Čarnogurský, which drew heavily on the experience of Catholic dissent. For them, the party's *raison d'être* was to be a close community of like-minded individuals with an explicitly Christian vision of society rather than to serve purely as a vote-winning machine. Second, there were nationalists such as Ján Klepáč and Viliam Oberhauser. The third group, which included Mikuláš Dzurinda and Ivan Šimko, wanted a more moderate party with greater electoral potential, but remained subservient until the mid-1990s.

In almost any democratic polity major political parties have to be 'big tent' parties, tending to contain within themselves significant variations of opinion albeit linked by core underlying values. Rather than adopt a strategy of inclusion, the powerful forces within KDH opted for purity. Indeed, it can be argued that the conservative Catholics who have been largely in control of KDH since the party's creation had by 2002 achieved their goal. The nationalists and the moderates had left, leaving a party unified around a conservative Catholic agenda, although one which manages to win only a tenth of the vote.

While that strategy might bode well for the prospects of KDH, it damaged the party's electoral potential in the early 1990s. Given Čarnogurský's strategy of a gradual increase of Slovakia's autonomy (which would end eventually in the country's independence within the European Union), the Catholic conservatives were unwise to divest themselves of the nationalist faction around Klepáč in the party. It is unclear whether Klepáč's faction would have remained for much longer in KDH in any case, and it is unclear how much pressure Čarnogurský himself exerted to force the departure of Klepáč and his allies; but we can state that Čarnogurský did nothing to persuade the nationalists to remain.[22] The nationalist faction (amounting to a third of KDH's parliamentary representation) left in March 1992 to form the Slovak Christian Democratic Movement. The KDH leadership welcomed the split, 'arguing that it freed the party to present itself as a true right-of-centre Christian Democratic party'.[23] Klepáč and his allies, however, won just over three per cent of the vote in the 1992 elections – votes that could have gone to KDH.

The experience of dissent and its impact on individuals needs to be factored in here. Čarnogurský, for example, was a man whose *Weltanschauung* was forged during the post-Prague Spring 'normalization'. His belligerence and unwillingness to compromise, laudable assets before the revolution, were not well suited to the give-and-take deal-making of liberal democracy. The character of Čarnogurský and his ilk helps explain why KDH did not have a more expansionary electoral strategy in the 1990s, and also helps explain why a number of leading party figures were not willing to be subsumed under the Slovak Democratic and Christian Union umbrella in 2000 (to which we will return below).

The desire for party purity on the part of Čarnogurský stands in direct contrast to the strategy employed by Vladimír Mečiar and his Movement for a Democratic Slovakia (HZDS). In 1989 there were four clearly defined ideological–political poles in Slovak politics: nationalists, ethnic Hungarians, the left (of both communist-successor and social-democratic variants) and the centre-right Christian democrats. Ironically, however, it was a fifth force that became the most successful party. HZDS's success was attributable to its ability to draw support from three of these camps (nationalists, leftists and Christian Democrats) thanks to its mixed bag of policies. HZDS, like KDH, also contained within in it various strands in the early 1990s. The key difference was that HZDS had a charismatic politician who tried (at least initially) to build a broad-church party, whereas KDH had a leader keener on the ideological purity of the sect than on ensuring success at the ballot box. The very fact that Mečiar realized the importance of building up a party with a broad base of support does add some weight to Saxonberg's arguments (discussed by Szczerbiak and Hanley in their introduction to this collection) concerning the incentive structures of parliamentary compared with semi-presidential institutional frameworks.[24]

Strategic Choices in a Time of Dynamic Change

The legacies of Catholic dissent may explain who was leading KDH's troops in the early 1990s, and the party's policies of purity help explain why KDH's army was not larger, but they do not explain everything on the political battlefield. Political battles were fought not just on transition issues (especially the speed and extent of economic reform): they were muddied and often subsumed by the national question – the future of Czechoslovakia.

Having examined the internal politics of KDH, we now turn to the interaction between KDH and the rest of the party political scene in the period 1990–92. The decline in KDH's popularity in 1991–92 owes much to three related strategic decisions: the removal of Mečiar from the prime ministership in 1991, the decision of Čarnogurský to become prime minister, and the policy package pursued by his government in 1991–92.

Vladimír Mečiar was removed from his position as Slovak prime minister in 1991 thanks not to the votes of the Slovak people in an election, but to a vote within parliament. Indeed, one of the great puzzles surrounding Čarnogurský is why he agreed to support the federalist wing of Public Against Violence, assist in the removal of Mečiar from power and become prime minister himself. Three plausible explanations can be advanced. First, Čarnogurský was no fan of Mečiar; he wanted to see Mečiar removed and took on the burden of the top job out of a sense of duty.[25] Second, Čarnogurský was a close friend of a couple of notable figures in Public Against Violence, including his fellow dissident Ján Langoš, who may have persuaded the KDH leader to back them. Third, although Čarnogurský is a man driven not solely by concerns of power or the trappings of office (in Müller and Strøm's schema, 'policy' drives him),[26] he is not immune to the lure of power. The Christian Democrats had decided in favour of Viliam Obhauser getting the top job, but Čarnogurský with the backing of KDH's coalition partners became prime minister. Were his motives, therefore, to put his rivals in their place?[27]

Čarnogurský's motives aside, his decision to assist in the removal of Mečiar in 1991 harmed KDH. When Mečiar was ousted from power both his personal and his government's approval ratings were staggeringly high (close to 80 per cent).[28] In a nascent democracy, such as Slovakia's in 1991, where many voters were only just beginning to learn the rules of the parliamentary game, the voting out of such a popular leader by a group of parliamentarians is hardly likely to endear the new prime minister to the country. Not only is the new man almost guaranteed to be blamed for what were perceived as the undemocratic machinations of people within Public Against Violence, but the electoral clock was against him: he had only a year to build up his own popularity before new elections while trying to introduce pain-inducing marketization measures. It would have been a tough task for any politician.

The participation of KDH in the Slovak government between 1991 and 1992 clearly harmed the party's prospects in the 1992 elections. Part of the 'failing credibility' of the government stemmed from the interminable discussions over Slovakia's place in Czechoslovakia,[29] but a large slice of the government's unpopularity was caused by the painful effects of economic reform. Čarnogurský's character can be factored in here. He declared his single-minded determination to push ahead with economic change, however hard the consequences.[30] The leader of KDH's position was captured in a cartoon by Boris Kusenda: an earnest-looking Čarnogurský is trudging up a mountain weighed down by a heavy rucksack labelled 'Government' on the path from *election 1990* to *election 1992*. Three of KDH's rivals (including the Mečiar-led HZDS), however, are ahead of the KDH leader having already reached the summit where they left their flags and are now making their descent towards the next elections unencumbered by the weight of office.[31] To those factors we can add the anecdotal observation that KDH appeared to be run almost by a clan: Čarnogurský and his brother Ivan were joined in top party positions by František Mikloško and his brother Jozef.

One of the interesting paradoxes of Čarnogurský was his desire to see a pure Christian Democratic movement, coupled with a willingness to compromise with his coalition partners during 1991–92, particularly over questions related to *the nation*. In contrast to Mečiar, who realized that a more nationalistic line (although stopping short of advocating independence) was a vote-winning stance,[32] under pressure from its pro-federation coalition partners KDH diluted its confederal stance and advocated a looser federation instead.[33] Čarnogurský's liability on the national question was the product of his reluctance to pursue his dream of an independent Slovakia. At times he even emphasized the similarity of KDH's goals with those of the separatist Slovak National Party.[34]

March 1994: The Critical Juncture for Slovak Party Politics

Arguably the most important critical juncture for party politics in Slovakia occurred in early 1994. Dispute within the ranks of HZDS and its coalition allies led to the collapse of the second Mečiar-led government in March 1994. The new government, including KDH and it arch-enemy the communist-successor Party of the Democratic Left, could have remained in place until the end of the parliamentary term (June 1996), but the decision was made to push for early, but not immediate, elections.

In retrospect this decision appears to have been a major mistake. HZDS was haemorrhaging support in the period 1992–94, falling to a mere 12 per cent in November 1993.[35] Removal from office by a parliamentary vote of no confidence enabled HZDS to re-group, relieve itself of the burdens of office, and blame the new government for the country's economic plight. The decision was not made by KDH leader Čarnogurský, but rather by the leader of the Party of the Democratic Left, Peter Weiss, who was buoyed by the success of the communist-successor parties in Poland and Hungary.[36] Blame cannot be placed solely on Weiss's shoulders, however, as KDH was happy to acquiesce in Weiss's plans.

The decision opened the door for Mečiar's return to power after the autumn 1994 elections, in part the result of a splinter grouping that broke away from the Party of the Democratic Left in disgust at what the deserters saw as the party's abrogation of its class interests. It was the 1994–98 Mečiar-led government whose actions sullied Slovakia's name and ensured the snubbing by NATO at the Madrid summit and the EU at the Luxembourg European Council in 1997.[37] This government was a major stimulus towards the reconstitution of the political scene in 1998 and for the creation of the Slovak Democratic and Christian Union in 2000.

Closer Co-operation and Merger: The Emergence of the Slovak Democratic and Christian Union

The seeds of the centre-right's dominance in Slovakia after the 2002 election were sown in the mid 1990s. Indeed the period 1996–2000 is significant for the development of the centre-right, not just because it culminated in the creation of a new, strong centre-right grouping, but also because the moderate wing of KDH became influential in the party. Although institutional factors played a role, political crafting is the key to explaining the cohesion and strength of the centre-right in this period.

Spurred on by Slovakia's increasing international isolation and the tendency towards the use of autocratic means by the Mečiar-led government, the opposition parties including KDH began to see the need for closer co-operation. The moderate wing of KDH, including Šimko and Dzurinda, fostered links with other opposition parties such as the Democratic Union and the Democratic Party with which KDH formed the loose 'Blue Coalition' in 1996. In May of the following year, however, the thwarted referendum on direct presidential elections and NATO membership persuaded the greens and the social democrats to join forces with the Blue Coalition in a broader electoral coalition.[38] The Slovak Democratic Coalition was created, in the words of Mikuláš Dzurinda, who became its leader, by 'smelting all the democratic forces in the country so that the group would be the strongest'.[39] Even though the cause appeared to be above party politics – for some it appeared to affect the very future of Slovak democracy – a number of KDH hardliners (from the Catholic conservative faction) were reluctant to throw their lot in with the other opposition parties. Because the KDH leadership wanted their views represented by the conservative wing, Šimko was even recalled from the working party set up to discuss co-operation with the other parties that were to form the Slovak Democratic Coalition.

Institutional factors play their part here. Thanks to the changes in the electoral law requiring all components of an electoral coalition to cross the five per cent threshold (what Dzurinda labelled rather hyperbolically as 'political terrorism'[40]), the constituent parties agreed to transform the electoral coalition into a single party. Even in the face of a naked attempt to disadvantage the opposition parties, the conservative wing of KDH was reluctant to agree to the creation of a single party. Five members of the party's presidium voted against the transformation of the Slovak Democratic Coalition into a party, even though it was to be a party created simply to achieve success in the 1998 election; the 'mother parties' were to remain intact.[41]

Although a slight exaggeration, it could be argued that the moderates saw the creation of the Slovak Democratic Coalition as an opportunity, while for the conservatives it was a threat. The conservatives' dominance had been demonstrated at the party congress in November 1996 when Čarnogurský defeated Dzurinda by 214 votes to 130. The creation of the Coalition, however, brought the tensions out into the open. The new electoral law, designed by Mečiar and his allies to inflict as much damage on their opponents as possible, contained a provision banning members of one party from being on another party list. KDH nominees to the Slovak Democratic Coalition, therefore, had to drop their KDH membership, an issue that came to the fore after the election.

The Slovak Democratic Coalition was successful in the 1998 elections, gaining 26.3 per cent of the vote and forming the mainstay of the new coalition government. Tensions between the moderates and the conservatives persisted, however. For many on the moderate wing the electoral coalition was not just a temporary solution to overcome the pitfalls of the electoral law: it represented the 'first step' towards the creation of a new party.[42] Indeed, Šimko and Dzurinda realized that co-operation was an alternative route to their goal: a strong, inclusive centre-right grouping. Šimko, for instance, frequently made positive reference to the German Christian Democratic Union's inclusivity, gathering Catholics, evangelicals, conservatives, liberals, Christian socialists and others under the party's umbrella.[43] On the other hand, Čarnogurský was no fan of sitting under a big tent with liberals.

The issue of double membership came to the fore again at a KDH party congress in April 1999. Dzurinda proposed that the KDH party constitution (*stanovy*) be changed in such a way as to allow double membership. Although the proposal received majority support (246 out of 465), it failed to achieve the necessary two-thirds.[44] A subsequent proposal introducing a limited version of double membership was passed, but this merely strengthened the position of the Catholic conservative faction, because it allowed dual membership only for those members who did not hold positions in the KDH leadership.[45] The newly elected leadership of KDH, therefore, contained only representatives of Čarnogurský's conservative Catholic faction, because all the significant moderates such as Dzurinda and Šimko were members of the Slovak Democratic Coalition. The battle of the 1999 congress is significant because it demonstrated two points. First, there were a significant number of KDH politicians from the Catholic conservative faction who were driven by a desire to maintain KDH at any cost: for them, what mattered was the Christian Catholic purity of values. Second, the moderates wanted to pursue a broad-church strategy and saw the Slovak Democratic Coalition as the vehicle not only to widen the appeal of the centre-right, but also replace the old guard. The 1999 congress, therefore, highlighted the fact that the battle between Catholic conservatives and moderates was both ideological and power-driven.

Many elected on the Coalition's list maintained strong ties to their 'mother' parties and advocated a return to the original five-party coalition form. This position, however, met with strong resistance from the Coalition's leader, Mikuláš Dzurinda, and a number of senior colleagues. After fruitless attempts to find an agreement, Dzurinda and seven cabinet ministers, together with other senior politicians from two of the Slovak Democratic Coalition's parties (KDH and the Democratic Union), announced in January 2000 that they were ready to offer the Slovak voters a new union of 'directions, streams and personalities'.[46]

Thanks to the provisions of the coalition agreement, the newly formed Slovak Democratic and Christian Union (SDKÚ) lived a strange existence until the 2002 elections. It was akin to a chrysalis, from which the butterfly fully emerged only when the 2002 election campaign began. Dzurinda and his allies knew that the new political entity was not a signatory of the coalition agreement. The leadership of SDKÚ, therefore, invented a *double membership* solution, allowing all members of the Slovak Democratic Coalition the chance to become members of SDKÚ as well. Moreover, Dzurinda was acutely aware that he had become prime minister thanks to his position as leader of the Slovak Democratic Coalition. By stressing that SDKÚ was a project not for now, but for the 2002 elections, he wanted to protect his position as prime minister. None the less as prime minister he hoped to capitalize on his popularity and visibility and persuade voters and centre and centre-right politicians to join his new gang.

SDKÚ declared itself to be unequivocally centre-right, advocating market reforms and lambasting 'socialist paternalism',[47] but the core messages were the threat posed by other political parties to Slovakia's less than secure democracy (hence the need for a strong party), and also the projection of the party as the sole guarantor of Slovakia's entry into NATO and the EU.

Although driven in part by the desire to create a strong centre-right party, the formation of SDKÚ proved ironically not to be a force for cohesion, but ultimately led to the split between the KDH moderates and conservative Catholics. The drive for a broad-church unity on the centre-right was resisted by several members of KDH. In response to SDKÚ's founding congress, which took place in November 2000, those Christian Democratic members of the Slovak Democratic Coalition's parliamentary party group who disagreed with the creation of the new party left the broad anti-Mečiar coalition and established an independent grouping in parliament that was recognized by other members of the coalition and formalized in a supplement to the coalition agreement.

The year 2000 saw significant developments for KDH. Not only did the organization re-establish itself at the parliamentary level and become a party to the coalition, but also Ján Čarnogurský decided not to stand for re-election as party chairman. In the leadership election the moderate Ján Figel' was convincingly defeated by Pavol Hrušovský. Although Hrušovský was a new leader, he was Čarnogurský's candidate and a man who represented continuity with the party's previous leadership. Hrušovský's victory, on top of developments in parliament, consolidated the position of the Catholic conservatives as the dominant force.

Explaining the Success of the Slovak Democratic and Christian Union and the Christian Democratic Movement in the 2002 Elections

The 2002 elections marked an important step in Slovakia's development, not least because the resultant government was palatable to both NATO and the EU. The election results have been explored in more detail elsewhere,[48] but a number of points relating to the success of the parties of the centre-right deserve to be mentioned.

These parties profited from the failure of the nationalist parties and the communist-successor left. The Slovak National Party, its splinter the Real Slovak National Party and the Party of the Democratic Left all failed to cross the five per cent threshold. If one of those parties had achieved more than five per cent, the four-party centre-right coalition would have been short of a majority in parliament. It is tempting, therefore, to make the case for the importance of this institutional factor in explaining the centre-right. The electoral system, however, was simply a contributing factor in explaining the failure of the Party of the Democratic Left. The party, which had been the second largest in the 1998–2002 government, achieved its ignominious result owing to a near-lethal cocktail of splits, scandals and strategic errors.[49]

The success of centre-right components and the failure of the left and centre-left components of the 1998–2002 government at the ballot box in 2002 can be explained in part by the fact that the government had to pursue a tough package of economic measures which were more palatable to a centre-right electorate than on the other side of the spectrum. The Party of the Democratic Left's Brigita Schmögnerová, as finance minister, was the visible face of many of the painful economic reforms, a fact that not only harmed the party's image but also exacerbated tensions within the party. Second, a large part of the appeal of the Slovak Democratic and Christian Union (SDKÚ) in 2002 lay not in its position on the left–right dimension, but rather in its role as the perceived guarantor of EU and NATO entry. Indeed, part of SDKÚ's success in 2002 can be reduced to *valence issues* 'associated with competence and an ability to achieve shared objectives and goals'.[50]

SDKÚ ran a well-organized campaign in 2002 contrasting the success of the 1998–2002 government, particularly in the international sphere, with its predecessor. The party portrayed the options before the Slovak voters in stark terms: the electorate had a choice between 'tolerance, partnership and international recognition' or a return to 'that which Slovakia rejected in 1998: a return to Vladimír Mečiar, to the politics of hatred, violence, intolerance and international isolation', or the 'so-called Third Way' of Smer and ANO for a future of 'experimentation and uncertainty'.[51]

All Right Now? Prospects for the Centre-Right in Slovakia

The Christian Democratic Movement (KDH) appears to be in a strong position after surviving the turbulent waters of the 1990s. The party stands like a solid statue that came through the violent storm of Slovak politics in the 1990s with a few scars but no major damage. The party has carved out for itself a niche on the Slovak electoral scene as a conservative Catholic party, and is not afraid to articulate its trenchant position on contentious issues, as its stance on abortion, homosexuality and the role of the Catholic Church in public life demonstrates. Although it is unwise to make predictions, KDH appears to have a loyal support base, which will stick to the party.

In contrast, SDKÚ shows signs of disintegrating (at the time of writing, February 2004). Part of the disintegration lies with Dzurinda himself, whose leadership style has become increasingly domineering. He has alienated many of his former allies. Chief among these is Dzurinda's comrade-in-arms through the struggles between conservative Catholics and modernizers, Ivan Šimko. After voting against the party line in cabinet, thanks to Dzurinda's initiative Šimko was stripped of the defence portfolio and removed from his position as vice-chairman of the party. In disgust Šimko led a breakaway faction of six colleagues who formed Free Forum in December 2003. SDKÚ's difficulties are also linked in to the valence factor. The party achieved its cherished goals of securing entrance tickets into the EU and NATO. With these goals reached, and the landscape of party politics changing thanks to the waning of the Mečiar-induced polarization of the 1990s, SDKÚ's future appears uncertain. Its appeal in 2002 was driven largely by one-shot factors. By 2006 (the next scheduled date for elections), Slovakia will be established in the European Union and NATO. Moreover, invoking the nightmare of a return to power by Mečiar is unlikely to wash. Ironically the support for a self-ascribed centre-right party (SDKÚ), with its themes of lower taxation and reducing the role of the state, is on the decline at the very time when the left–right divide has come to be dominant on the Slovak political scene.

The centre-right agenda being pursued by the government is engendering unpopularity. Although SDKÚ is only one of the coalition partners, it is the most visible face of reform: not only does the party hold the prime ministership, it also holds the portfolios of finance and social affairs. Cuts in public spending and reform of the pension system may be deemed necessary by their ministers, Ivan Mikloš and Ľudovít Kaník, but they are unpopular. Thanks to this reform agenda plus the crackdown on the power of corporatist bodies, the government has lost popularity in certain circles. Indeed, the trade unions organized a series of large-scale protests in 2003 and collected sufficient numbers of signatures to call for a referendum on early elections. Whereas in the first Dzurinda government of 1998–2002 leftist elements acted as a brake on such reforms, the government can now push ahead relatively unhindered, although changing parliamentary arithmetic due to defections has complicated matters. It is worth stressing that KDH has remained remarkably immune to the drop in support for the government and SDKÚ. We would argue that this is the product both of KDH's solid support base and of the party's decision to take portfolios such as justice and the interior ministry, where the party can pursue tough but popular policies against crime, thanks in part to KDH's component ministers such as the justice minister, Daniel Lipšic.

Conclusion

Legacies, the dynamics of the transition and institutions all contribute to explaining the level of success achieved by the centre-right in Slovakia since 1989, but we argue that political crafting and strategic decisions at critical points are central to an explanation. Indeed, the Slovak case appears to give credence to a modified path-dependent explanation. Although such an approach probably works better to explain the limited success of the communist-successor Party of the Democratic Left,[52] we suggest that it may be the best explanatory framework to understand the fate of the centre-right.

Employing the language of modified path-dependency, agency's role was important at key critical junctures. Such junctures become critical because 'once a particular option is selected it becomes progressively more difficult to return to the initial point when multiple alternatives were still available'.[53]

We do not deny the importance of context (particularly in terms of the dynamics of the early transition), but context provides opportunities and constraints for political actors. Some actors exploit these opportunities; others make strategic errors. We contrasted the decisions made by Mečiar and Čarnogurský in the period 1990–92. Čarnogurský and his conservative Catholic faction in KDH pursued a policy of purity, whereas Mečiar opted for a strategy of inclusion. Moreover, Čarnogurský's role in the removal of Mečiar from the prime ministership in 1991 was a strategic error. Mečiar's political crafting helped to bring his party to power in 1992 and led to the break-up of Czechoslovakia. Two years later, Mečiar was again removed from the top job through a parliamentary vote of no confidence, but the decision made by the new government to push for early elections in the autumn was unwise. It gave Mečiar a chance to regroup and the parties in government insufficient time to produce palpable results. That decision largely accounts for Mečiar's return to power in 1994 and set Slovakia on a path of polarized politics that dominated the political scene until the end of the decade, producing (thanks in no small part to the changes in the electoral law) an ideologically broad political party (the Slovak Democratic Coalition) which leading figures in KDH agreed to support with varying degrees of enthusiasm.

The Coalition did spawn a centre-right party, the Slovak Democratic Christian Union, but SDKÚ's appeal lay less in the party's programme than in its role as the guarantor of Slovakia's entry into international clubs and as a bulwark against the unpalatable getting their hands on power. Indeed, once the SDKÚ had secured Slovakia's entry into NATO and the EU, the centre-right components of its programme – such as flat-rate tax, lower public spending and reform of public services – plus the increasingly domineering style of Dzurinda caused support for the party to fall. In contrast the reconstituted KDH appears electorally secure. It seems that a policy of purity may not bring instant rewards, but the strategy may subsequently bear fruit.

ACKNOWLEDGEMENTS

The authors are grateful to Seán Hanley, Aleks Szczerbiak and Vladimír Bilčík for their comments on earlier drafts.

NOTES

1. For detailed accounts of voting patterns and the support bases of political parties in Slovakia see Vladimír Krivý, *Politické orientácie na Slovensku – skupinové profily* (Bratislava: IVO, 2000); and Vladimír Krivý, Viera Feglová and Daniel Balko, *Slovensko a jeho regióny: socio-kultúrne súvislosti volebného správania* (Bratislava: Nadácia Média, 1996).
2. Martin Chren and Martin Thomay, *Verejný audit volebných programov politických strán a hnutí* (Bratislava: Nadácia F.A.Hayeka, 2002), available at <http://www.napri.sk/web/hayek/slovak/downloads/Audit2002web.pdf>.
3. Thomas Rochon, 'Mobilizers and Challengers: Towards a Theory of New Party Success', *International Political Science Review*, Vol.6 (1985), pp.419–39; see also Tim Haughton, '"We'll Finish What We've Started": The 2002 Slovak Parliamentary Elections', *Journal of Communist Studies and Transition Politics*, Vol.19, No.4 (2003), pp.78–9.
4. *Sme*, 25 Aug. 2003.
5. *Narodná obroda*, 3 July 2003, p.3; *Sme*, 3 July 2003, p.2.
6. Tim Haughton, 'HZDS: The Ideology, Organisation and Support Base of Slovakia's Most Successful Party', *Europe–Asia Studies*, Vol.53, No.5 (2001), pp.745–69.

7. Vladimír Mečiar (with Dana Podracká and Ľuba Šajdová), *Slovenské tabu* (Bratislava: Silentium, 1996); Marián Leško, *Mečiar a mečiarizmus: politik bez škrupúl', politika bez zábran* (Bratislava: VMV, 1996).
8. Tim Haughton, 'Explaining the Limited Success of the Communist-Successor Left in Slovakia: The Case of the Party of the Democratic Left (SDL')', *Party Politics*, Vol.10, No.4 (2004), pp.177–91.
9. Vladimír Krivý, 'Náboženské prejavy v 90. rokoch', in Oľga Gyárfášová, Vladimír Krivý, Grigorij Mesežnikov and Michal Vašečka, *Krajina v pohybe: Správa o politických názoroch a hodnotách ľudí na Slovensku* (Bratislava: IVO, 2001), p.266.
10. Abby Innes, 'The Breakup of Czechoslovakia: The Impact of Party Development on the Separation of the State', *East European Politics and Societies*, Vol.11, No.3 (1997), p.407.
11. Barbara J. Falk, *The Dilemmas of Dissidence in East–Central Europe: Citizen Intellectuals and Philosopher Kings* (Budapest and New York: CEU Press, 2003), p.101.
12. Milada Vachudová, 'Right-wing Parties and Political Outcomes in Eastern Europe', paper presented to the American Political Science Association annual meeting, San Francisco, 2001.
13. Janusz Bugajski, *Political Parties of Eastern Europe: A Guide to Politics in the Post-Communist Era* (Armonk, NY and London: Sharpe, 2002), p.305.
14. 'Prejav na zakladajúcom sneme KDH', reprinted in Ján Čarnogurský, *Videné od Dunaja* (Bratislava: Kalligram, 1997), pp.217–20.
15. *Stanovy Krest'anskodemokratického hnutia*, ratified at the KDH congress, Liptovský Mikuláš, 10 April 1999, article 2; *národnost'* can also be translated as 'nationality'.
16. Ján Čarnogurský, 'Prejav na sneme v Žiline', 9 Nov. 1991, reprinted in Čarnogurský, *Videné od Dunaja*, p.234.
17. Ján Čarnogurský, 'Obrana KDH' (originally published 16 November 1992), reprinted in Čarnogurský, *Videné od Dunaja*, p.336.
18. Ján Čarnogurský, 'Dve úlohy KDH', reprinted in Čarnogurský, *Videné od Dunaja*, pp.229–33.
19. Vladimír Krivý, *Čo prezrádzajú volebné výsledky? Parlamentné voľby 1992–1998* (Bratislava: IVO, 1999), p.79.
20. Ibid., pp.123, 124, 126.
21. Čarnogurský, 'Obrana KDH', p.338.
22. František Mikloško, *Čas stretnutí* (Bratislava: Kalligram, 1996), p.181.
23. Innes, p.419.
24. Steven Saxonberg, 'The Influence of Presidential Systems: Why the Right is So Weak in Conservative Poland and So Strong in the Egalitarian Czech Republic', *Problems of Post-Communism*, Vol.50, No.5 (Sept.–Oct. 2003), pp.22–36.
25. The argument is Karol Ježík's: see Marián Leško, *Ľudia a ľudkovia z politckej elity* (Bratislava: Petrex, 1993), p.21.
26. Wolfgang C. Müller and Kaare Strøm (eds.), *Policy, Office, or Votes? How Political Parties in Western Europe Make Hard Decisions* (Cambridge: Cambridge University Press, 1999).
27. Leško, *Ľudia a ľudkovia z politckej elity*, p.22.
28. *Slovensko – júl 1991: Analytická štúdia* (Bratislava: Ústav pre sociálnu analýzu Univerzity Komenského, 1991), p.21.
29. Innes, p.413.
30. Ján Čarnogurský, 'Prihovor v STV 23. aprila 1991', in Čarnogurský, *Videné od Dunaja*, pp.169–70.
31. Leško, *Ľudia a ľudkovia z politckej elity*, p.23.
32. Innes.
33. Bugajski, p.306.
34. Ján Čarnogurský, *'Princíp gyroskopu'* (interview), *Smena*, 11 Oct. 1990, reprinted in Čarnogurský, *Videné od Dunaja*, pp.271–2.
35. Zora Bútorová and Martin Bútora, *Slovensko po rok: cesty a križovatky nového štátu očami jeho obyvateľov* (Prague: Sociologicke nakladatelstvo, 1994), pp.9, 10, 31.
36. Haughton, 'Explaining the Limited Success'.
37. Marian Leško, 'Pribeh sebadiskvalikacie favorita', in Martin Bútora and František Šebej (eds.), *Slovensko v šedej zóne? Rozširovanie NATO, zlyhania a perspektívy Slovenska*

(Bratislava: IVO, 1998), pp.15–85; Karen Henderson, 'Slovakia and the Democratic Criteria for EU Accession', in Karen Henderson (ed.), *Back to Europe: Central and Eastern Europe and the European Union* (London and Philadelphia, PA: UCL Press, 1999), pp.221–40.

38. Lubomír Kopeček, 'Slovenská demokratická koalice – vznik, geneze a charakteristika', *Politologický časopis*, Vol.3 (1999), pp.248–70.
39. Mikuláš Dzurinda, *Kde je vôľa, tam je cesta: môj maratón* (Bratislava: Koloman Kertész Bagala, 2002), p.11.
40. Ibid, p.12.
41. Ibid, p.13.
42. Marek Rybář, *Slovak Political Parties Before Parliamentary Elections 2002* (Bratislava: Friedrich Ebert Stiftung, 2002), p.6.
43. Ivan Šimko, *Dobrá správa pre krestanskú demokraciu a pre Slovensko: Programová esej* (Bratislava: Nadácia pre európske štúdie, 2000) p.53.
44. Grigorij Mesežnikov, 'Vnútropolitický vývoj a systém politických strán', in Miroslav Kollár and Grigorij Mesežnikov (eds.), *Slovensko 2000: Súhrnná správa o stave spoločnosti* (Bratislava: IVO, 2000) p.6.
45. Ibid.
46. Rybář, p.7.
47. SDKÚ, *Programové východiská Slovenskej demokratickej a krest'anskej únie*, at <http://www.sdkuonline.sk>; see also Grigorij Mesežnikov (ed.), *Vol'by 2002: Analýza volebných programov politických strán a hnutí* (Bratislava: IVO, 2002).
48. See Grigorij Mesežnikov et al., *Slovenské vol'by '02: výsledky, dôsledky, súvislosti* (Bratislava: IVO, 2003); Geoffrey Pridham, 'The Slovak Parliamentary Election of September 2002: Its Systemic Importance', *Government and Opposition*, Vol.38, No.3 (2003), pp.333–56; and Haughton, 'We'll Finish What We've Started'.
49. Haughton, 'Explaining the Limited Success'.
50. Aleks Szczerbiak, 'Old and New Divisions in Polish Politics: Polish Parties' Electoral Strategies and Bases of Support', *Europe–Asia Studies*, Vol.55, No.5 (2003), p.731.
51. SDKÚ election newspaper, *Modré správy*, Sept. 2002.
52. Haughton, 'Explaining the Limited Success'.
53. James Mahoney, 'Path Dependency in Historical Sociology', *Theory and Society*, Vol.29 (2000), pp.507–48.

What Is the Right Way in East–Central Europe? Concluding Remarks

PAUL G. LEWIS

In these concluding remarks, we turn to see how far the case studies presented in this volume have contributed to a general answer to the questions that inform it: Why have some post-communist centre-right formations been electorally and organizationally more successful than others? Why have strong and cohesive centre-right parties developed in some post-communist states but not in others? More concretely, this has meant identifying the roots of electoral success and specifying the conditions under which Solidarity Election Action (AWS) won the 1997 Polish election with 33.8 per cent of the vote, far exceeding the 12–13 per cent ever won by broadly defined right-wing parties like the Democratic Union and Freedom Union or the 13 per cent gained by Civic Platform in 2001; accounting for the 25–30 per cent of the vote regularly gained by the Civic Democratic Party (ODS) in the Czech Republic between 1992 and 2002 (with no other single right-wing force ever having gained more than ten per cent) and the 29 and 41 per cent received by Fidesz in recent Hungarian elections; and explaining the prominence of the role played by the Christian Democratic Movement (KDH) and Democratic and Christian Union (SDKU) in Slovakia. Consideration of the record of these parties has also involved investigation of the extent to which such leading centre-right formations have succeeded in dominating the right of the mainstream party spectrum in these countries more generally, as well as the overall conditions for their institutional development (or lack of it) during the post-communist period as a whole. The striking failure of some right-wing parties (notably in Poland) has also been analysed. In this respect there has been considerable variation among the countries of Eastern and Central Europe and there remains, as a particular task for this conclusion, scope for further comparative analysis and discussion of the major factors involved.

In each case the question posed has, therefore, a distinct national dimension. In the case of Poland, for example, why have right-wing forces often been so weak in electoral and institutional terms, and the development of parties on this side of the political spectrum so problematic compared with the steady growth and strong electoral record of the Democratic Left Alliance (SLD)? Why was the reconstitution of the right so effective, on the other hand, in Hungary and how did Fidesz succeed in transforming itself and dominating that sizeable portion of the political area? How did Klaus, similarly, manage to keep the Civic Democratic Party (ODS) so dominant for a considerable period of time both on the right of the Czech spectrum – and even, despite certain electoral and other setbacks, in the political system as a whole? How strong has it been and is it likely to be in the future with his departure from the party's leadership? By what means did the KDH and SDKU survive the lengthy period of Mečiar's dominance in Slovakia and finally succeed in coming to power? What prospects do they have for retaining their place in government and for effective future development? There is also a general question to be posed about right-wing developments in the whole of Eastern and Central Europe: to what extent have strong and cohesive centre-right parties developed at all, and how does the development of the post-communist right as a whole compare with that of the left? Despite the relative success of the centre-right parties examined here, for example, it must also be recognized that in three of the four countries concerned the right has been out of power from 2002 to the time of writing in 2004 and that it is the centre-left that has had the greater electoral success in recent years.

Contributions of the Explanatory Approaches

The answers provided in the case studies presented here offer somewhat different explanations for these developments. A range of alternative explanatory approaches are identified by Szczerbiak and Hanley in the Introduction:

1. historical–structural approaches that favour legacy-based explanations have been influential in this area but now, it is argued, have limited relevance when answers are sought to questions about the varying strength and cohesion of centre-right parties across Eastern and Central Europe or concerning the different patterns of post-communist political development seen across the region;
2. accounts that emphasize the role of choice exercised by political agents at critical junctures of the transition phase, particularly during 1989–91;
3. institutional approaches that direct attention to a range of structural factors and different features of the political environment, such as:
   a) the nature of the electoral system – relating, for example, to the proposition that less proportional systems are more likely to produce strong and more cohesive parties;

   b) the existence of parliamentary regimes that are more likely to produce
      coherent political blocs than more presidential systems;
   c) organization of the centre-right from a political centre and institutiona-
      lization on the basis of territorial penetration rather than diffusion;
4. elite-focused explanations that emphasize the importance of political
   actors, as well as the role of ideological and social cohesion in providing
   an effective vehicle for party leadership.

Most, if not all, these factors have been discussed in each of the four case
studies contained in this volume and a certain measure of agreement reached
on the usefulness of the different explanatory approaches, although different
emphases emerge according to national context.

In Poland, micro-institutional factors (mainly in terms of party origins and
their lasting impact on the course of institutional development) are seen to
play an important role, and combine with significant leadership failure
(that is, political agency) to explain its weak performance in government
and crushing defeat in the 2001 election. Other factors, such as the electoral
mechanism, may have played some part in encouraging fragmentation in
1991 and then, once a five per cent threshold was introduced, in providing
incentives for the centre-right to combine around the AWS after a punishing
defeat in 1993. But the effects of the original mechanism may have reflected
existing divisions rather than created new ones, and there remains the question
of why this factor did not exert an equivalent influence on the centre-left. Electoral mechanisms, too, are devised and chosen by the very politicians who
operate according to their requirements. The role of political agency also
appears to be an important one in the survival and subsequent success of
the centre-right in Slovakia. Particular significance is ascribed to political
crafting and the taking of appropriate strategic decisions at critical points,
pointing in this context to the utility of a modified path dependence explanation – that is, the right decisions being taken at key critical junctures.
Mention is again made of macro-institutional factors such as the electoral
mechanism when, for example, the requirement was introduced in 1998 for
all members of an electoral coalition to cross the five per cent threshold, a
move that led directly to the transformation of the Slovak Democratic
Coalition into a party itself.

Some linkage between centre-right development and the emergence of
political cleavages on the basis of post-communist marketization, on the
other hand, is detected in the Czech Republic in association with a strong
element of successful political entrepreneurship at a critical juncture of the
post-communist transition. In distinction to Poland and Hungary, for
example, Czech voting behaviour showed stronger signs of a growing correlation between social class and party choice – thus lending some support to

the historical–structural analysis undertaken by Herbert Kitschelt and the prominence he assigned to electoral competition on the left–right plane in the Czech Republic. But even here a structural–legacy approach does little to explain the particular strength of the free market Czech New Right after 1989 – or its subsequent decline in the latter half of the 1990s. Once again, the role of agency is very important and the impact of the 'Klaus phenomenon' highly significant. Political strategy and the choices made at critical junctures of the transition in the period 1990–92 also had a key importance. Aspects of leadership are again emphasized in the Hungarian case and particular attention is directed to the positive role played by such factors as ideology and elite unity – in marked contrast to Poland, for example, where these were for various reasons areas of notable weakness. In general, then, all these interpretations play down the explanatory power of structural–legacy approaches, broad institutional factors, and even transition dynamics, thus tending to emphasize the role of micro-institutional factors, choice and political agency, and effective leadership.

Such explanations of right-wing developments thus contrast with several accounts of the successful survival and transformation of many former communist parties[1] and, indeed, of conditions for the overall development of party systems in early post-communist Eastern and Central Europe,[2] which both place considerable emphasis on the role of historical–structural factors. On the face of it this may seem rather puzzling, particularly as parties of the right and left inherited the same broad historical legacy and inhabit the same political space. More value from this kind of historical–structural approach may be derived, though, by developing a closer focus on specific institutional and organizational legacies – which indeed seemed to give former communist and other regime parties something of a head-start in terms of resources, membership and personnel. Nevertheless, as Radosław Markowski has pointed out, even here it is strange that these assets did not prove their political worth (at least in cases analysed here) when they were most needed, in the very early phase of the post-communist regime. Much of SLD's success in post-communist Poland was in fact seen to derive from the failures of the right and the party's capacity to adapt its behaviour to the new democratic procedures – a view very much in line, in fact, with that presented in the case studies discussed here.[3] This was also the phase when anticommunist, broadly right-wing forces had greatest impact and achieved a uniform political success, even if it was to prove short-lived in many cases. A focus on broad historical legacies does not, therefore, prove to be very helpful here in explaining the fate either of the centre-right or the left in terms of the political dynamics of the post-1989 period. It is time, as Szczerbiak and Hanley emphasize in the Introduction, to bring politics back into the analysis of Eastern and Central European parties.

The Range of Institutional Explanations

Other kinds of structural factors and features of the institutional environment seem to play a more important part in the analysis, however. Electoral mechanisms are clearly significant, but the precise nature of any influence on the fate of the centre-right remains uncertain, particularly as (again) such arrangements applied to the left in exactly the same way. It is only in Hungary, where there was a distinctively majoritarian factor in play, that the mechanism promoted a significantly bipartisan outcome. But even here it was not possible just to 'read off' the emergence of a coherent centre-right and its relative success from the electoral system. The successive changes in the Polish electoral mechanism also had an impact on the fate of the centre-right in that country and produced dramatic shifts in political representation, both punishing the right in 1993 but then producing such a left-wing parliamentary dominance that the defeated forces were driven to unite within Solidarity Electoral Action. The view of the complex role post-communist electoral systems have played that is presented in the case studies is in line with detailed comparative analysis that 'found that post-communist electoral design was an iterative, recursive process that both formed political actors and was formed by them'.[4] In a general discussion of the influence of electoral systems, although with particular reference to post-communist Poland, it was also noted that 'It takes many elections with the same electoral rules before their systematic effects stabilize'.[5] Recognition of this uncertainty is reflected in the importance assigned to the electoral mechanism applied in the Eastern and Central European cases discussed here, as well as by general agreement that its role has not been determinant for the fate of the centre-right.

Little direct attention has been directed in the case studies, on the other hand, to the similarly important issue of the legal requirements for party registration – or, more significantly, to the changes that were made in them in the course of the 1990s. This was a factor of some importance in Poland, where it particularly concerned Solidarity Electoral Action, whose electoral success in 1997 was achieved precisely on the basis of its activity as a coalition rather than a unitary actor and under the leadership of a trade union rather than a conventional political party (both aspects are fully explored in the relevant article in this collection). The new party law that came into effect later the same year, however, introduced major changes in the political and legal conditions under which parties could operate. The minimal demands previously made had done little to encourage the development of stronger parties with more coherent organization and did little to prevent the proliferation of weak and unstable parties in the early post-communist period. More stringent organizational requirements for registration were now established with the inducement of more regular and generous state funding for institutions that complied with these demands. This was a further reason for the decision to set up the Solidarity Electoral Action Social Movement in November, as described by Aleks Szczerbiak, but it was still clearly not designed to be a standard political party and it remained ambiguously linked with the trade union, conditions that were fatal to its subsequent development (in contrast to the far smoother and more successful transformation of the Democratic Left Alliance into a more standard party institution).

Another factor to which relatively little explanatory power is ascribed in these studies is that of transition dynamics – although the attention directed to path dependence does highlight the particular importance of 'critical junctures' in Slovakia while key turning-points are also referred to in the Polish context as significant milestones in the course of centre-right development. Elections emerged as critical junctures for party development in the Czech Republic, while coalition choice is identified as being a similarly significant factor in Hungary. Some further progress in constructing a general explanatory model might indeed be made by paying more attention to the role of *specific* institutional legacies and conditions, and how they have impinged on the transition dynamics of particular countries.

The attempt to construct a broader and more theoretical account of the success of the centre-right in Eastern and Central Europe might also benefit from more extensive examination of established institutional approaches to party development in the context of a broad comparative analysis. The important work of Angelo Panebianco in this area has been noted in the Introduction, and his analysis of the deleterious effects of external sponsorship for party institutionalization is clearly relevant to the discussion of Poland in Szczerbiak's article.[6] Analysis within the framework of Panebianco's genetic model of the decline of the parties that had developed within the Solidarity camp during the early phase of post-communist party politics in Poland between 1989 and 1993 was conducted at the time.[7] His account of the role of major factors in party institutionalization was convincing in terms of the early failure of Solidarity and clearly pointed to relevant conditions for the later decline of AWS (although the lack of territorial penetration to which he directs attention is not explicitly emphasized here) – and in this context it is as much the resurrection of Solidarity forces in the form of AWS during 1996 that requires explanation as its subsequent demise. The early application to Poland of Panebianco's model also pointed to the more promising developmental path apparently taken by the Confederation for Independent Poland (KPN), a small party but one that had political significance as the only clearly right-wing party to be represented in the 1993 parliament. The analysis carried out at the time, however, proved to have limited predictive value as KPN turned out to be far from institutionally robust and began to fragment in 1994, splitting decisively (and fatally) two years later. This suggests that a firmer grasp on the conditions for centre-right party success may require analysis of a range of such parties, small and large, stable and unstable.

The experience of such parties and insights derived from this institutional perspective are, of course, not limited to Poland. The promising institutional beginnings of the Christian Democratic Movement in Slovakia may equally be linked with the bottom-up origins of the party noted by Haughton and Rybář in their article, which in turn recall the strategy of territorial penetration identified by Panebianco as opening up positive organizational pathways. While the KDH has indeed survived and appears to be electorally secure in 2004, it remains to be seen whether it will develop any further in institutional terms and build on the rather limited eight per cent of the vote it gained in 2002. The Confederation for Independent Poland achieved a similar level of support at some stages of its career, too, but found it impossible to progress further and was finally swallowed up by AWS. Another party whose trajectory might provide something of a negative model for the Slovak KDH is the not dissimilar Hungarian Christian Democratic Party (KDNP), which also appeared to have found an equivalent political niche during the 1990s as a stable sub-cultural party.[8] Its decline and subsequent amalgamation with Fidesz is duly noted in Brigid Fowler's article on Hungary. Fidesz thus represents a model of centre-right party success, which many other small parties have been unable to emulate.

One factor that does not receive separate attention in the case studies, and one that has clearly had some influence on the fate of the centre-right, is that of government performance and issues of policy formation and implementation more generally. Differences in policy and government performance have not been greatly emphasized as discrete factors in the cases discussed here, although there have clearly been some major contrasts between the different countries that affected the position and survival potential of particular centre-right parties. The four flagship reforms implemented by Solidarity Electoral Action in government were seen by Polish citizens as 'poorly conceived, hastily introduced and incompetently managed'. Even if these were not regarded as a major reason for AWS losing the level of support it had commanded in 1997, such views could hardly be seen as much of a boost for the popularity of the centre-right party in government or a solid basis for it to contest the subsequent election.

Government policies are rarely, if ever, wholly successful but those in the other countries of Eastern and Central Europe certainly seemed to be more positively accepted than they were in Poland. The political fortunes of the Civic Democratic Party were linked to its ability to act as a vehicle for successful post-communist transformation in the Czech Republic; centre-right politicians during the mid-1990s were able to produce coherent policy programmes that commanded considerable popular support in Hungary; while centre-right forces in the Slovak coalition that governed during the late 1990s produced a tough package of economic measures that at least had some attraction for a critical portion of the electorate. Decisions on policy priorities, the formulation of policy and capacities to implement it effectively all come, of course, under the heading of political agency and relate to individual questions of political entrepreneurship, but the signal failure of the Solidarity Electoral Action policy initiatives does deserve special attention in the comparative context of the analysis conducted here.

Questions of Party Cohesion

Other institutional studies have directed attention to the prominent issue of party cohesion. Solidarity Electoral Election presents, again, a paradigm case of the lack of organizational cohesion, but it was far from alone in experiencing such problems in the course of its institutional development. Seán Hanley shows how the Civic Democratic Party faced major problems in the Czech Republic after the crisis that erupted after the party funding scandal of 1997 and the split that led to the founding of the Freedom Union soon afterwards. ODS was not then able to form a government after either the 1998 or the 2002 elections. The generally positive account of Slovak centre-right party developments presented in the article by Haughton and Rybář is also cast in a less positive light by the observation that 'the SDKU appears to be disintegrating'. In fact, problems of organizational cohesion have been a widespread, major dimension of the general obstacles placed in the way of successful centre-right party development in Eastern and Central Europe and the challenges they have faced in the course of institutional growth. In the context of the well-known issues of political instability and party fragmentation in the region, problems of cohesion have been a major feature of the uneven process of party development.

Patterns of institutional development have, however, not always followed the model that established western-based theory might suggest. The parliamentary origins of many parties and the top–down mode of party formation might have promoted the view that it would be the parliaments that would afford new parties a viable and easily available organizational base. But a comparative study of party organization in new democracies of both Eastern and Central and Western Europe finds rather unexpectedly that the 'party in public office' does not predominate within the party organization, that the extra-parliamentary party is remarkably powerful, and that the party executive occupies a particularly strong position. It is an outcome that is directly attributed to the cohesion-seeking strategies employed by parties in new democracies, but one that is quite different from what might have been expected from the elite-focused accounts of party origins in post-communist Europe.[9] It casts further light on the singular experience of the AWS in Poland (a country that did not form part of van Biezen's research set) and the outcome of an organizational model based on trade union and parliamentary party. Since issues of party unity and cohesion have been prominent in the discussion of factors contributing to the success of the centre-right, this is a topic that deserves close study and one path that further comparative research might take.

In this context it is also necessary to acknowledge, as the contributors to this volume have done by sharing major doubts about the usefulness of historical–structural approaches to the explanation of centre-right success, that the value of established models of formation and organizational development for parties in newly established democracies is often quite limited.[10] The surprising dominance of the party central office in several new democracies provides one example of how established party theory would have predicted a quite different outcome from those actually observed. The rich empirical accounts of centre-right development in the cases examined here also uncover some of the specific ways in which this problem has been approached and solutions applied, with varying degrees of success, in the different countries of Eastern and Central Europe.

The most acute variant of the party cohesion problem is that of Poland, as exemplified by the rise and fall of Solidarity Electoral Action. The decision to base a resurrected centre-right party on the extensive organization of the Solidarity trade union and to give it a clearly hegemonic role had undoubted attractions; but, as suggested earlier in terms of discussion of the institutional dangers of external sponsorship and party weakness in terms of territorial penetration, it was a model with marked drawbacks. Organizational cohesion, as Szczerbiak points out, was limited to little more than the exercise by the Solidarity leader Krzaklewski of an almost dictatorial role on the Polish right. Even if he had exemplary powers of leadership and political judgement (which was not the case), this was a role very difficult for Krzaklewski to perform and a strictly limited basis on which to secure the party's cohesion. Much of this task consequently rested on the shoulders of Prime Minister Jerzy Buzek, who had very few resources at his disposal to hold the party together. The use of patronage and resort to an increasingly clientelistic style of politics – often interpreted in purely moral or even criminal terms by much of the public, and therefore highly unattractive in electoral terms – thus became a distinctive structural response to the organizational problems of an unwieldy and fundamentally ill-formed AWS. The legal status of the party as an electoral coalition barred it from some of the state funds that had become available to formally constituted parties, which further restricted the influence of the party leadership and gave the cash-strapped small parties that made up part of the coalition yet more encouragement to make the most of the financial opportunities that government office provided them with.[11]

From one point of view, this had the clear appearance of a lack of organizational self-discipline and an absence of the necessary political skills to build and maintain parties for which much of the Polish elite seems to have acquired a well-deserved reputation. From other perspectives such behaviour was a rational response to the structural incentives embedded in the particular form that Poland's major centre-right institution had taken, and a distinctive response to pressing problems of organizational cohesion. But it is also necessary to recognize, of course, that AWS itself arose in this form on the basis of a sequence of personal choices and individual perceptions (or perhaps misperceptions). Ideas of agency and choice are, therefore, not quite so distinct from those of structure and institutional framework as they sometimes appear. It makes sense to ask where the values and perceptions that shape choice have come from, as well as how individuals or groups come to be in the position to make the influential decisions they do. As pointed out in the discussion of Grzymała-Busse's work in the Introduction, there is a tension between structure and agency that is never fully resolved; and a focus on successful decision making, suggested by the prioritizing of agency explanations, inevitably involves consideration of the legacy of political skills that politicians have inherited from the previous communist regime and other historical periods. We need to turn, therefore, to look at the factors involved in the operation of agency and choice and re-examine some approaches that place greater emphasis on aspects of historical legacy, after all.

The Operational Context of Agency and Political Choice

Broadly speaking, the analyses presented in this volume tend to favour agency over structure, choice over legacy, and action rather than institutions. Wise choice and a capacity to operate effectively in the new party environment have generally been suggested as major factors in securing the success of centre-right party formation and development. But we are then impelled to seek the origin of these organizational skills and political proclivities. Where do the broadly pro-party attitudes detected in Hungary and the Czech Republic and anti-party sentiments widely noted in Poland have their source? If they are attributed to political culture it is necessary to investigate where these values and normative orientations actually come from, and to consider how far past experience imposes constraints on contemporary behaviour. A conception of historical legacy that enables some account of where contemporary cultural orientations might come from might be well worth examining, although it should also be recognized that this involves an approach rather different from the more deterministic approach emphasizing socio-economic structure discussed and broadly criticized in the Introduction to this volume.

Clearly, some quite subjective judgements are involved here, although it is not particularly difficult to identify unique historical characteristics and the particular conjunctures of national development that have exerted an influence on the origins and nature of the contemporary Central European state. The account of Hungary points out, for example, that centre-right elites have been able to look back to quite positive experiences in the political life of the inter-war and pre-1914 periods. Hanley, on the other hand, refers to the historic weakness of the Czech right, although it should also be recognized that the political class as a whole had enough capacity for party building and sufficient organizational skills to build and sustain the only viable parliamentary system of inter-war Central and Eastern Europe. Taking the Polish case, however, the re-formation of a nation-state after the First World War, when its territory had been partitioned for more than a century among neighbouring powers, emerges as a prominent historical factor that can easily be understood to have exerted a formative influence on the striking Polish susceptibility to issues of unity and fragmentation.

The problems of forming a cohesive state out of the diverse territories formerly ruled by Russia, Germany and Austria-Hungary, peopled by various national groups and having developed under quite different economic regimes, were indeed considerable and quite different from the longer history of statehood and pluralist politics that formed part of the Hungarian pre-communist legacy, as Fowler makes clear in her article. Many Poles held a strong desire for integration and national unity, but it was an outcome that the country's recently established political system had great difficulty in delivering. Much of the blame for this was attributed to the incoherent party system of the new democracy and the fragmentation of its parliament, which in 1925 included 32 different parties and 18 separate political clubs. In this context the military coup d'état headed by Marshal Piłsudski the following year had considerable popular support, with many Poles appearing to share the marshal's reported extreme intolerance of party politics.[12] Polish experience during the early years of the modern state helped entrench, therefore, a strong desire for national and political unity combined with a dominant belief that this was not to be achieved through the foundation and activity of political parties.

Experience during the communist period did little to dispel the dislike of party politics, as well as the politics of the (single) communist party, and this was a further reason for the mobilization of anti-communist opposition within the framework of a trade union and social movement, a development that Poland shared to some extent with several other Central and East European countries. The strength of Poland's Solidarity movement was unique, however, and it emerged far earlier than any comparable movement in the region. Its formation in 1980 and dominance of the transition process in 1989 and 1990 accorded well with established Polish preferences for a unified national institution and non-party form of organization. Despite the growing need for institutionalized expression of political diversity, and a more formally organized base for government and parliamentary activity, too, leading Polish activists were more opposed than those elsewhere to the subsequent establishment and development of conventional political parties.

The Solidarity leader Bronisław Geremek thus expressed the view that older party structures had served their purpose and that 'something new' was emerging in the political sphere; when forming the pro-Mazowiecki ROAD organization in 1990 Zbigniew Bujak was remarkably evasive about whether or not it was a political party (maintaining, like Geremek, that this was something that belonged in the nineteenth century); and even when such leaders formed the Democratic Union they did not assign great importance to membership recruitment and remained relaxed about questions of organization growth.[13] The problems of institutional development and stable party growth on the Polish centre-right was due, therefore, not just to the fact that politicians often seemed to lack the skills to build political parties but also to the marked disinclination of so many of them to undertake the task in the first place. From this perspective, then, the emphasis on political agency and individual choice as a basis for explanatory analysis of the centre-right phenomenon is not wholly convincing, and some conception of political and cultural legacy can helpfully be factored in to provide a full account. The different kinds of legacy may therefore be usefully distinguished, and it should be noted that we have here been concerned with those derived from the imperatives of state building – which have therefore particularly shaped the values and perceptions of the political class – rather than the broader impact of patterns of socio-economic development.

Critical Junctures and the Role of Political Sequence

Analysis of the role of Solidarity also points to a particular difficulty in distinguishing historical–structural legacies from transition dynamics and the onset of critical junctures of early post-communist political life – and, indeed, from a micro-institutional perspective on party growth as well. The formation of Solidarity as far back as 1980 raises particular problems in this respect and places Polish developments in a different category from those elsewhere in the region, where opposition movements and independent party development indeed developed during the closing phase of communist rule but could be seen as early signs of transition rather than as central elements of contestation within the continuing dynamics of a communist

system. Such problems of analysis and explanation can be at least partly miti-
gated by the inclusion of a focus on questions of *sequence* in the progressive
collapse of communist rule, the dynamics of the transition process itself and
the pattern of early post-communist politics.

It is, of course, a perspective with a lengthy pedigree in the comparative
analysis of party development and of democratization more generally.
Robert Dahl drew attention to the importance of sequence in terms of the
need for patterns of contestation between factions or early parties to
develop within an exclusive political system before the political arena was
opened up to mass competition if the structures of stable democracy were
to develop.[14] In the post-communist context, attention has been directed to
the democratization of state institutions and the pluralization of civil
society, the sequence of these processes having an impact on party system
fragmentation and the capacity of former communists to retain power.[15]
Opportunities for party patronage have also been linked to the relative
timing of democratization and state bureaucratization.[16] Questions of
timing and the sequence of political developments can similarly be seen to
have played a major part in the development of a Solidarity-dominated
and unstable centre-right in Poland.

The pioneering, though only partially free, election of 1989 provided the
independent trade union with a limited capacity to challenge communist
rule but had consequences that were largely unforeseen in bringing about
the end of communist hegemony over the region as a whole. This combination
of circumstances, and the sequence in which further key changes occurred,
had distinct, and generally negative, implications for party development.
The limited opening that initially presented itself meant that the incipient
parties that existed at the time had little opportunity to mount any political
challenge, while the extent of the victory that it soon became apparent that
Solidarity had actually secured meant that party activity seemed to be of
little relevance when the amorphous movement, or at least some of its representatives, moved so quickly into the key positions of political authority. Party
development, albeit of a highly personalized nature, nevertheless got under
way as the presidential contest began to dominate the political arena in
mid-1990. As Fowler points out, this was a very different situation from
that which developed in Hungary. By this stage, however, the growing fragmentation of the Solidarity movement meant that many groups were fearful
of establishing a threshold in forthcoming elections that might lead to their
political extinction – this being a view that was shared for similar reasons
by the rump communist party. The situation at this point thus represented a
critical juncture at which a majority of competing political forces shared an
interest in promoting a proportional electoral system that perpetuated
the high degree of pluralism then apparent. It was on this basis that a highly

fragmented parliament populated as much by a diverse range of political cliques as by formally constituted parties emerged after the 1991 election.

Poland thus saw two 'exceptional' elections rather than the single 'founding' election seen in Hungary and Czechoslovakia, a direct consequence of Poland's position at the head of the sequence of developments that brought about the end of communist rule in the region. Both elections were moreover conducted through unusual – though quite different – institutional mechanisms that facilitated the emergence of a form of political competition that was essentially factional rather than party-based for as long as four years, until 1993. The sequence of Polish developments in this sense can be related to discussion about the emergence and nature of party systems in Western Europe that continues to be linked with the 'freezing hypothesis' originally proposed by Lipset and Rokkan in the 1960s.[17] The sequence of elections in Poland (though not in other Eastern and Central European countries), on the other hand, can thus be understood to have produced conditions for the early freezing not so much of cleavages and their reflection in terms of party systems but of factional inclinations, a view that directs attention to the influence of transition dynamics and institutional arrangements for the early transition, as well as the decisions taken at critical junctures of the 1989–91 period. They had the effect of holding back the institutional development of the centre-right in Poland yet further.

Summing Up

Considerable attention has now been paid to the four or more distinct approaches that can be identified to explaining the emergence and fate of the centre-right in four countries of Eastern and Central Europe; some factors identified to which relatively little attention was previously paid in some contexts (questions of party registration, the role of cultural rather than socio-economic legacies, and the precise sequence of political developments); and suggestions made about some possible links between relatively distinct approaches. One tentative general conclusion that might be advanced at this stage is that, while perhaps two of the theoretical approaches outlined seem to been identified in the case studies as contributing more to explaining the overall success of the centre-right than the others, it is not possible to rule out any one of them completely for failing to make any contribution at all. While major doubts are expressed in the Introduction to this collection about the value of the historical–structural approach, it is by no means clear that the role of agency and political choice as an explanatory factor has great strength in the absence of *some* linkage with ideas of cultural and historical legacy.

In short, there are a number of possible explanations for the emergence and relative success of the centre-right in the different countries of Eastern and

Central Europe. There is moreover some degree of overlap between the different perspectives and a measure of ambiguity about the weighting of different factors. But it is difficult to see how things could be otherwise in a pioneering study of the nature and role of the centre-right in post-communist developments. The collection as a whole admirably succeeds in moving on from a historical–structural perspective that places prime emphasis on the role of deep-rooted legacies in explaining post-communist developments. It directs attention to the emergence of the post-communist countries as a prime arena of *political* activity – and thus as a sphere of behaviour subject to major uncertainties and the influence of human volition.

More than a decade and a half have now passed since some of the key events in the transition, and there has been ample opportunity for different patterns of party activity to develop. This has been as true (if not more) for organizations of the centre-right as for any others. The challenge of producing any simple explanation for what has happened becomes so much more difficult an exercise – and, indeed, one that appears to be increasingly inappropriate. It is tempting in this context to echo the view expressed by Radosław Markowski on the equivalent exercise of attempting to account for the divergent trajectories of communist successor parties, that 'there is simply too much variation among the independent macro-variables and too few cases'.[18] There is at least some danger, as Fowler observes in the comparison of Hungary and Poland, of over-determining the differences observed. Nevertheless, considerable progress has been made in the case studies presented here in gaining a deeper insight into the dynamics of centre-right party politics and understanding the reasons for the particular fate of individual organizations. Together they make an original and highly distinctive contribution to the study of post-communist party development in Eastern and Central Europe.

The wealth of country-based analysis presented in this volume also has the merit of providing indicators for further comparative work. The selection of countries examined here is certainly a limited one, and fuller explanation of centre-right developments would be gained by extending the focus at least to include countries at similar levels of democratic and socio-economic development – a group whose members would include in the first instance the other countries joining the European Union in 2004: Estonia, Latvia, Lithuania and Slovenia. All, for example, have their key centre-right parties (understood in broad terms) identified in Hanley's article on 'Getting the Right Right' in this volume. But this in itself raises some interesting questions. How authentically centre-right is Slovenia's main party, the Liberal Democracy? Its origins and international affiliation (ELDR) actually point in rather different directions, while all the main centre-right formations discussed here have been members of the more clearly right-wing European People's Party. The obviously right-wing formations like the Slovenian People's Party and Christian Democrats have also lost support since the mid-1990s, so questions about the strength and position of the centre-right in Slovenian politics raise interesting issues. On the face of it, the fate of centre-right parties also seems to vary considerably across the Baltic counties – they are clearly strong in Latvia, less so in Lithuania, and somewhere between the two in Estonia. There are new perspectives to be opened up with further comparative research, and an analysis that encompasses more countries of post-communist Europe certainly promises to cast further light on the centre-right phenomenon and enhance our understanding of its role in contemporary politics.

NOTES

1. A. Bozóki and J.T. Ishiyama (eds.), *The Communist Successor Parties of Central and Eastern Europe* (Armonk, NY: Sharpe, 2002), pp.422–4.
2. H. Kitschelt, Z. Mansfeldova, R. Markowski and G. Tóka, *Post-Communist Party Systems: Competition, Representation, and Inter-Party Cooperation* (Cambridge: Cambridge University Press, 1999), pp.383–9.
3. R. Markowski, 'The Polish SLD in the 1990s: From Opposition to Incumbents and Back', in Bozóki and Ishiyama, p.81.
4. S. Birch, F. Millard, M. Popescu and K. Williams, *Embodying Democracy: Electoral System Design in Post-Communist Europe* (Basingstoke: Palgrave, 2002), p.178.
5. R. Taagepera, 'How Electoral Systems Matter for Democratization', *Democratization*, Vol.5, No.3 (1998), p.86.
6. Angelo Panebianco, *Political Parties: Organization and Power* (Cambridge: Cambridge University Press, 1988).
7. P.G. Lewis, 'Political Institutionalisation and Party Development in Post-communist Poland', *Europe–Asia Studies*, Vol.46, No.5 (1994), pp.779–99.
8. Z. Enyedi, 'Organizing a Subcultural Party in Eastern Europe: The Case of the Hungarian Christian Democrats', *Party Politics*, Vol.2, No.3 (1996), pp.377–96.
9. I. van Biezen, *Political Parties in New Democracies: Party Organization in Southern and Eastern and Central Europe* (Basingstoke: Palgrave, 2003), pp.214–17.
10. I. van Biezen, 'On the Internal Balance of Party Power: Party Organizations in New Democracies', *Party Politics*, Vol.6, No.4 (2000), p.410.
11. P.G. Lewis, 'Recent Evolutions of European Parties East and West: Towards Cartelization?', *Central European Political Science Review*, Vol.3, No.8 (2002), pp.16–17.
12. R.F. Leslie (ed.), *The History of Poland Since 1863* (Cambridge: Cambridge University Press, 1980), p.166.
13. Lewis, 'Political Institutionalization and Party Development', pp.785, 791–2.
14. R.A. Dahl, *Polyarchy: Participation and Opposition* (New Haven, CT: Yale University Press, 1971); see also R. Grew, 'Crises and Their Sequences', in R. Grew (ed.), *Crises of Political Development in Europe and the United States* (Princeton, NJ: Princeton University Press, 1978), pp.3–39.
15. J. Simon, 'Electoral Systems and Regime Change in Central and Eastern Europe, 1990–1994', *Representation*, Vol.35, Nos 2/3 (1998), pp.122–36.
16. D. Perkins, 'Structure and Choice: The Role of Organizations, Patronage and the Media in Party Formation', *Party Politics*, Vol.2, No.3 (1996), pp.355–75.
17. S.M. Lipset and S. Rokkan (eds.), *Party Systems and Voter Alignments: Cross-National Perspectives* (New York: Free Press, 1967).
18. Markowski, p. 52.

Index